Judith L. Irvin

Julie Meltzer

Melinda Dukes

TAKING
ACTION
on Adolescent Literacy

An Implementation Guide for School Leaders

Association for Supervision and Curriculum Development
Alexandria, Virginia USA

D0129484

Association for Supervision and Curriculum Development
1703 N. Beauregard St. • Alexandria, VA 22311-1714 USA
Phone: 800-933-2723 or 703-578-9600 • Fax: 703-575-5400
Web site: www.ascd.org • E-mail: member@ascd.org
Author guidelines: www.ascd.org/write

Gene R. Carter, *Executive Director;* Nancy Modrak, *Director of Publishing;* Julie Houtz, *Director of Book Editing &*
Production; Deborah Siegel, *Project Manager;* Greer Beeken, *Senior Graphic Designer;* Keith Demmons, *Typesetter;*
Dina Murray Seamon, *Production Specialist/Team Lead*

This publication was made possible (in part) by a grant from Carnegie Corporation of New York. The statements
made and views expressed are solely the responsibility of the authors.

Printed in the United States of America. Cover art copyright © 2007 by ASCD. ASCD publications present a
variety of viewpoints. The views expressed or implied in this book should not be interpreted as official positions
of the Association.

All Web links in this book are correct as of the publication date below but may have become inactive or otherwise
modified since that time. If you notice a deactivated or changed link, please e-mail books@ascd.org with the
words "Link Update" in the subject line. In your message, please specify the Web link, the book title, and the page
number on which the link appears.

PAPERBACK ISBN: 978-1-4166-0541-6   ASCD product #107034   s6/07
Also available as an e-book through ebrary, netLibrary, and many online booksellers (see Books in Print for the
ISBNs).

Quantity discounts for the paperback edition only: 10–49 copies, 10%; 50+ copies, 15%; for 1,000 or more
copies, call 800-933-2723, ext. 5634, or 703-575-5634. For desk copies: member@ascd.org.

Library of Congress Cataloging-in-Publication Data
Irvin, Judith L., 1947-
  Taking action on adolescent literacy : an implementation guide for school leaders / Judith L. Irvin, Julie Meltzer,
and Melinda S. Dukes.
      p. cm.
  Includes bibliographical references and index.
  ISBN 978-1-4166-0541-6 (pbk. : alk. paper) 1. Reading (Middle school)--United States. 2. Reading
(Secondary)--United States. 3. Language arts (Middle school)--United States. 4. Language arts (Secondary)--
United States. I. Meltzer, Julie, 1963- II. Dukes, Melinda S., 1971- III. Title.

  LB1632.I785 2007
  428.4071'2--dc22

                              2007004988

18 17 16 15 14 13 12 11 10 09 08 07   1 2 3 4 5 6 7 8 9 10 11 12

TAKING *ACTION* on Adolescent Literacy

An Implementation Guide for School Leaders ⭐

PREFACE

This book was developed for middle school, high school, and district leaders who want to help students improve their academic achievement through a focus on literacy. In it we describe a Leadership Model for Improving Adolescent Literacy whose components can and should be included in any literacy improvement effort to ensure that the effort is systemic and sustainable. The model is designed to illustrate how principals' traditional areas of responsibility, when seen through the lens of literacy, can be used to improve students' reading, writing, speaking, and thinking skills and have a positive effect on student achievement.

In addition to principals, others involved in the effort—including literacy coaches, assistant principals, team leaders, and department chairs—will find the information, vignettes, suggestions, resources, and key messages in this book helpful as they work to improve students' literacy habits and skills. District-level leaders who need to understand and support school improvement efforts can use this book as a guide as they work with schools. Prospective school leaders will appreciate the discussion of the components of schoolwide change with a focus on literacy.

We have had extensive experience working with middle and high school educators across the United States and have learned a great deal from school leaders working to improve literacy in their schools. We have seen pockets of excellence where teachers and administrators "put it all together" and create a literacy-rich environment that pervades the school and classrooms. It is our intention to share what we have learned from literacy leaders throughout the nation in a readable and useable form. We hope it is helpful to you in your work to improve literacy and learning for all of your students.

ACKNOWLEDGMENTS

Writing this book was a collaborative effort in thinking and writing. We have attempted to capture and distill the advice and experience of many educators across the United States who share a commitment to the support and development of adolescent literacy. The voices and efforts of hundreds of people are echoed in these pages.

First and foremost, thanks to Andres Henriquez at the Carnegie Corporation of New York, who began the conversation several years ago with Judith Irvin about the need for tools for school leaders to use to improve literacy and learning among their students and who championed resource support for the development of the model and the writing of this book. His powerful vision continues to inspire our work.

We wish to thank the dozens of school and district leaders whom we interviewed about successful practices they used in their literacy improvement efforts. We also drew from our work across many schools and our conversations with middle and high school educators and began to discuss what a model for literacy leadership would look like. The Leadership Model for Improving Adolescent Literacy began to take shape, and the model was sketched out, discussed, and revised. The emerging model was presented at several regional and national conferences, and again educators shared their feedback and suggestions, noting where the model truly represented their work or helped to spotlight an area for concern. Then the real writing began—three authors who had not written together before, attempting to write a book with a common tone, theme, and point of view.

The project's advisory board, made up of scholars and practitioners, met twice to guide the development of the model and the book to ensure content rigor, practicality, and viability. Their invaluable guidance and insightful questions sharpened our thinking and ensured we stayed on track. The following individuals served as members of the advisory board:

- Judy Buchanan—Deputy Director, National Writing Project, Philadelphia, Pennsylvania
- Doug Buehl—Adolescent Literacy Support Teacher, Madison Metropolitan School District, Madison, Wisconsin
- Amy Correa—Reading Specialist, Chicago Public Schools, Office of Literacy, Chicago, Illinois
- Agnes Crawford—Assistant Executive Director, Program Development, Association for Supervision and Curriculum Development, Alexandria, Virginia
- Andres Henriquez—Program Officer, Carnegie Corporation of New York, New York City
- Carol Jeffers—Literacy Coach, Pinellas County Public Schools, St. Petersburg, Florida
- Jerryelyn Jones—Principal, Curie Metropolitan High School, Chicago, Illinois
- Keith Lenz—Senior Research Scientist, Center for Research on Learning, University of Kansas, Lawrence, Kansas
- Melvina Phillips—Literacy and Professional Development Practitioner, National Association of Secondary School Principals, Reston, Virginia
- Barbara Scott Nelson—Director, Center for the Development of Teaching, Education Development Center, Boston, Massachusetts
- James P. Spillane—Professor, Northwestern University, Evanston, Illinois

We used a two-step review process to ensure applicability and content validity of the model and the book. By April 2006, 21 reviewers had provided extensive feedback, including nine current or former middle school or high school principals. Round-one reviewers had substantive content knowledge or practitioner experience or both: Nancy Dean, John Meinecke, M. Jan Mickler, Suzie Shapiro, Robert Spear, and Susan Ziemba. Round-two reviewers included two principals and a district literacy coordinator who represented our targeted audience for the book. Thanks go to Timothy Gadson, Mark

Hatch, and Jennifer Hester Schalk. Their suggestions and thoughtful critiques greatly improved the manuscript.

We also wish to acknowledge the support and contributions of our colleagues at Florida State University, the National Literacy Project, and the Public Consulting Group's Center for Resource Management. Last, but not least, we wish to thank our family members who waited patiently for us to finish the manuscript. Thanks especially to Julie's son and daughter, who gave up a lot of attention while their mom worked on this book.

We dedicate the book to our families and to all of the educators who are working hard to make a difference in the literacy lives and futures of the adolescents they serve.

INTRODUCTION

This book is for school and district leaders who want to make a difference in the lives of their students through a focus on literacy. What does literacy have to do with high dropout rates, low test scores, frustrated teachers and students, and irate employers? Just about everything.

Adolescent literacy is in a state of crisis. A sense of urgency pervades local and national conversations on the topic. The Alliance for Excellent Education estimates that as many as 8 million middle and high school students read below grade level (Joftus, 2002). The number at risk is far higher when we talk about the literacy habits and skills that students will need to meet 21st-century demands: core subject knowledge, 21st-century content, learning and thinking skills, information and communications technology, and life skills (Partnership for 21st Century Skills, 2006).

Students are dropping out of school in large numbers, many because they do not have the academic literacy skills to be successful in school. Limited literacy skills are a barrier to getting and retaining good employment and participating actively as a citizen. A substantial percentage of high school graduates need remedial classes in reading and writing when they get to college. Businesses spent more than $3 billion in a recent year to provide basic writing classes to employees (College Board, 2004). Scores on the National Assessment of Educational Progress (NAEP) remain flat. The bottom line is that many students in the United States are leaving high school unprepared to read, write, speak, listen, and think at a level needed for college, careers, or citizenship.

Many school leaders are daunted by the size and complexity of the task. Systemic development of literacy influences—and is influenced by—all aspects of school including curriculum, instruction, assessment, policies and structures, resource allocation, teacher professional development, and school culture. Therefore, it is understandable that many middle and high school leaders wonder where to begin and what is involved in the process of improving literacy achievement for all students.

What can school and district leaders do? Actually, a lot. In fact, savvy principals use a systemic focus on literacy as a lever for school improvement.

The central feature of this book is a Leadership Model for Improving Adolescent Literacy that outlines the components essential to any literacy improvement effort. We assume that school leaders know how to be effective managers and instructional leaders. The model shows how principals can improve student literacy and increase student achievement in general by approaching their traditional areas of responsibility with a new focus on literacy.

Our goal in this book is to help middle school, high school, and district leaders address the challenge of improving students' skills in reading, writing, speaking, and thinking. School and district leaders need to know what they can do to reverse the cycle of failure experienced by so many students in the areas of reading and writing and how schools can be organized to prepare all students to meet the literacy demands of 21st-century life, be it in school, in the workplace, or as a citizen. In the broadest sense, school and district leaders need to take three important steps:

1. Develop and communicate a literacy vision. Work toward a shared understanding of literacy goals, and create a schoolwide literacy vision that will inspire faculty, students, parents, and the community to motivate and engage students in becoming competent readers, writers, speakers, and thinkers. (Chapter 1 presents strategies for motivating and engaging students and addresses the connection between motivation and achievement.)

2. Translate the literacy vision into action. Establish and lead a schoolwide literacy team that includes representatives from all content areas who will work to develop and implement a schoolwide literacy action plan. Provide quality teacher professional development and expect all teachers to provide literacy support in the content areas. Ensure that literacy interventions are in place to help struggling readers and writers. Set up procedures to monitor progress. (Chapters 2 and 3 address classroom contexts and instruction; Chapter 5 provides data-driven approaches for how to develop a literacy action plan; Chapters 6, 7, and 8 provide tools for how to support and monitor teachers, use data effectively, and build leadership capacity to take action; and Chapter 9 addresses allocation of resources.)

3. Create and sustain a supportive, literacy-rich environment. Promote an academically oriented, orderly, and purposeful school climate with literacy as the central focus. (Chapter 4 provides specific strategies for creating a literacy-rich environment.)

In addition to practical ideas and suggestions, the book contains fictional vignettes based on our actual experiences in schools across the United States. The vignettes are not case studies of specific schools; rather, they illustrate the points we discuss (see Appendix D for references to actual case studies of middle and high schools engaged in efforts to improve literacy). In some of the chapters describing the action steps we suggest tools to use with your schools. These tools can be found in Appendix C. Each chapter closes with key messages.

In the next section of this Introduction, we briefly discuss how adolescent literacy reached the level of a crisis, the challenges of literacy development in the information age, and how school leaders can become more informed about literacy. We then present a vignette of a literacy-rich high school to help readers visualize what can be accomplished through a sustained literacy improvement effort, followed by an overview of the Leadership Model for Improving Adolescent Literacy.

A History of Neglect: Literacy Support in Middle and High Schools

Recent policy reports such as *Reading Next: A Vision for Action and Research in Middle and High School Literacy* (Biancarosa & Snow, 2004), *Reading to Achieve: A Governor's Guide to Adolescent Literacy* (National Governors Association, 2006a), *Reading Between the Lines: What the ACT Reveals About College Readiness in Reading* (ACT, 2006a), *Writing Next: Effective Strategies to Improve Writing of Adolescents in Middle and High Schools* (Graham & Perin, 2007), and *Double the Work: Challenges and Solutions to Acquiring Language and Academic Literacy for Adolescent English Language Learners* (Short & Fitzsimmons, 2007) have helped to focus attention on the fact that many middle and high school students are not reading and writing at levels that enable them to compete in a rapidly changing information age. However, secondary schools have largely neglected literacy instruction. Most people would consider it ludicrous to stop teaching mathematics when students finish the elementary grades. Yet students in the United States have generally not received systematic or consistent instruction in literacy beyond grade 5. While in kindergarten through 3rd grade, students learn the structure of stories, a basic sight vocabulary, phonics, and fluency with simple stories. However, even students who were successful readers and writers in the early grades may experience difficulty as the demands of text become more challenging (Snow, 2002). Four reasons underlie why adolescent literacy development has been neglected in middle and high schools:

- decision makers do not understand the complex nature of literacy learning,
- secondary teachers are not trained to support students' literacy development,
- resources have been put into early literacy reform efforts to the neglect of adolescent literacy, and
- literacy demands are higher than ever before.

Decision Makers' Lack of Understanding

Those who decide what is taught in schools, such as state- and district-level personnel and school board members, have typically not understood the complex demands of literacy placed on students as they enter the middle grades and mistakenly assume that students do not need continued support in reading and writing. But "middle and high school students [must] build on the literacy strategies they learned in the early grades to make sense of abstract, complex subjects far removed from their personal experiences" (Moore, Bean, Birdyshaw, & Rycik, 1999, p. 4). Success in the middle and high school classroom requires increasingly complex reading, writing, and thinking habits and skills. Students entering a middle or high school speaking a language other than English (Garcia, 2000) or students struggling with basic reading and writing abilities face almost insurmountable literacy tasks every day in every classroom. The assumption has often been that students learn to read in elementary school; the effort in middle school and high school has been remedial or limited to the English/language arts curriculum, if it occurs at all (Peterson, Caverly, Nicholson, O'Neal, & Cusenbary, 2000). The reality is that many students who have basic reading and writing skills will require ongoing assistance in the forms of modeling, explicit instruction, and ample practice opportunities to develop the proficient reading and writing skills required for academic success. Others will need continued assistance in basic skills. Appropriate programs, policies, and approaches to address the various needs of students must be put into place. When decision makers do not understand the complexity of literacy development and the interconnections between literacy and content-area learning, the result has been that little support is available to help students develop the academic literacy skills they need to be successful in school and in life.

Teachers' Lack of Preparation

Most middle and high schools have few teachers (or administrators) with any degree of confidence or competence in teaching reading and writing. Most secondary teachers lack knowledge about content-area literacy because they majored in English, math, social studies, science, music, or art. Subject area teachers often feel unprepared to assist students in negotiating difficult and content-dense books (Cooney, 1999). Most do not feel confident about how to teach students effective writing or higher-order thinking skills, and although they may *assign* writing or reading, they do not know how (and are sometimes unwilling) to assist students with reading their textbook, or how to model quality writing, or how to teach problem solving using reading and writing. In addition, fewer than 10 percent of middle and high schools have literacy specialists in their buildings to work with students and other teachers in any capacity (Southern Regional Education Board, 2002). This lack of onsite expertise in literacy in most middle schools and high schools severely limits efforts to improve the academic literacy skills of students.

Favoring Early Literacy at the Expense of Adolescent Literacy

As noted in a joint position paper by the International Reading Association and the National Middle School Association,

> Young children must get off to a good start in reading; however, it is a serious mistake to assume that a good start is sufficient for producing competent readers. The ability to comprehend a variety of texts, to use sophisticated comprehension and study strategies, to read critically, and to develop a lifelong desire to read is not acquired entirely during the early years. A good start is critical, but not sufficient. (National Middle School Association, 2001, p. 1)

The efforts directed toward literacy learning for primary grade students implemented over the past decade are beginning to bear fruit, but structures are needed to support students' continued growth as readers and writers. Funding for reading at the middle school and high school levels is much lower than at the elementary levels, and this condition has existed for many years.

Adolescent literacy is just beginning to receive the understanding, attention, funding, and support traditionally directed toward early reading development. Educators and stakeholders at large are increasingly recognizing the urgent need to provide consistent and sustained support in literacy beyond the elementary grades. With national attention now being turned to the needs of secondary school students, one can only hope that in the next few years, resources and programs will be put in place for improving adolescent literacy.

Unprecedented Literacy Demands

In the 21st century, higher literacy levels are required than has been the case in the past (Moore et al., 1999). Some educators and community members mistakenly believe that being able to read and write narrative text (stories) is sufficient to succeed in school and in life, that reading is the same no matter what you read. But the challenge of reading and writing varies with the type of text and the purpose. Reading for pleasure is different from reading an instruction manual or reading an informational Web site. Writing a letter to a friend requires different skills than writing a research report, a business plan, or a letter to the editor. Basic reading and writing skills—such as those taught in elementary school—are not sufficient to succeed in high school, college, or the workplace.

In middle and high school, students are expected not only to read and understand increasingly difficult text, but also to remember and organize information to demonstrate what they learned. Content-area standards are filled with literacy-based demands to describe, analyze, discuss, and synthesize content. Yet study after study reveals that students are not being taught to do this type of high-level reading, writing, and thinking in most middle and high school classrooms (Schmoker, 2006). Basically, there appears to be a gap between what we assess and what we teach (Sturtevant et al., 2006).

Well-meaning teachers discouraged by students who cannot, do not, or will not read may actually enable their resistant readers to read less, exacerbating the problem (Schoenbach, Greenleaf, Cziko, & Hurwitz, 1999). By receiving the content through other means such as hands-on projects, videos, and lectures, students may learn the content but be unable to go on to learn more on their own; they become more dependent on the teacher to feed facts, concepts, and generalizations to them because they have not learned the skills required to access, evaluate, and synthesize information themselves. Comparing the reading and writing expectations in college-preparation tracks and in Advanced Placement and other advanced classes with those in general or non-college-preparation tracks reveals a startling gap in the amount and quality of assigned reading and writing. Students in the general and the non-college-prep tracks appear to get less practice and little support to develop the skills necessary to their success in life, work, and school (Gamoran & Kelly, 2003). Schools need to address this problem, with skill development incorporated into the fabric of teaching and learning across the content areas.

Teachers need to understand the literacy demands of their content areas and be able to teach their students how to meet the requirements of state standards that insist on students reading like historians, writing like scientists, and thinking like mathematicians. Different content areas require different literacy habits and skills. Reading a play is not the same as reading a math textbook or a primary source or a technical manual; writing a letter is not the same as writing an essay or a lab report; and presenting a dramatic reading is different than explaining a science fair project or participating in a debate. Teachers who explicitly teach students to present, to read, and to write in all of these different disciplines enable their students to become independent learners.

Literacy in an Information Age

The world of adolescents today constitutes a media-rich, information-dense context for literacy. Most middle and high school teachers spent their own school years in a completely different technological era and perhaps have difficulty understanding how the information age and the technology resources available today change the milieu for learning. For example, writing a report on a country 20 or 30 years ago (still a standard assignment for today's students) entailed consulting the encyclopedia and a few library books for facts and somewhat sterile information, making note cards, developing an outline, and writing the paper. In contrast, a Google search of a country name— "Ireland," for example—can produce literally millions of Internet references, including information on maps, universities, art, literature, sports, food, travel, and politics. To find out more, a student could join a chat group about Ireland or with Irish people, view Irish TV online, and listen to authentic Irish folk music. These are potentially powerful ways to get insight into a culture and to gain hands-on experience that was simply not available to earlier report writers. In this technological context, it is important that an assigned investigation such as a country report be focused and relevant to the learners and that they be taught skills for selecting, analyzing, organizing, and summarizing information—a much more complex task given the mass of information available.

Teachers across the content areas are increasingly aware of the potential of technology to enrich teaching and learning. But they may not be aware of how these technologies (and adolescents' comfort with them) change the very nature of reading, writing, and learning. "Teachers need to engage directly in these new textual cultures... of mass media. Without this, we risk producing literacies that have little salience and critical purchase on the real worlds where adolescents live their lives" (Elkins & Luke, 1999, p. 214). No one can deny the new technologies that are available, but few middle and high school educators are prepared to incorporate these technologies into their task of developing academic literacy for a wide variety of learners. Technology can, and some say *must*, be an integral part of this central task, especially because the world of work and learning that these students will participate in as adults will include technology as an ever-present reality.

Understanding the relationship between literacy and technology means that schools should examine

- what types of academic literacy habits and skills are needed to prepare students for the future they face;
- how contexts for conducting research, learning, reading, and writing have changed because of the available technologies; and
- how assignments, teaching goals, and understandings about literacy have shifted.

For example, the need to critique information sources has never been more important; word processing can support the writing process as never before; and reading and writing hypertext is very different in terms of process, genre, and structure from reading and writing conventional linear prose. Those with convenient Internet access can easily connect to experts and to mountains of information, raising questions about validity, plagiarism, criteria for adequate performance, and the digital divide. Technology can also be a powerful tool for assisting those with reading difficulties to improve their decoding, fluency, and comprehension skills. In addition, technology can help teachers and school leaders improve their knowledge base about literacy, and they can use technology to motivate students to complete reading and writing tasks by providing motivating contexts for learning. Technology can also provide access to content-area texts at many reading levels, something that most educators have not been able to offer until now.

Developing Literacy Expertise

I had to learn about literacy myself . . . my background was as a business teacher. I built my own background knowledge right alongside of my teachers. I had to ask myself . . . what do I need to know to lead this effort?

—High school principal

Literacy refers to the communication modes of reading, writing, listening, speaking, viewing, and representing. Helping students to understand, analyze, and respond to the challenging texts that they find in content-area classes is essential to the development of academic literacy habits and skills. Of course, *thinking* is essential for all communication systems. Although our main focus in this book is academic literacy—types of literacy that students need to be successful in school—we recognize that students have multiple literacies that they use in and out of school settings for various reasons.

The first step in any literacy improvement effort is to become more knowledgeable about the literacy learning process (conceptual knowledge) and effective instructional support for literacy (pedagogical knowledge). Obviously, it is impractical to expect every middle and high school principal to become a literacy expert. But because secondary schools typically do not have many teachers and administrators with professional training in literacy, school leaders need to find ways to increase their own and their teachers' knowledge base and to provide teachers with strategies to motivate and teach students to read and write proficiently.

School leaders we talked with noted the benefits of collaboration and critical dialogue with other administrators, literacy coaches, reading specialists, and teachers. Some schools and districts employ outside consultants to provide the conceptual and pedagogical knowledge about literacy. Other schools and districts create professional learning communities or establish peer-coaching structures in which teachers support one another while trying out literacy support strategies in classrooms. In some schools, teachers and administrators engage in study groups.

In all cases, it is important to develop a common understanding about what is meant by specific literacy terms, which may be unfamiliar or may have a specialized meaning or may be used inconsistently in the field. For example, in this book, we refer to *literacy coaches* as those teachers who work primarily with other teachers and who do not have a student assignment, and *reading specialists* as teachers who work in intervention classes with students. But in some publications, these terms are used interchangeably. (To clarify the meaning of terms and to provide the basis for a common understanding, a glossary of literacy terms appears in Appendix B.)

Whatever the vehicles used, learning about literacy is the necessary first step to developing and implementing a literacy improvement effort in a middle or high school. And expertise in literacy is most beneficial when held collectively by the entire school community. (See Appendix D for a list of resources for further learning and Appendix E for a selected set of research reviews that informed our thinking as we developed the Leadership Model for Improving Adolescent Literacy.)

But leaders should beware—collective knowledge about literacy is not enough. The gap between knowledge and practice must be bridged. Therefore, it is important for school and district leaders to establish expectations and to provide the necessary follow-up in classrooms to implement effective instructional practices. (See Appendix C for a set of practical tools for leaders: a Teacher Knowledge Inventory, a Classroom Observation Guide, and a Literacy Assessment Review Tool.)

Creating a Vision

Principals often ask us, "What does a literacy-rich school look like? How is it different from what is going on at our school?" It is difficult to develop a vision without having some sense of the goal. This entire book is about turning a vision into a reality—creating a literacy-rich middle or high school that successfully develops the academic literacy habits and skills of all students. Reading through the book, reflecting upon how the descriptions of a literacy-rich school resemble or do not resemble schools with which leaders are familiar, and discussing the ideas with colleagues will help the vision become more real. Leaders will also come to understand how these components might be implemented at their school.

Another activity that leaders can do is to facilitate a discussion with faculty around what their school would look like if the literacy initiative were successful. What would students be doing? What would teachers be doing? What would the environment be like? The responses can be compiled and used as a guide for action and a litmus test for progress.

Can a schoolwide focus on literacy *really* make a difference? In his book *Results Now*, Mike Schmoker (2006) makes a cogent, powerful case for focusing on literacy as a lever for school improvement. He discusses the power of "generous amounts of close purposeful reading, rereading, writing, and talking" as the essence of authentic literacy:

These simple activities are the foundation for a trained, powerful mind—and a promising future. They are the way up and out—of boredom, poverty, and intellectual inadequacy. And they're the ticket to ensuring that record numbers of minority and disadvantaged youngsters attend and graduate from college. (p. 53)

Consider the following fictional vignette. Like others throughout the book (including four in Appendix A), it is a composite based on our experience, not a case study. But reading it may provide a sense of what we mean by a school that is systemically developing student literacy; it may inspire you to action. Of course, it is only one description of how a successful literacy improvement effort might look. Another school might be very different. This vignette is based on a high school. A middle school vignette can be found in Appendix A. The journey is not about copying what someone else is doing but about enacting a vision that achieves the goal of motivating and engaging students to improve their reading and writing proficiency, provides teachers with the knowledge and support to provide quality literacy instruction as part of content-area teaching and learning, and, therefore, raises student achievement.

Walking into Liberty High School gives one the impression that this is an unusual place. A TV monitor in the hall is running school announcements: activities scheduled for tonight include meetings of the speech club and of the editors of the literary magazine, a play rehearsal, and various sports team practices; a poetry jam will be held on Friday; and the words of the week are nefarious, curmudgeon, draconian, viscosity, *and* definitive. *Student artwork is prominently displayed, and various contraptions are set up on a table in the foyer—a sign says they are data collection instruments being used as part of a science inquiry into the building's environment. A student almost runs you over as he delivers the weekly school paper to people in the office; after apologizing, he offers you a copy.*

You notice that the newspaper, as well as all of the signs in the office, is in English and Spanish; more than 40 percent of Liberty students speak Spanish at home. The principal greets you and says that today is "just an ordinary day—you may not see anything special in terms of literacy," but you are welcome to look around and come back and talk with him after the tour.

After you get your visitor's pass, two students appear and announce that they are your tour guides. You start off with them down the hall to the history wing. The topic of study in every classroom is obvious from the words on the word wall, displays of student work, or discussions taking place. Every classroom has "bell work" posted on the board—a quick-write or something to read. In one or two classrooms, a teacher is at the front of the room explaining something, but in the other eight classrooms, it is sometimes difficult to find the teacher. Classrooms look well stocked with theme-related books at a variety of reading levels. Students are reading, writing, discussing, or working on the computer alone or in pairs. You ask students what they are doing, and the answer varies:

> *We are working on our research project on the economic costs of malnutrition.*
> *We have to come up with a response to the problematic situation the teacher gave us on taking sides in the Revolutionary War.*
> *We are learning our part of the chapter so we can do a jigsaw.*
> *We are comparing our answers on last night's anticipation guide for the reading we did.*
> *We are practicing our Renaissance character monologues.*

You move on to the English wing of the building, where you find an equally diverse array of activities: students are working in small groups on a Romeo and Juliet Web quest requiring them to rewrite a scene in contemporary language and a specific style, doing reciprocal teaching with a section of The Grapes of Wrath, *conducting peer reviews of essays, working in pairs to code parts of* Fever, *comparing and contrasting the film version of* The Joy Luck Club *with the novel. In another room, students are doing "book commercials" that the audience rates using a rubric. Student writing is posted everywhere.*

You assume that in the math classrooms things will be more staid, but you are wrong. In one geometry class students are reading and discussing a section of Flatland; *in another they are demonstrating to the class how they solved problems using Geometer's Sketchpad; in a third classroom they are completing a lab on finding the volume of irregularly shaped objects such as bananas. In one algebra class, students are reading and coding the text in pairs; in another, they are working together to develop problems that will be included on an upcoming test. Every classroom has a word wall; triple-entry vocabulary journals are evident on many students' desks. In an Algebra II class the teacher is handing back work to the students; a closer look reveals that stapled to each student's written description of how to solve the problem is a problem-solving rubric with indications of how the student and the teacher rated the problem on each dimension: clarity, mathematical accuracy, logic and coherence, and use of mathematical vocabulary. The teacher mentions that using the problem-solving rubric is new for him this year, but he cannot believe how well it is working and how much better problem write-ups are getting.*

In the science wing, even more is going on. In one class, the small-engine repair teacher and the physics teacher are coteaching; later you see the students' projects in the vocational wing of the building. In another class, students are on their way out to collect more data on stream pollution; in a third, students are using a computer-modeling program to develop a theory in genetics class. Students are working in groups to create summaries of articles related to aspects of habitat and biodiversity, working in pairs to fill out a semantic feature analysis on characteristics of diseases, or working on their own to write persuasive essays about the pros and cons of genetically altered foods. Words, books, and discussion are evident everywhere. The voices are those of the students, not the teacher, and just about everyone seems to be on task.

When it is time for schoolwide sustained silent reading, everyone in the building pauses. Secretarial staff, custodial staff, educational technicians, students, teachers, and administrators relax and read for 20 minutes. Many students eagerly read the new issue of the school newspaper. Some wear headphones. Your guides apologize and explain that you need to stop the tour and read. You enter a classroom and select a paperback from a rack—you do not want to be the only person not reading!

After 20 minutes, you notice a low hum. Your guides mention that after the reading period, people talk about what they are reading—what it made them think about, if they recommend the book, and so forth. As you continue your tour, you notice book lists with ratings on every classroom door. You pass two computer labs where students are using programs to improve their reading skills. Your guides point out several classes where one of the teachers of English language learners is coteaching with a content area teacher. You realize that almost half of the classes you observed had two teachers. When you ask about it, the guides say that special education teachers and the literacy coaches often coteach classes, and also that on many occasions two classes will combine—an art class and a social studies class, or a career and technical education (CTE) class and an English or a science class—and then both teachers will be in the classroom. The guides say that this is great because then students have more than one person to go to for help, and it "mixes it up a little" and makes class more interesting.

The emphasis on vocabulary, reading, and writing continues to be evident when you tour the unified arts and CTE classes. Students are reading and discussing articles, creating repair manuals, writing art critiques, completing nutrition logs, and writing reports on work samples. One of the teachers explains the emphasis on authentic tasks in the unified arts and CTE classes and tells about the many commissioned works being undertaken for the community. She adds that students read, write, and talk about everything. The focus is on quality, problem solving, and professional presentation. You observe that students seem to read and write more in the CTE class than in their English class. They all have to complete portfolios.

A student comes up to you and asks where you are visiting from and if you have formed a "definitive" opinion about the school. You stress that you are just visiting, not evaluating, and the student laughs and asks you to sign a card "certifying" that she used one of the "words of the week" appropriately in conversation. You are happy to sign. Now that she brings it to your *attention, you realize that you have heard the words* nefarious *and* viscosity *more than once today and that this was not coincidental.*

On the way back to the office, you pass a literacy coach working with three teachers on how they can use their word walls more actively. In the auditorium, students are practicing for a debate on whether coal and nuclear energy or alternative fuels are the route to energy self-sufficiency for the United States. In another room, a student is videoconferencing with his elementary school reading buddy—together they are reading and discussing Frog and Toad. *Your guides explain that some kind of literacy-related community service is expected of everyone in 10th grade. Choices include reading the newspaper to blind people, creating books on tape for the elementary school students, having an elementary reading buddy, tutoring in the after-school program, working on the school newspaper, translating and recording school newsletters for parents who do not speak English or who do not read, writing letters for nursing home residents, and translating health information at the local clinic for Spanish-only speakers.*

You return to the office, where your guides leave you to discuss what you observed with the principal. "Yeah, I tend to forget all we now have in place here," the principal says. "The scores are going up, but I think the energy you mention is even more important—kids know when they come here that they are going to have an active, interesting day learning, reading, writing, and thinking. Teachers are much more creative than they used to be, and the standards are higher. The literacy team is the most popular standing committee! The community is more supportive, too, because they see what the students can do. Students provide reading and translation services, fix cars and repair small engines, create graphic logos for businesses, create Web sites for local organizations, and conduct research on local issues.

"We had to get the intervention piece right, too. That took a while. At first we merely offered a reading course for students scoring below grade level. But we realized that one course was not enough. We then made sure that students with literacy learning needs were supported throughout the day. We began our summer reading camp three years ago. That did a lot to provide additional support for students who scored at the lowest levels.

"Of course, not all of this happened overnight. In fact, the students resisted at first. They were quite used to 'getting by.' These changes meant that they had to work more. We did a lot of discussing and visioning; we had a number of book discussion groups; we developed a literacy plan that we continue to monitor and revise; and we did a lot of teacher professional development. We worked it out with the district so that content-area teachers could get inservice points toward their recertification for the professional development they were doing.

"Our media center has been integral to the whole effort as well. Circulation is way up, and the librarian/media specialists have been wonderful about getting curriculum materials for

teachers to support units of study. The teachers see them as real resources—especially when it comes to issues of plagiarism and citing online sources.

"I had to be out there leading the charge. Of course, I was lucky that I have two good literacy coaches and that my district was supportive of the changes we wanted to make. The community was helpful, too. We're not a rich school—we needed help. You know, there are still a few people who are not really on board. But we hold them accountable, and members of my administrative team do regular literacy walk-throughs and check in with folks. Literacy support for students has become part of the culture of Liberty High School—part of the way we do things around here."

This book clarifies and describes the roles, responsibilities, and actions that leaders of middle schools and high schools can take to enact a vision similar to that depicted in the vignette. We do not envision literacy development as an "add-on." Rather, we discuss leadership roles and responsibilities through the lens of literacy to make it clear how literacy development relates to the areas for which school leaders are already held accountable. We developed the Leadership Model for Improving Adolescent Literacy through a review of the research, interviews with school leaders, careful examination of the roles of leaders in successful schoolwide literacy efforts, and ongoing discussions with school and district leaders. The model is based on the assumption—borne out by the efforts of many middle and high school leaders throughout the United States—that a well-designed, thoughtfully implemented literacy action plan can serve as a lever for school reform, and that the ultimate goal of literacy improvement is student motivation, engagement, and achievement.

Through our extensive work with school leaders, we noticed that effective leaders for literacy focused on certain types of tasks and worked in similar ways. We believed that if accurately captured, the work of those leaders could guide others attempting to support literacy development for adolescents. Further, it became clear that literacy action plans that yielded results had common components. We found, however, that knowing about these components did not necessarily mean that school leaders were confident in moving forward or that they understood their role in the process of literacy improvement.

Improving students' reading and writing ability is a task that requires the dedication, knowledge, and skills of the entire school community. It is tempting to buy a program here, sponsor an inservice activity there, or offer a special course in reading. These isolated attempts to improve literacy seldom make a lasting difference or sufficiently affect the literacy development of most students. Example after example shows that successful school leaders engage in a process that accesses the expertise of all and develops a sense of shared responsibility for ensuring that all students can read, write, and think proficiently. In schools that enact and sustain comprehensive and coordinated literacy programs, leaders at both the district and school levels play significant roles in leading for literacy improvement.

In the following overview of the Leadership Model for Improving Adolescent Literacy, we describe each component and indicate where the components are addressed in the book. The quotations included throughout the overview are from middle and high school principals and literacy coaches whom we interviewed as we were developing the model.

Overview of the Leadership Model for Improving Adolescent Literacy

Improving student reading and writing requires the active participation of teachers across the content areas, reading specialists, special education teachers, teachers of English language learners (ELLs), school and district administrators, parents and community members, and the students themselves. But it is school leaders who can best lead the charge for literacy improvement. To do this, leaders benefit from knowing what actions to take. The Leadership Model for Improving Adolescent Literacy provides this guidance.

The components of the model are synergistic and interdependent; they are separated here only to provide an initial understanding of what is involved in leading for literacy. For example, using data to make decisions cannot be separated from improving teaching and learning or from the interventions implemented for struggling readers and writers or from developing an effective literacy action plan.

The model, which appears on page 17, has both *goal* and *action* components. The three *goals* are

- *student motivation, engagement, and achievement* (center of the figure);
- *integrating literacy and learning* across content-area classrooms and through use of literacy interventions (inner band); and
- *sustaining literacy development* by including the school environment, parents and the community, and the district (outer band).

The five *action steps*, indicated by the points of the star in the figure, provide leaders with roles and responsibilities for leading a schoolwide literacy improvement effort. The *action steps* are

- *implement a literacy action plan,*
- *support teachers to improve instruction,*
- *use data to make decisions,*
- *build leadership capacity,* and
- *allocate resources.*

Leadership Model for Improving Adolescent Literacy

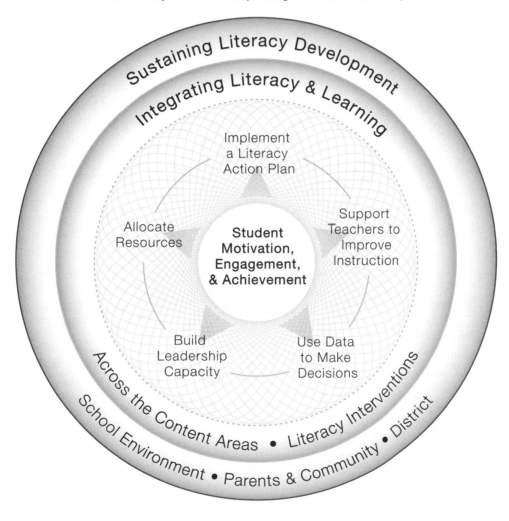

Student Motivation, Engagement, and Achievement (Chapter 1)

> When I visited classrooms, the students were not engaged in learning. Three or four hands were up, but for the most part, students were merely going through the motions to finish assignments. Where was the real learning?
>
> —Middle school literacy coach

Student Motivation, Engagement, and Achievement occupies the center of the graphic of the model. The ultimate goal of a schoolwide literacy improvement effort is increased student motivation, engagement, and achievement. If students are not motivated to actively engage with reading, writing, and thinking, they will not have the opportunity to improve their literacy habits and skills and they will not be successful as learners. While students are engaged, teachers have the opportunity to provide coaching and instruction, thus improving student competence and confidence. School leaders have an important obligation to understand the well-researched connections between motivation, engagement, and achievement. Equally important are understanding and carrying out the leadership roles and responsibilities required to ensure that all classroom contexts address what is known about successful adolescent literacy and learning. It is appropriate that students are in the center of the model. The entire model is focused upon their success.

Integrating Literacy and Learning (Chapters 2 and 3)

> I hear teachers say, "I don't want to teach reading," and I know they are just uncomfortable because they do not feel prepared. So I had to help teachers understand that literacy learning in our school was not optional.
>
> —Middle school principal

Integrating Literacy and Learning is the inner band on the graphic. This component concerns what happens in classrooms with teachers and students and is of paramount importance. All students need support to meet the demands of increasingly complex texts used in content areas. In addition, some students who struggle with reading and writing need extra time and instruction to develop their literacy skills.

Literacy development across the content areas. Much has been written about the effectiveness of literacy practices in content-area classrooms and the reciprocal connection between a focus on content-area literacy and standards-based instruction. Teachers who successfully integrate literacy into content-area instruction help students to use reading and writing on a daily basis to improve learning. Curricula and instruction that are connected to state standards and assessments require teachers to use literacy strategies regularly and purposefully to scaffold and differentiate instruction. It is essential for school leaders to establish and reinforce expectations that all teachers embed literacy development into content-area instruction. It is also critical that leaders provide effective professional development so that teachers can meet these expectations in ways that improve student learning while addressing state content standards.

Literacy interventions for struggling readers and writers. It has become clear that many students in middle and high schools need intensive support to strengthen their reading and writing abilities. Moreover, the literacy needs of students vary. School leaders need guidance in designing, implementing, and monitoring specific interventions to meet the needs of struggling readers and writers. Critical issues for intervention strategies include the identification of students in need of further support; the appropriate format, structure, content, and focus of remediation/acceleration options; qualified instructors; and appropriate assessment measures. Struggling readers and writers can only be helped when all of their teachers recognize and support them.

Sustaining Literacy Development (Chapter 4)

One of my teachers brought it to my attention that there wasn't one reference to our new literacy focus on our Web site. I started looking around and realized that we needed literacy to be more visible to parents, visitors, district personnel, and students.
—High school principal

Sustaining Literacy Development occupies the outer band on the graphic. School leaders benefit from understanding the implications and opportunities inherent in creating a literacy-rich environment, involving parents and community members, and garnering support from the school district.

School environments should reflect a focus on literacy. What is in the physical environment that communicates that a school is a reading/writing/thinking community? Schoolwide initiatives such as sustained silent reading time, a read-aloud program, daily book commercials, or a community read can enhance efforts and give a clear message to students that literacy is important. It is imperative that school structures and policies such as the master schedule support the literacy improvement effort. Aligning school structures and policies changes the very culture of the school to one that focuses on literacy improvement. The media center can play an important role as well.

Parents and community members are necessary partners in improving literacy; they can enable critical connections for students and bring authenticity to the importance of reading and writing proficiently. Most parents want to understand how they can help with literacy efforts for their child and for the school. In addition, community members can help by serving as positive adult role models, mentoring students, offering resources and apprenticeship opportunities, and promoting the literacy effort.

School districts play an essential role in the everyday management of schools. Beyond that function, however, school districts can provide instructional leadership support for principals and other school leaders, align and interpret the curriculum, support school-based coaching and mentoring, and collect and analyze data so that school personnel can use it to make instructional decisions. School districts can help or hinder the literacy improvement effort underway at a school, and school leaders need to be able to work with the district to advocate for site-based decisions and support.

Implement a Literacy Action Plan (Chapter 5)

> Developing a literacy plan seemed like just one more exercise until we got the whole faculty involved. Then it became the vehicle to examine how we actually do business in this school. It now guides the decisions we make every day.
>
> —Middle school literacy coach

Implement a Literacy Action Plan is the first action step, represented by the top point of the star on the graphic. After a review of the relevant data and discussions, a literacy team or other teacher-leader group writes a plan to meet the literacy needs of students. This plan is shared in teams or departments to seek faculty input. It includes goals and objectives, and it specifies who is responsible for what and outlines specific available resources required for implementation. Once the plan is developed, it can be evaluated, updated, and readjusted as programs and interventions are implemented. The literacy action plan is a strategic tool for leaders because it provides a customized blueprint for a schoolwide literacy improvement effort. The plan should guide decisions about instruction, curriculum, and resource allocation on a daily, semester, and annual basis.

Support Teachers to Improve Instruction (Chapter 6)

> My assistant principal and I are constantly monitoring what is going on in the classroom. My teachers were not used to being observed. In fact, one teacher said to me, "What are

you doing on the third floor?" I just said, "I'm here because that is where your classroom is . . . and I'll be back here again tomorrow."

—High school principal

Support Teachers to Improve Instruction is the second action step, located on the upper-right point of the star on the graphic. Students benefit from sustained engagement with purposeful reading, writing, and thinking tasks coupled with ongoing strategic assistance to develop the skills they need to become independent learners. School leaders should support and guide teachers as they strive to improve instruction and, ultimately, student learning. Professional learning communities, coaching, teacher professional development, and making the work public are strategies that school leaders can use. In addition, school leaders have the responsibility to ensure that best practices are actually implemented in classrooms; they can do this through classroom observations, literacy walk-throughs, teacher evaluation, and new teacher induction.

Use Data to Make Decisions (Chapter 7)

We analyzed the classroom assessments, and they were very elementary; but students have to take the state test at the high school level. We saw clearly that there was a mismatch between what students were expected to do in class and what they were expected to perform on the state test.

—Literacy team member

Use Data to Make Decisions is the third action step, represented by the lower-right point of the star on the graphic. School leaders at all levels benefit from understanding how different types of data can inform decision making. Teachers and administrators who analyze data to understand the literacy and learning needs of their students and use the data to make curricular decisions are generally more successful in implementing improvement efforts and sustaining them over time. School leaders benefit from knowing the different types of existing data available to them, other forms of data they can collect, and ways to analyze and use data to inform reading and writing instruction. Further, it is to their advantage to know how to connect data to the school's literacy goals and objectives to improve content-area learning and to identify students who need to be placed in intervention classes.

Build Leadership Capacity (Chapter 8)

> I realized when I started at this school that I needed instructional leaders to work side by side with me. So I chose the department chairs—they were the group I decided to invest in. I started with the people who were open to people coming into their classrooms.
>
> —High school principal

Build Leadership Capacity is the fourth action step, represented by the lower-left point of the star on the graphic. Principals need the support of other leaders in the school community, including the members of the literacy team, the literacy coach and reading specialist, the curriculum coordinator, the media specialist, the department chairs, and the teachers. A literacy team can be fundamental in developing a literacy action plan, and a literacy coach can play an essential role in building collective competence in literacy instruction by providing leadership and support. Successful schools make provisions for all teachers to develop expertise in literacy and to work in vertical as well as horizontal teams to guide and support quality teaching and learning. To sustain literacy improvement efforts over time, shared leadership is important.

Allocate Resources (Chapter 9)

> I knew we needed a literacy coach to move this effort forward, but the money just wasn't there. I took the problem to the literacy team, and we brainstormed ways of getting the support for teachers. By changing the schedule some, we were able to free up two teachers for one-half day each to act as mentor teachers.
>
> —Middle school principal

Allocate Resources is the fifth action step, represented by the upper-left point of the star on the graphic. Schools and districts will benefit from focusing the allocation of their limited resources in support of literacy improvement efforts and creatively apportioning time, space, personnel, support for professional development, materials, technology, and funding.

Time and space for collaboration and reflective dialogue are essential for teachers and students. A schedule that gives students extended time for literacy-connected learning every day is necessary for them to develop reading and writing fluency, vocabulary, and skills in strategic reading and comprehension.

Personnel such as the media specialist, reading specialists, and literacy coaches obviously play key roles in implementing the literacy plan. However, it is important that the school principal be at the center of the efforts to improve literacy.

Professional development, including time for teachers and administrators to learn about, reflect on, and implement best practices, is essential. All educators involved in the effort can learn the process and components of literacy learning and how to modify instruction to support literacy and learning in their classrooms.

Materials that students can and want to read have to be available to students both in the media center and in classroom libraries. Students should be encouraged to read a wide variety of texts (narratives, expository works, poetry, magazines, newspapers, and electronic text).

Technology such as software packages, the Internet, and media tools can be an invaluable tool for literacy and learning.

Funding is essential in an effort to improve literacy in terms of books and reading materials, test protocols, software, professional development, and, perhaps, additional teaching or resource staff. School leaders can list the goals and objectives in the school literacy plan in order of priority and search the budget for ways to direct funding toward literacy efforts.

Our Purpose

Through this book, we hope to facilitate the work of school and district leaders to help *all* students read and write at high levels and to do so using a wide variety of texts. We believe that *all* students in grades 6 through 12 need ongoing literacy support—those who struggle, those who read on grade level, those whose academic skills are strong, those for whom English is not their first language, those who have special learning needs, and those who feel unmotivated and disenfranchised. Although some of the approaches, types of programs, and support for each of these groups of learners may vary, the essentials of what school leaders need to know and be able to do to facilitate their growth and success do not change. Young and older adolescents (approximately ages 11 through 19) attend school in a variety of settings, including traditional elementary, middle, or high schools; magnet schools; career and technical education centers; and special needs centers. We hope to help the leaders in all of these settings to see literacy support as central to, not peripheral to, students' academic success. Literacy is not something to add to an already overcrowded plate; literacy **is** the plate.

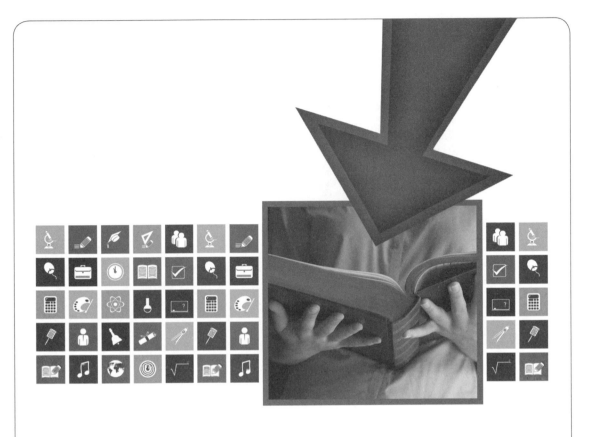

⭐ PART 1:
GOALS

1 Student Motivation, Engagement, and Achievement

Why is this component important? Becoming skilled readers, writers, speakers, listeners, and thinkers requires ample opportunity for practice, authentic reasons for communicating, and effective instructional support. To achieve competence in literacy, students must be motivated to engage with literacy tasks and to improve their proficiency as readers and writers. Instruction and practice then provide the coaching and feedback necessary to gain competence. Increased competence inspires continued motivation to engage. This cycle supports improved student achievement. The role of school leaders is to ensure that this cycle of engagement and instruction is provided by all teachers to all students.

Literacy is a big part of the everyday world of adolescents. They pass notes, read e-mail, write in journals, share stories, study the driver's manual, decipher train schedules, search the Web, send instant messages to one another, read reviews of video games, discuss movies, post blogs, participate in poetry jams, read magazines and novels, and so much more. Yet many middle and high school teachers and administrators lament that students just do not read and write anymore, often blaming today's TV and video game culture.

We maintain that many, perhaps most, teenagers are actually highly motivated readers and writers—just not in school. For school leaders who want to improve the academic literacy skills of students so that they will be more successful in school, this situation poses a challenge. Addressing this challenge is the key to a literacy improvement initiative. Helpful questions for school leaders to ask include the following:

• What evidence do we have of students' out-of-school literacy skills that we can build upon to encourage completion of reading and writing assignments in school?

• What motivates and engages students to read and write, and how can we include these types of opportunities throughout the school day and across the content areas?

• What kinds of coaching, instruction, and practice develop proficiency in reading and writing, and how can leaders support teachers to provide these?

Many researchers have explored the richness, competence, and depth of adolescents' out-of-school literacies (see for example, Alvermann, 2003, 2004; Lee, 2005; Smith & Wilhelm, 2002). The motivation for students to read and write outside of school seems to be threefold: (1) the topic needs to be something they feel is important to communicate about; (2) the topic needs to be something they feel strongly about or are interested in; or (3) the reading or writing needs to take place when they want to do it, or "just in time." Add to this a feeling of competence with the language, topic, or genre and multiple authentic opportunities for feedback and practice. These conditions produce situations in which adolescents are highly engaged with reading and writing.

Consider, for example, this instant message (IM) conversation between two teens who rarely read or write in school. Note the participants' high level of fluency with a code that many adults do not understand:

JZ: what's the 411 on tonight
LilK: we r abt2 hit the mall
JZ: which 1
LilK: TM

JZ: now?
LilK: yeah—going 2 get som p-za n then p/u a movie. u coming?
JZ: may-b. which movie?
LilK: dky—there r a few dope ones. what do you want 2 c
JZ: idk
LilK: what about wolfcreek
JZ: str8 J y? that what you want
LilK: j/c
JZ: what time? Go alap
LilK: Y
JZ: bcoz got 2 do some family stuff. hit my numbers b4 u go
LilK: a-rite
JZ: g2g
LilK: k
JZ: cul8r
LilK: c ya

If adolescents have reading and writing skills as we claim, why is it so difficult to get many of them to read a chapter in the history text or finish a short story in a literature anthology? Several issues are at play. First, out-of-school literacy skills may not be adequate for, or easily transferable to, academic reading and writing tasks. Second, many teachers do not build upon or bridge from out-of-school literacies to develop academic literacy skills because they may assume that because students *will not* read and write that they *cannot*. Third, most academic reading and writing assignments are not particularly motivating or engaging. And fourth, many middle and high school teachers do not have the expertise to provide reading and writing instruction in the content areas.

Many students approach assignments as something to get through without understanding the relevance of those assignments to their lives. Many try to avoid assigned reading because for them reading is an unpleasant, arduous, and unrewarding task; for some middle and high school students, their decoding and basic fluency skills are too limited to read grade-level textbooks. For far more students, the content of the textbook, article, or trade book is too difficult or too irrelevant to their experience, and encountering the information on the page is not sufficient for understanding. These students need to talk, write, and connect the content to what they already know to make sense of the material on the page. Other students do not see the relevance of the assigned reading to their lives and are not interested in putting forth the effort to complete the task. Often, however, many of these same students are able to persevere with difficult

reading if they are interested in the subject at hand and if they get appropriate help—
that is, if they can be motivated and supported to *engage* with the task.

Engagement with learning is essential, because it is engagement that leads to
sustained interaction and practice. Coaching, instruction, and feedback become critical
to ensure that students develop good habits and increase their proficiency. Increased
competence typically leads to motivation to engage further, generating a cycle of
engagement and developing competence that supports improved student achievement.

In the Leadership Model for Improving Adolescent Literacy, the interconnected
elements of *Student Motivation, Engagement, and Achievement* make up the central goal
of a schoolwide literacy improvement effort and are represented as the center circle on
the graphic that depicts the model. In this chapter, we describe the well-researched
connections between motivation, engagement, and achievement. Then we present
strategies for motivating students to engage with literacy tasks, followed by a discussion
of how engagement is connected to development of proficiency and what leaders
can do to promote student motivation, engagement, and achievement. Two vignettes
illustrate aspects of motivation and engagement, first through relationship building, then
through instructional context. In both, the classroom itself is used as an intervention
to get disengaged students motivated and involved in reading and writing for authentic
purposes. We conclude the chapter with key messages.

Why Motivation and Engagement Are Important

Until recently, most middle and high schools in the United States have not included a
focus on improving academic literacy skills—reading, writing, speaking, listening, and
thinking—as a primary educational role. People have largely assumed that students
are supposed to arrive in middle and high schools with adequate reading and writing
skills that they can then apply to assignments involving increasingly complex reading
and writing tasks. If, by chance, students do not arrive with these skills, educators
sometimes prescribe remediation. More often, students are able to get through classes
without reading and writing much at all. Well-meaning teachers may focus on alternate
methods—showing and telling as opposed to reading and writing—to ensure that
students are "fed" the content and not "penalized" for having low literacy skills. The
result is that the students with the weakest skills often get the least amount of practice.

Other teachers assign reading and writing tasks and give low or failing marks to
students who do not complete the assignments, assuming that motivation, not ability,

determines if the work is turned in. The mindset of many teachers and administrators is that if students do not have the requisite reading and writing skills by middle or high school, it is simply too late. A number of educators speculate that some students just do not like to read and write—"that's just the way it is." Additionally, many middle and high school teachers do not know how to provide explicit reading and writing instruction. Specific literacy instruction, as part of content-area learning, tutoring services, learning centers, or study skill classes, has been virtually unknown in many middle and high schools.

For students with poor academic literacy skills, this lack of embedded and explicit literacy support results in a downward spiral that can lead to academic failure. It is especially important to motivate students who arrive in middle and high school classrooms with a history of failure as readers or writers. People are understandably reluctant to persist at behaviors that they do not enjoy or that make them feel incompetent—adolescents even more so. Adolescents with poor literacy skills will sometimes go to great lengths to hide their deficiency; some of them devote considerable energy to "passing" or to distracting attention from their struggles, and the effort required is a major reason why many drop out of school.

Yet discussions with teens who are struggling readers and writers do not suggest convictions such as "we are proud of not being able to read and write well" and "we should be left alone to reap the lifelong consequences of leaving school with inadequate literacy skills to face the workplace and the responsibilities of citizenship." Many of these students understand that poor literacy skills place them at a distinct disadvantage economically, personally, vocationally, and politically. They want to be better readers and writers, but in addition to their weak literacy skills, other serious barriers interfere, such as

- minimal and often inappropriate help,
- alienation from uncomfortable school environments and curricula that seem irrelevant to their lives, and
- unreceptive environments for admitting the level of vulnerability they feel.

Motivation and engagement do not constitute a "warm and fuzzy" extra component of efforts to improve literacy. These interrelated elements are a primary vehicle for improving literacy. Until middle and high school educators work strenuously to address all of the barriers, and thereby motivate students to become engaged with literacy and learning, in the words of one student we interviewed, "I can tell you it just ain't gonna happen, you see what I'm sayin'?"

The Connection Between Motivation, Engagement, and Achievement

By the time students reach middle and high school, many of them have a view of themselves as people who do not read and write, at least in school. It is often difficult for teachers to know if middle school and high school students *cannot* or *will not* do the assignments; often all they know is that students *do not* do them. Herein lies the challenge for teachers and administrators: how to *motivate* middle and high school students to read and write so that they *engage* in literacy tasks and are willing to accept instruction and take advantage of opportunities to practice and accept feedback, thereby improving their academic literacy skills that will, in turn, improve their content-area learning and *achievement*.

This is not an either/or proposition. Instruction without attention to motivation is useless, especially in the case of students who are reluctant to read and write in the first place. As Kamil (2003) points out, "Motivation and engagement are critical for adolescent readers. If students are not motivated to read, research shows that they will simply not benefit from reading instruction" (p. 8). In other words, adolescents will take on the task of learning how to read (or write) better only if they have sufficiently compelling reasons for doing so.

Because motivation leads to engagement, motivation is where teachers need to begin. Reading and writing, just like anything else, require an investment by the learner to improve. As humans, we are motivated to engage when we are interested or have real purpose for doing so. So motivation to engage is the first step on the road to improving literacy habits and skills. Understanding adolescents' needs for choice, autonomy, purpose, voice, competence, encouragement, and acceptance can provide insight into some of the conditions needed to get students involved with academic literacy tasks. Most successful teachers of adolescents understand that meeting these needs is important when developing good working relationships with their students. However, many teachers have not thought of these needs in relation to their potential consequences for literacy development, that is, to what extent they meet these needs in the classroom through the academic literacy tasks they assign and the literacy expectations they have for students.

Motivating students is important—without it, teachers have no point of entry. But it is *engagement* that is critical, because the level of engagement over time is the vehicle through which classroom instruction influences student outcomes. For example, engagement with reading is directly related to reading achievement (Guthrie, 2001; Guthrie & Wigfield, 2000). Engagement—with sports, hobbies, work, or reading—results in opportunities to practice. Practice provides the opportunity to build skills and gain confidence.

However, practicing without feedback and coaching often leads to poor habits. Coaching—or, in this case, explicit teaching—helps refine practice, generates feedback, creates structured exercises targeted to specific needs, and provides encouragement and direction through a partnership with the learner. Note that more modeling, structure, and encouragement are often needed to engage students who are motivated to begin but who have weaker skills and therefore may not have the ability or stamina to complete tasks on their own.

Sustained engagement, therefore, often depends on good instruction. Good instruction develops and refines important literacy habits and skills such as the abilities to read strategically, to communicate clearly in writing or during a presentation, and to think critically about content. Gaining these improved skills leads to increased confidence and competence. Greater confidence motivates students to engage with and successfully complete increasingly complex content-area reading and writing tasks, and this positive experience leads to improved student learning and achievement.

Thus, teachers have two primary issues to contend with when trying to improve the literacy skills of unmotivated struggling readers and writers: (1) getting them to engage with academic literacy tasks, and (2) teaching them how to complete academic literacy tasks successfully. Proficiency is developed through a cycle of engagement and instruction (Guthrie & Wigfield, 1997; Roe, 2001). Figure 1.1 shows a Literacy Engagement and Instruction Cycle that exemplifies the interrelatedness of teaching and learning within the context of literacy.

This cycle represents the learning conditions and support required for literacy learning to take place. Teachers and administrators who understand what this cycle looks like within the content-focused classroom can support the activation and maintenance of the cycle for all students. The vignettes in the next two sections of this chapter illustrate how teachers can make this happen and what types of learning environments are effective for motivating students to engage with academic literacy tasks. For leaders, the challenge is how to support teachers to develop these types of classroom experiences and contexts so that they become typical practice, rather than the exception.

1.1 **The Literacy Engagement and Instruction Cycle**

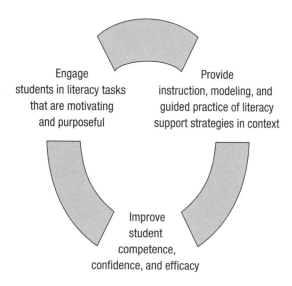

Engage
students in literacy tasks
that are motivating
and purposeful

Provide
instruction, modeling, and
guided practice of literacy
support strategies in context

Improve
student
competence,
confidence, and efficacy

Source: From *The Literacy Engagement and Instruction Cycle,* by J. Meltzer, 2006. Copyright 2006, Public Consulting Group, Inc. Reprinted with permission.

Breaking the Cycle of Failure

Breaking the cycle of failure for struggling readers and writers and engaging all students to participate actively in their own literacy development requires the use of classroom environments themselves as interventions. In some cases, it is the classroom culture that prompts or supports reluctant readers and writers to *want* to engage with literacy tasks, resulting in their being more open to instruction. Such classroom environments provide motivation to read, multiple opportunities and authentic reasons to engage with text, and safe ways to participate, take risks, and make mistakes. In these classrooms, students feel that the teacher really cares about them and their learning. The following vignette illustrates how this type of classroom context worked to encourage the literacy and learning of one student.

Carly arrived at high school reading at the 5th-grade level. During middle school, she got involved with a rough crowd that did not care much about doing schoolwork, and figured that no one cared much anyway, so why should she try? She used to like books about real people and stories that the teachers in elementary school read aloud. In elementary school, she had been a pretty good student.

During the first week of 9th grade, Carly's English teacher told her that she would like Carly to join the mentoring club. Carly told her, "No disrespect, but I don't think so." The teacher, Ms. Warren, persisted. Furthermore, she read all of Carly's papers, checked in with her daily, and had a frank talk with Carly about how she had a lot of potential, was very smart, and needed to get her reading and writing up to speed.

The books and short readings that Ms. Warren assigned in English were interesting and relevant to Carly, describing real events and people with dilemmas, but they were hard for her to read. Students in Ms. Warren's class were encouraged to share their opinions and ideas—but they always had to back them up with what they had read in the text. Ms. Warren taught her students multiple strategies for approaching different types of texts and always connected what they were reading to important themes in students' lives—power, cheating, love, violence. Carly tried the strategies and found they helped a lot.

Carly began to work hard—but just in that one class. She agreed to join the mentoring club because Ms. Warren just wore her down and kept asking her again and again. To her surprise, Carly found she loved tutoring younger students, and the experience made her work harder on her own reading and writing skills so she could be a good role model for Tyanna, the 4th grader she met with after school. Carly's attendance improved because when she skipped school, both Ms. Warren and Tyanna got on her back about it. She started working harder on her papers because Ms. Warren commented on them and scheduled time to meet with her one on-one to revise them. She asked Carly questions about her intent as though she were a real author. Later Carly admitted, "At the beginning I didn't think about what I was writing; I just wrote something down to turn in. But then I started thinking more about it." Carly also liked that Ms. Warren always gave students a choice of what to write about.

Midway through the year, Ms. Warren told Carly that she had a lot to say and suggested that she submit one particular essay to the school literary magazine, The Mag. Carly balked, but Ms. Warren submitted it anyway and it was accepted. Kids whom Carly did not even know came up to her and commented on how much they liked it. When she was asked to be on the editing committee for The Mag, she was surprised. She started to think that maybe she wasn't so stupid after all and went to the Learning Center for help with algebra. Her grades started to improve.

The following year, when she was asked what made the difference for her, Carly responded immediately: "It was Ms. Warren, Tyanna, and that darn piece she [Ms. Warren] submitted to The Mag. Kind of a combination. I'm still not so good at math. I have trouble sometimes reading my history book, and I hate biology—it's gross. But now I know that I am smart and that what I do matters and that I am just shooting myself in the foot if I don't try. I never thought about college before, but now I think I want to go."

Middle and high school leaders can reverse the downward spiral of failure many students experience by creating a literacy-rich environment throughout the school (see Chapter 4 for suggestions), establishing classroom environments as described in this vignette as the norm, and expecting all content-area teachers to provide literacy instruction in the content areas. Although Ms. Warren was apparently well versed in strategies for improving reading and writing, most content-area teachers, including many English teachers, are not. School leaders can support teacher learning about content-area literacy instruction through frequent, high-quality, job-embedded professional development and by providing opportunities for strategy sharing, feedback, and coaching. Content-area teachers must accept the challenge of integrating literacy and learning for their students.

Likewise, students cannot be expected to develop skills when the contexts for engagement and support for instruction are not in place. As described in the vignette, Carly was unengaged in school and not willing, at first, to participate in her own literacy development. She needed to see that someone cared, needed to have authentic and motivating reasons to read and write, and needed support to improve her literacy skills. None of this was likely to magically happen just because the educators in the school system announced that they believe in high standards for all students. But Ms. Warren knew how to create a classroom culture that supported literacy development. For Carly, as for many students, motivation and engagement led to increased literacy skills and higher self-esteem as a reader, writer, and learner, which led, in turn, to improved academic achievement.

Conditions for Engagement

The literature is full of examples of how the climate and conditions of the classroom really can make a difference in whether or not adolescents choose to engage in literacy tasks. We know that the learning environment and culture within each classroom play a part in supporting or undermining the chances that middle and high school students will participate in, and therefore benefit from, literacy development through the engagement-instruction cycle. This is the case with students at all literacy levels, including struggling readers and writers, English language learners, reluctant readers and writers, and *aliterate* students (those students who have adequate reading and writing skills but typically choose not to read or write). This understanding means it is well worth paying attention to the elements of classroom culture and environment to ensure that the conditions for literacy learning are in place. The following vignette describes students' engagement with a variety of literacy tasks when these were assigned within a motivating and supportive learning environment coupled with effective instruction.

The 8th grade students on the Dream Team at Lincoln Middle School were studying the topic of water quality. For this interdisciplinary unit, Kamal, Ayan, Mara, and Erika were put into a group. None of them really understood why watersheds were important when they began the project. The first assignment was to read and discuss a chapter in the science book. The terminology was hard, and they really did not understand what the chapter was about even after previewing it. But the science teacher provided strategies for learning the vocabulary and reading the text, so even though the group members were not inspired, they were able to complete the assignment.

Members of Kamal's group became more interested when they saw the results of a local survey of waste disposal habits of businesses and households. The results indicated that "really disgusting stuff" was being dumped near the city's main supply of drinking water. Students listened to a local scientist and a government official talk about watershed and water treatment issues—policies, pollution, protections, and current threats. Students then took a tour of the local water treatment plant. In social studies class they debated the pros and cons of bottled water in terms of environmental and equity issues. Based on additional research and responses to e-mail questions submitted to the speakers, the students created a physical model of the watershed and the water treatment facility and discussed possible areas of concern.

Each team of four identified key questions and went into the field to conduct tests of water and soil for the presence of pollutants. Then they learned to read government charts representing safe levels of these substances in the public water supply and technical documents describing the treatment plan for the city. Kamal's team carefully compared its test results with the information on the charts. What they found was disturbing. Levels of certain toxic substances and bacteria were high in the reservoir, but the water treatment facility was not addressing the problem by changing the treatment of the water, suggesting that the city's drinking water may not be safe. The teachers encouraged the students to report their findings using PowerPoint presentations. Students were given a specific format for presenting their questions, data, conclusions, and recommendations. Together with teachers, the students developed a rubric for each component of the presentations. The two presentations with the highest scores based on the rubric would be presented to the city council.

The members of Kamal's team worked hard on their presentation—harder than they had ever worked before. Kamal and his fellow group members checked and rechecked facts, read and reread articles, discussed and debated what the recommendations should be, and revised and edited their presentation. To make sure they understood what they were reading, the group took the articles to the Learning Center during lunch, where a teacher showed them some strategies for finding facts and taking notes. They used these strategies to tackle some tough text, including findings from a scientific report. The two students with limited English proficiency in the group, Ayan and Mara, asked the others repeatedly if what they wrote was "OK." Kamal, usually apathetic when it came to school, saw this issue as important—he had four younger brothers and sisters, and his family used tap water for cooking and drinking all the time; he wanted it to be safe. Erika, who was usually shy in class but who really liked music, made up a theme song about water safety to accompany their presentation.

When Kamal's team's presentation was chosen as one of the two to be shared at the city council meeting, their classmates were surprised. But Kamal and his teammates were not—this was an important opportunity to be heard. In their minds, this was much more important than the rest of the stuff they usually did at school—and they were willing to put in the time and effort to do it right. When a staff writer from the local newspaper attended the presentation and pressured the city to respond to the students' findings, the students knew their effort had been worthwhile.

In this vignette, several key factors relating to motivation inspired Kamal's team to engage with much more rigorous reading and writing than was typically the case. The students were working together on an issue they thought was important; they had choice and autonomy in the decisions about how to gather and present the information; and the presentation was for an authentic audience beyond the teacher or their peers. In Guthrie and Knowles's 2001 review of the empirical literature and their three-year study of K–12 classroom events that prompted sustained literacy interactions, they outline seven principles for promoting motivation to read:

- use of conceptual themes to guide inquiry,
- real-world interactions as springboards for further inquiry,
- encouragement of self-direction,
- the existence of a variety of texts,
- support for the use of cognitive strategies,
- social collaboration, and
- opportunities for self-expression.

Guthrie and Knowles see this network of variables as those "likely to spark and sustain the long-term motivation required for students to become full members in the world of engaged readers" (p. 173). Like many researchers and practitioners, Guthrie and Knowles stress the connections between the affective, social, and cognitive aspects of reading. Although this research was not solely focused on adolescents, all of these factors were in place during the water quality project described in the vignette, and they contributed greatly to the engagement and success of Kamal's group.

Strategies to Engage Students

One extensive review of the literature related to adolescent literacy (Meltzer, 2002; Meltzer & Hamann, 2004) generated three promising practices that teachers can use to motivate students, including English language learners, to read, discuss, and strengthen literacy skills across content areas:

- *making connections to students' lives*, thereby connecting background knowledge and life experiences to the texts to be read and produced;
- *creating safe and responsive classrooms* where students are acknowledged, have voice, and are given choices in learning tasks, reading assignments, and topics of inquiry that then strengthen their literacy skills; and
- *having students interact with text and with each other about text* in ways that stimulate questioning, predicting, visualizing, summarizing, and clarifying, preferably in the process of completing authentic tasks (tasks with a personal purpose or for a larger audience than the teacher).

Adolescent motivation in general is highly variable and is often dependent upon purpose and context, including relationships with peers, parents, teachers, and others. Therefore, a variety of motivational entry points need to be present to spur student engagement with literacy. Content-area classrooms that implement these three practices tend to be well stocked with books, magazines, technology resources, and a variety of other types of texts and materials. The next sections describe what each of these practices looks like in the classroom.

Making Connections to Students' Lives

In classrooms that promote motivation, teachers continually make connections between texts and the life experiences of students, films, other texts, previous school experiences,

and the topic at hand. Before assigning a piece of text to read, teachers provide students
with a purpose for reading, and they consciously activate students' prior knowledge.
Teachers use a variety of approaches—demonstration, film, field trips, picture books,
discussion—to build students' background knowledge and regularly ask students to
present similarities and contrasts between their own life experiences and what is in
the text. For example, students might participate in hands-on activities that they then
actively discuss and analyze before completing related reading and writing. Motivation
to read and write is enhanced by their new knowledge and experience and by the
discussion that precedes the reading and writing. Students feel as though their life
experiences are relevant and appreciated and that they are expected to use their own
and others' experiences to make sense of text and content. They view the content they
are learning as meaningful and connected, not isolated and foreign. Reading, discussing,
analyzing, and creating texts become primary formats for learning and expression.

Establishing a purpose for reading is also related to improved comprehension. When
students have a purpose for reading, have adequate background knowledge, and make
personal connections to what they are reading, they can persevere through challenging
text. Helping students to make connections is essential because student engagement is
determined by the personal purpose for reading, the particular texts being read, and the
links between the texts and students' personal circumstances. Helping students make
connections between their own goals and their choices of texts is also important for how
students develop the ability to use text to learn.

In the vignette, Kamal and his team were able to make connections between what
the speakers said, what the textbook said, what articles and reports revealed, and the
field trips they took. They had opportunities to discuss what each meant and allowed the
connections being made and the conclusions being drawn to spur further inquiry.

Creating Safe and Responsive Classrooms

In safe and responsive classrooms, teachers respond to adolescents' needs for choice
and flexibility and offer clear expectations and support for higher achievement. Teachers
are also responsive to differing cultural and socioeconomic perspectives, making their
appreciation of these perspectives clear through their facilitation of discussion, choices
of literature, structuring of assignments, and assessment strategies. Teachers who
successfully build upon the multiple literacies that students bring with them to the
classroom learn about these literacies and help students understand how the forms of

argumentation, categorization, and rhetoric that they commonly use out of school are similar to and different from those commonly encountered in academic texts.

Most important, teachers must understand that engagement feels like a high risk for many students. For those with low literacy self-esteem, the motivation to read and write depends on their judgments regarding whether teachers will give up on them or believe that they are worth the investment of time and encouragement. Teachers who persist in trying to reach resistant or reluctant learners continue to repeat invitations to join in the discussion, valuing small contributions and allowing students to participate at their own pace. Teachers must make clear to students that they care about their learning and their development of literacy skills, as well as their well-being as individuals. It is okay to make mistakes in these classrooms—the teacher acknowledges explicitly that learning is a continuum and that the role of students in a learning community is to improve their own skills and help others to improve theirs. When possible, teachers incorporate a choice of topic or format and, sometimes, goal setting and self-assessment into reading and writing assignments to accommodate varying student interests and learning styles and to engage students in developing their proficiency as readers and writers.

In the vignette, Kamal's group clearly felt that the classroom was a safe environment in which to learn, question, and present ideas. The team was encouraged to make choices, follow lines of inquiry, and use a variety of sources of information. The teacher validated a personal reason for pursuing the topic and encouraged various means of expression. Resources were provided and support was available to help the students as needed.

Having Students Interact with Text and with Each Other About Text

In classrooms that support motivation, students frequently work in small groups and pairs to analyze texts and to edit one another's writing assignments. Teachers structure learning experiences to help students develop deeper comprehension through discussion, to debate using text-based reasoning, and to understand various points of view. A collaborative learning experience within the context of a classroom environment that welcomes and supports diverse perspectives is the norm across the content areas. The multiple literacies that students bring to the classroom are viewed as a capacity and a resource. Teachers might encourage students to compare and contrast how a scene could be described using first language, home dialects or vernacular English, or IM script. Different ways of approaching and solving problems in math and science and writing are discussed and appreciated. When students share how situations similar to those being studied in social studies or read about in English would play out within their own cultural contexts, teachers value their contributions as additional insight into the topic at hand, not a distraction.

Kamal and his team members were able to discuss their project with one another from its inception through its presentation. They were able to discuss texts and to use their native languages when necessary to understand or explain to one another or to find out how to express something in English. Class activities encouraged discussion and debate and exploration of multiple, often conflicting, texts and points of view.

Focusing on Authentic Literacy Tasks

Authenticity is often the hidden key to motivating reluctant readers and writers to engage in academic literacy tasks. Yet in many middle and high school classrooms, authentic literacy tasks, if they occur at all, tend to be infrequent events. Moreover, many teachers consider *simulated* performance tasks to be authentic—a perspective students often do not share. Adolescents want their work to matter, and they want to conduct inquiry for reasons other than it being an assignment or an exercise. Authentic literacy tasks play into adolescents' needs to do things that are *real* and often prompt new effort for rehearsal, comprehension, discussion of content, planning, revision and editing tasks, summarizing, and other literacy skills because these activities are being carried out for purposes other than "just passing it in to the teacher." This phenomenon was evident in the vignette; the fact that water quality was a real issue that mattered to Kamal and his teammates led to much more rigorous effort than standard textbook reading assignments had elicited.

Other authentic literacy tasks include adolescents reading with younger students or creating books on tape or authoring books for them, designing Web sites, writing newspaper articles, and conducting and reporting upon inquiries that reflect real societal concerns (such as neighborhood crime, pollution, teen issues, or school or city policies that affect them or their families). These strategies often motivate and engage students to persist with challenging or extended reading or writing tasks (Alvermann, 2001).

Encouraging Critical Literacy

Helping students to analyze bias, perspective, audience, and the underlying assumptions and purpose of a piece of writing is an authentic approach for studying texts because it empowers students to understand that texts are not infallible. As vehicles for communicating the point of view of the author, texts are infused with subjectivity and based on assumptions. Understanding the larger political, historical, and economic contexts within which texts are produced allows students to comprehend why certain perspectives are valued above others, what assumptions underlie the author's words, whose ideas gain currency, and why this might be the case. Students can apply these understandings to their reading of an article about a scientific discovery, primary sources, history textbooks, novels, newspaper stories, and many other types of text. For many students, this approach to studying text is motivating and meaningful and leads to greater engagement with text. For Kamal and his teammates, understanding the texts so they knew if the water system was at risk was an important reason to persevere through challenging material.

Using Technology

The use of technology is often highly motivating to adolescents in terms of getting them to read and write more carefully and with more effort. The ability to revise on the computer, to add effects (color, graphics, sound) to presentations, and to code or mark text using word processing features such as highlighting motivates many students, especially when this capability is combined with an authentic purpose to read and write. Some students are much more likely to persevere with skill development if it is presented through a computer program or to complete an inquiry assignment if it is structured as a Web quest.

In the vignette, Kamal and his teammates used a PowerPoint presentation to successfully present their case. The technology was a useful and easy-to-use tool that helped communicate their ideas to their audience.

Connecting Engagement to Improved Proficiency

Although it may be easy to see how these learning conditions stimulate motivation and engagement, the connection to how they build literacy skills and improve literacy learning may be less clear. Obviously, willingness alone does not make one competent. As previously shown in the engagement-instruction cycle (Figure 1.1), when coupled with support and instruction, engagement with literacy tasks that one perceives are worth completing allows for guided practice. Because skillful coaching improves performance during practice, practice allows for improvement to take place.

But just as responsive classrooms do not happen by accident, neither does literacy learning for the vast majority of students. Most students need skillful literacy instruction within the context of content-area learning to support their ongoing literacy development, including explicit instruction in reading strategies and skills and how these can be applied to various genres and contexts. In Chapters 2 and 3, we present, in detail, the types of strategies and skills that reading and writing instruction should include as part of both content-area instruction and intensive interventions for struggling readers and writers.

In the following sections we describe three additional types of academic literacy habits and skills that the research stresses as being necessary for all students to develop to become independent learners: metacognitive skills, vocabulary development, and the ability to generate questions. Competence in each of these three skill areas supports students' abilities to learn content. Teachers' conscious development of each of the three, coupled with attention to motivation, will support engagement with academic literacy tasks and improve reading and writing proficiency. Students' academic success is dependent upon developing competence with each of these, whether or not they are used in conjunction with reading or writing.

Developing Metacognitive Skills

Metacognitive skills allow students to monitor their own comprehension effectively. That is, learners realize when they do not understand something or when something does not make sense. Students with good metacognitive skills can use a variety of "fix-up" strategies when reading or listening, like rereading, listing or visualizing, questioning the text, relating the content to personal background, or using text aids to assist with comprehension. Weaker readers can learn the metacognitive strategies that stronger readers use. These strategies help weaker readers improve reading comprehension and, therefore, improve their content area learning. Being able to use metacognitive strategies independently as needed to strengthen and deepen literacy and learning is the de facto definition of an "independent learner." This sense of having more control over one's reading and learning through the development of metacognitive skills typically motivates students to sustain engagement.

Developing Vocabulary

Vocabulary development is intertwined with reading comprehension and content-area learning. Students need a variety of strategies they can use to learn and remember the many technical terms, key concepts, and academic vocabulary that they encounter in the study of various disciplines. There is no evidence that "assign, define, and test," the most prevalent approach used in middle and high school classrooms for learning vocabulary, is effective in helping students to learn words. According to Allen (1999), teachers in each content area should implement purposeful vocabulary instruction to

- increase reading comprehension,
- develop knowledge of new concepts,
- improve range and specificity in writing,
- help students communicate more effectively, and
- develop deeper understanding of words and concepts with which students are only nominally familiar.

Struggling readers and writers and most ELL students also need purposeful attention to the study of words (root words, affixes) and the development of academic language (non-content-specific words found in printed directions, forms, textbooks, novels, and other publications). Throughout the literature, vocabulary development is stressed as a key component of literacy.

Generating Questions

Finally, students need to learn how to generate good questions. Questioning is effective for improving comprehension because it provides students with a purpose for reading, focuses attention on what must be learned, helps develop active thinking while reading, helps monitor comprehension, helps review content, and relates what is being learned to what is already known (Armbruster, Lehr, & Osborn, 2001). Having students generate their own questions about a text has also been shown to be an effective strategy for improving reading comprehension—questioning becomes a vehicle for connecting the text to their own prior knowledge.

Questioning is a part of several other learning strategies. For example, writing-to-learn strategies, written responses to higher-order-thinking questions, engagement in Socratic discussion, use of analytical graphic organizers, inquiry-based learning, and collaborative routines for text study all involve asking and answering questions, and all have been proven effective in improving literacy habits and skills, including reading comprehension. Developing metacognitive skills requires asking oneself if a particular text is making sense, and if not, why not. Activating prior knowledge, described in the literature as an essential way to connect students with text and improve reading comprehension and the ability to learn from text, requires asking questions. Many stages of the writing process, from choosing a topic to developing an outline, revising, and publishing, also require the ability to ask questions. Completing research is highly dependent on identifying key issues and framing good questions to guide inquiry. Again, the premise that students need to be able to ask effective questions is not one that is found in many middle and high school classrooms, where the focus is typically on answering questions asked by the teacher or the text.

Explicitly teaching students these literacy habits and skills and providing multiple opportunities to practice them across content areas will ensure that students develop competence in these three areas. For example, teachers can focus on vocabulary development with each unit of study, or teach how to complete a research paper and present research findings through a focus on questioning. As the engagement-instruction cycle (Figure 1.1, p. 34) illustrates, this increased competence will further motivate students to engage with reading and writing tasks and will lead to improved student achievement.

Connecting Learning to Adolescents' Needs, Interests, and Dispositions

Adolescents are not passive recipients of information who have few skills. They are, instead, actively curious young people with background knowledge and a wide range of literacy skills that they may or may not be using in school. Improving their skills involves gaining their participation. Sometimes teachers and administrators spend considerable energy fighting with adolescents instead of harnessing their abilities and skills in the service of improving their literacy and learning. To help adolescents improve their academic literacy habits and skills, teachers and administrators can build on needs, interests, and dispositions that adolescents have, such as those presented in Figure 1.2.

What Leaders Can Do

School leaders know that most academic learning in middle and high schools takes place within classrooms. Leaders who are aware of the options teachers have to promote student motivation and engagement with literacy tasks can ensure that these options are in place in every classroom. Principals can work with teachers to identify a vision for what classrooms where students are motivated to engage with literacy development would look like. What would teachers be doing? What would students be doing?

What would the classroom environment be like? Then teams of teachers can define what immediate steps they can take to move toward this vision. The vision can be reintroduced during the year to check on progress and remind teachers of this priority. When principals do walk-throughs or visit classrooms, their feedback to teachers might include references to aspects of the learning environment, assigned tasks, or instructional

1.2 Linking Instruction with Needs, Interests, and Dispositions	
Adolescents' Needs, Interests, and Dispositions	Possible Instructional Response
Need for control/autonomy	Provide choices in • Assignment topics • Assessment modes • Books to read • Order of completing work
Interest in technology/media	Use technology to support • Communication • Presentation • Research
Need to be heard	Provide authentic audiences, expectations, and opportunities for writing/speaking for an audience beyond the teacher
Disposition to debate	Plan many opportunities for • Debate • Text-based discussion • Opinion boards • Blogs • Letters to the editor • Student correction of content/format errors
Need to make a difference	Set up opportunities for • Reading to/tutoring others • Research into real issues • Apprenticeships • Creating informational Web sites • Writing articles for publication • Peer editing
Need to belong	Create a classroom culture and reinforce classroom norms that support the development of a community of readers, writers, and thinkers
Sense of accomplishment	Teach students how to participate in • Literacy goal setting • Progress monitoring • Use of rubrics • Collaborative teaming for completion of literacy tasks

support that appeared motivating to students. Principals should also provide feedback about how many students appeared to be actively engaged in learning so that teachers can monitor their progress in reaching and involving increasing numbers of students. Leaders can provide opportunities for teachers to share strategies for motivating and engaging different types of learners so these strategies are used more widely across classrooms.

School leaders also should think about the school environment in its entirety. How would visitors know that this is a school that values and encourages reading, writing, and thinking? Establishing a literacy-rich schoolwide culture that is focused on student motivation, engagement, and achievement will make it easier for teachers to feel supported to make changes, will reinforce key messages to students and parents about the importance of reading and writing, and will clarify to teachers that school leaders are willing to "walk the talk." (We present more ideas on what a schoolwide culture and environment look like in Chapter 4.)

A primary role of school leaders is to motivate teachers to engage in the professional development necessary for them to learn how to support the literacy development of their students more effectively. As long as teachers see a lack of engagement as "the students' fault," they will not be provoked to change their own classroom practices to focus on motivation and sustained engagement with reading, writing, and thinking. If they do not know strategies that support literacy in the content areas, they cannot be expected to incorporate them into classroom teaching and learning. School leaders need to motivate and engage teachers to make necessary changes in classroom learning environments and instruction through high-quality professional development, establishing an expectation that this will occur and providing support. (We describe strategies for providing the support that teachers need in Chapter 6.)

School leaders may want to survey students about their attitudes toward reading and writing and solicit students' suggestions on what types of classroom environments and support they would find helpful to their learning. Sometimes hearing what students say is motivating to them is helpful to teachers who do not understand the challenges of literacy development from the students' point of view.

Relevance, relationships, and rigor are the rallying cry of middle and high school reform efforts (Daggett, 2005). Through an unwavering focus on literacy improvement, all three can be achieved. School leaders need to understand the goal—student achievement—as well as the primary route to that goal—increased motivation and engagement of students and teachers, leading to improved teaching and learning and higher self-efficacy of teachers and learners. The end result will be greater student success.

Key Messages

This chapter discussed the critical relationship between student motivation, engagement, and achievement and how school leaders can use classroom environments and contexts as intervention tools, interrupting a cycle of failure. Some students arrive at middle or high school with the hard shells of resistant readers or writers, but, underneath, no student wants to fail. Enacting the engagement-instruction cycle is essential to ensuring that all students have a chance for success. Helping students to become active participants in their quests to become competent, confident readers, writers, speakers, and thinkers requires classroom contexts that motivate and engage students, coupled with explicit literacy instruction that supports the improvement of their skills. The following are the key messages from this chapter:

- A focus on motivation and engagement is the key to any effort to improve adolescent literacy habits and skills.
- Sustained engagement in reading and writing tasks coupled with effective instruction leads to improved learning.
- Three strong strategies for improving motivation and engagement are authentic tasks, critical literacy, and use of technology to support literacy development.
- Students' motivations to read and write are highly variable and dependent on purpose, perceived value, self-efficacy, interest, and context.
- Focusing on instruction without attention to motivation is not likely to be successful with adolescents.
- Classroom environments and teacher actions can sustain and encourage, or undermine, student motivation and engagement in academic literacy tasks. Three important instructional practices are having students make connections, creating safe and responsive classrooms, and having students regularly interact with text and with one another about text.
- Increasing students' competence through explicit literacy instruction within the context of a supportive learning environment will increase student engagement and improve student achievement.

Literacy is an integral part of adolescents' identities. Many struggling readers and writers have decided that improving their reading and writing skills is not worth the effort. Teachers may not know what to do when confronted with students who do not or will not read or write. When school leaders are aware of the connection between student motivation, engagement, and achievement, and know the strategies and practices that have been effective in breaking through students' resistance, they can support necessary changes in classroom environments, instructional practices, and school culture. Principals can support teachers' professional development, sponsor discussions among teachers about what they can do to infuse their content-area teaching with the effective practices mentioned in this chapter, and ensure that classroom environments and instruction include a strong focus on student motivation and engagement. Caring teachers, along with instructional and environmental supports, can go a long way to turning around a history of failure for many adolescent readers and writers.

2 | Integrating Literacy and Learning
Across the Content Areas

Why is this component important? To meet 21st-century literacy demands, students need to be proficient readers and writers of a variety of types of texts. All students deserve frequent opportunities to read and write and quality instruction as part of their learning of content. Teachers who provide explicit instruction and opportunities to practice content-specific reading and writing tasks help students become independent learners. It is the role of school leaders to ensure that this type of instruction and opportunity for guided practice occurs in every content area.

"An excellent teacher without a well-coordinated program can do only so much. In these situations, even the best of teachers can offer students only isolated moments of engrossed learning and rich experience in an otherwise disconnected series of classes" (Langer, 2002, p. 11). Langer's quotation speaks to the central message of this chapter: to reap maximum benefit from a literacy improvement effort, students must receive support in every classroom and from every teacher. This support is essential for students who struggle with reading and writing tasks, but it is important for average and strong readers as well.

The role of school leaders is to ensure that students experience regular, consistent, and high-quality instruction in content-area literacy. It is not enough to say that a school has some teachers who are "on the literacy bandwagon," some teams who are "on board," or one or two departments that "do a good job with literacy." What about all of the students who do not have those teachers to guide their learning? It is not equitable that some students get daily access to support in content-area literacy while others, just because of the quirks of the schedule, do not. It is likely that most schools have some content-area teachers who have attended workshops or conferences or taken courses and have committed to infusing literacy support into teaching and learning. It is equally likely that the vast majority of middle and high school teachers have not. This tends to result in a sort of "Swiss cheese" instruction in which some students encounter multiple teachers who focus on providing literacy support and extensive guided practice in reading and writing while other students may be in only one or two classes that provide this support during grades 6 through 12. This is not adequate, especially for struggling readers and writers, average readers and writers, and English language learners. School leaders have the responsibility to make sure this haphazard approach to literacy support does not happen.

Teachers and administrators, however, are often overwhelmed by the task of improving the literacy and learning of students. For one thing, many teachers and administrators are not convinced that content-area teachers actually need to provide this support. (We discuss this issue later in this section because it is crucial that the responsibility for literacy development not be delegated to a reading specialist or assumed to be addressed by the English department.) In addition, most middle and high school teachers and administrators lack the expertise in literacy to address the needs of their students. Some middle school teachers may have graduated from a generalist elementary education program, but most attended secondary teacher preparation programs that concentrate on a specific content area (English, social studies, math, science, art, music). Preparation for literacy instruction in these programs is often limited to one course on how to teach reading in the content areas, which is hardly sufficient to support the literacy development of students. In some cases, colleges waive even this single course. This situation creates a definite challenge when teachers and administrators face large percentages of students who cannot read and write on grade level, and it limits what teachers can do to support ongoing literacy development so that all students continue to improve their academic literacy habits and skills.

Literacy Across the Content Areas accounts for one-half of the component "Integrating Literacy and Learning" in the Leadership Model for Improving Adolescent Literacy, represented by the inside band of the model graphic. This chapter illustrates literacy learning and teaching with three vignettes—through the eyes of a student, a teacher, and a principal. We address the basic components of the literacy learning process along with examples of best instructional practices. We highlight the importance of two types of literacy knowledge: (1) conceptual knowledge about the reading, writing, and learning process; and (2) pedagogical knowledge about how to use literacy support strategies in the content-area classroom. Understanding why content-area teachers are essential to the effort and what content-area literacy support looks like is the first step toward supporting all teachers in this endeavor. The chapter includes a description of best practices in content-area literacy and concludes with key messages.

Why Content-Area Teachers Are Essential

Why do content-area teachers need to be the ones to provide the bulk of literacy support and development? Isn't that the responsibility of the reading specialist or the English/ language arts teacher? What is so different about reading and writing in different content areas that explicit instruction is required? If someone knows how to read and how to write, what more is needed? If school leaders are to make literacy across the content areas a priority—and expect everyone to buy in—then they need concrete answers to these questions. Quite simply, four reasons explain why content-area teachers are essential to a literacy improvement effort:

- content-area teachers know the content;
- content-area teachers know the reading, writing, speaking, and thinking demands of the content they teach;

- content-area teachers have the access and the opportunity; and
- content-area teachers collectively have the power to make a difference.

Knowledge of Content

The statement "content-area teachers know the content" sounds obvious. But it is critical for leaders to understand the connection between content area knowledge and content area literacy development. Deep knowledge of content is what helps teachers determine what concepts are important to teach, reinforce, connect with one another, and build upon. Knowing how a discipline is organized allows teachers to set teaching goals and objectives, present material in a variety of ways to make a point, and understand what is important to assess. Most content area teachers enjoy the subjects they teach and continue to learn about the content, and they model this enjoyment and ongoing love of learning for students. Good content knowledge allows a teacher to translate state standards and local curriculum goals to unit and lesson plans. Content-area teachers who know their discipline are able to choose and integrate literacy tasks and instruction that best support, not distract from, content area learning. For example, when choosing vocabulary development strategies, content-area teachers know the vocabulary that is most essential for students to learn within a given unit of study. When supporting students to interact with text through coding, teachers can select codes that help students think about the content most productively. When choosing graphic organizers for students to use to plan their writing, content area teachers can select those that support the types of thinking that they want students to perform in conjunction with the subject matter. When literacy instruction and content area instruction are blended in this way, students become stronger learners who are able to understand and retain more sophisticated content. Teachers can learn new literacy support strategies (discussed later in this chapter), but these are most effective when integrated skillfully into content area teaching and learning.

Knowledge of Reading, Writing, Speaking, and Thinking Demands

Content-area reading, writing, and presenting vary in terms of genre, formats and conventions, structures, and purposes of the different types of text in each field. Students need to learn how to read the different text structures of various genres differently and understand how these structures vary in terms of how connected ideas are presented. Then students need to be able to develop their ideas and present them verbally or in writing using these content-specific text structures, conventions, and formats. The skills and strategies students use to write a short story, to present a science project, to formulate a business plan, to draw conclusions from primary sources related to controversial issues in history, or to develop a geometric proof are quite different. Students need to know and be able to use a variety of generic and discipline-specific literacy strategies to plan, organize, revise, edit, and present a piece of writing or a presentation. Content-area teachers are the best ones to assist with this instruction because they know the content area reading and writing demands of their content area. For example, science students need to be able to read and evaluate journal articles, science textbooks, and Web sites. Business students need to be able to read business plans, trade magazines, and stock tables and reports. Math students need to be able to read word problems, graphs and charts, and math textbooks. English students need to be able to read short stories, novels, and reviews. Writing and presenting vary similarly across disciplines. A science fair project is a different sort of speaking opportunity than a debate on social issues, a dramatic monologue, a campaign speech, or a marketing presentation. Writing an analytical essay is quite different from writing an autobiographical essay, a letter to the editor, a manual, a description of an approach to solving a math problem, an art critique, a work order, or a lab report. Obviously content area teachers are in the best position to provide instruction in how to read, write, and speak in formats and genres specific to their content area.

Access and Opportunity

Teachers see their students on a regular basis, typically daily or every other day. From a scheduling standpoint, this makes content-area teachers the natural choice if a school leader is trying to increase the amount of reading and writing—and reading and writing instruction—that students experience. Learning skills and habits in context is very powerful, so it makes sense to teach and practice reading and writing skills within— not separate from—the context of content-area classroom teaching and learning. In addition, as we saw in the first vignette in Chapter 1, it is sometimes the relationship that a teacher has with students that motivates adolescents to improve their reading and writing proficiency. Content area teachers often have good relationships with students that could include support, encouragement, and instruction to engage students in improving their literacy skills.

Collective Power to Make a Difference

Students are in content-area classes during most of their time in school. Although one or two teachers doing their best might not make enough of a difference in developing the content-area reading and writing skills that all students need, if all teachers across all content areas are focused on literacy development, the cumulative effect can be powerful. If students have only one or two opportunities in their high school careers to do formal presentations or research papers, for example, it is unlikely that they will get proficient in these areas. If, however, students have opportunities to do these in two content-area classes every year, accompanied by instruction and modeling in how to create quality products, opportunities for practice and revision, and clear criteria for performance, that quadruples the amount of experience and instruction every student receives to develop these critical skills. If one 9th grade teacher provides instruction and modeling in strategic reading but none of the others do, it is unlikely that most of this teacher's students will become proficient at this skill. It is even more unlikely that these students will transfer these skills to their reading in other genres. But if these same students experience instruction in strategic reading from several teachers and are asked to apply it to a variety of types of text, it is far more likely that these students will actually practice these skills enough to internalize them and be able to transfer them to future reading. The Partnership for 21st Century Skills (2006) makes it clear that being able to learn through reading, writing, and thinking; to communicate clearly in speaking and writing; and to problem solve is essential if we intend to adequately prepare students to meet the literacy demands of the 21st century, as is being able to transfer those skills to learning new content or in new formats, including the use of new technologies.

Once school leaders are clear about why content-area teachers—and content-area literacy instruction—are so critical to a literacy improvement effort, it is easier to focus energy on ensuring that students get quality literacy instruction daily or weekly in all content areas. (Suggestions for how to mentor and support teachers and get teachers on board are presented in Chapters 6 and 8.)

What Proficient Readers Do

To be effective leaders of a schoolwide literacy improvement effort, school leaders need to understand and communicate to their teachers what constitutes quality content area literacy instruction. Therefore, it is important for leaders to understand what proficient readers and writers do and how this differs from what struggling readers and writers experience when assigned a reading or writing task. The next vignette describes how a proficient reader experienced her World History class. (For vignettes of quality literacy support in other content areas, see Appendix A.)

Alesha strolled into her social studies class still thinking about the poem they had just read in English class. She loved poetry and admired how Langston Hughes could say so much in just a few lines. The metaphor of stairs in "Mother to Son" was so compelling when he began the poem by saying that life for the mother "ain't been no crystal stair." Hughes described the mother's life with such harsh images: "boards torn up," "tacks," and even "splinters." Alesha thought that she would like to try to write a poem about her life using a powerful metaphor, but here she was in social studies—what was the topic for today?

On the board was written "The Importance of Pompeii"—oh! Why should she care about a city so far away? Where was Pompeii, anyway? Alesha thought they were starting a unit on Greek and Roman Culture. She assumed that they would study gods and goddesses—again— and wars, in which she did not have a lot of interest. But she liked Ms. Dean, so she opened her notebook and was willing to give her the benefit of the doubt. Maybe this wouldn't be as boring as she assumed.

Ms. Dean began the class with an activity that helped Alesha make predictions about why the city of Pompeii was important to what we know about early Roman culture. This activity helped Alesha understand this city and caused her to think of some new questions. Although she would rather be reading and writing poetry, she began reading the assigned pages in the textbook.

Alesha began her assignment by thinking about the type of text she was to read—a social studies passage, which is obviously read differently than a poem. Next, she flipped through the selection, noting that it was three pages long. The major headings were "Vesuvius Buries the City," "Lost for 16 Centuries," and "Unique Snapshot." She immediately started to imagine what life was like at that time and wondered what teenagers did for fun and what happened to Pompeii. She realized that she would have to remember a lot of information. Finally, she decided to try the two-column note-taking system with the three major headings on the left. She would write the details in the right column. At the top of the page, she wrote the question: What was the significance of Pompeii?

As she began reading, she understood that Pompeii was a typical city in AD 79, but it is unique because it was perfectly preserved after Vesuvius erupted. She wondered why the people did not escape when they felt the earth tremble. The pictures of people caught covered with ash were eerie. She wished the author had talked more about how people lived during that time.

What did they eat? What did they wear? She read that the city was covered with "the pyroclastic flow" from Vesuvius. She inferred that pyroclastic was the hot stuff that came out of a volcano because she knew pyro had something to do with fire.

At the end of class, Ms. Dean discussed the importance of Pompeii because of the well-preserved ruins and how it was a thriving port city in AD 79. Some tried to flee the city, and others seemed to think the danger from the volcano would pass, because they stayed in their homes. Alesha added this information to her notes. Then students were asked to get into small groups and use their notes to create a group summary of the material addressed in today's class, including what they heard from Ms. Dean and discussions with their classmates. In creating the summary with her classmates, Alesha was struck by how much one student knew about earthquakes and how another student was wondering what people would say about the culture and lifestyles of people today if their city were buried like Pompeii. Perhaps she would write a poem about Pompeii. Alesha decided that the theme for her poem would be "Catastrophe."

Alesha displayed impressive competence in this reading task. She understood that the literacy demands of English class were different from those associated with social studies. Although she would have preferred to continue to think about poetry, she switched strategies to read her social studies text. While she previewed the text, she demonstrated metacognitive skills by determining the most important ideas, and she reflected on her prior knowledge of early Roman history. She organized her thoughts for reading by using two-column notes. During her reading, she made inferences and generated questions centering on the important ideas. When she encountered a word whose meaning she did not know, she made a logical inference based on the context of the text. She summarized the main ideas of her reading and the subsequent class discussion through her notes and the group summary. Alesha displayed the characteristics of a good reader and writer (see Figure 2.1).

The Frustration of Struggling Readers

Few students display the reading and writing competencies of Alesha. In fact, more students are like Cody, who appears in the following vignette. Cody typically struggles with reading and writing tasks; he lacks prior knowledge to approach most content material, has limited content vocabulary, and expends great effort to stay motivated to complete assignments. These challenges make it hard for Cody to engage with the difficult content-area text he is often assigned to read. The vignette continues with a glimpse into how Cody experienced the same social studies class described earlier.

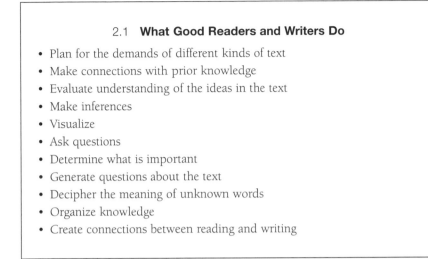

2.1 **What Good Readers and Writers Do**

- Plan for the demands of different kinds of text
- Make connections with prior knowledge
- Evaluate understanding of the ideas in the text
- Make inferences
- Visualize
- Ask questions
- Determine what is important
- Generate questions about the text
- Decipher the meaning of unknown words
- Organize knowledge
- Create connections between reading and writing

Cody sauntered into the classroom wishing he had a pass to skip class. He had done his homework but was pretty sure he would get a lousy grade on it because he really didn't get what the article was about. Ms. Dean was cool, though; she always helped him out when they had to read in class, and she was a fair grader. But she always made him read and write so much— and he just wasn't so great at that stuff. Oh, well; 80 minutes to lunch. Might as well open up the book—it might distract him from his growling stomach. At least they were talking about a volcano eruption today, which is better than all of the trade stuff they discussed yesterday.

The Literacy Learning Process

It is important for middle and high school educators to understand why students have difficulty with reading, writing, thinking, and presentation skills. In elementary schools, students receive instruction in how to read and write, typically within the context of a narrative text. But after the primary grades, many students receive little or no ongoing instruction to help them negotiate meaning with increasingly challenging expository texts. Students may have trouble reading progressively complex texts for many reasons. Often it is a combination of these reasons that thwarts students from becoming proficient readers and writers. Understanding the ways in which middle and high school students have difficulty with school-based literacy tasks is an essential first step for school leaders so that they can develop and implement a plan to meet the needs of students.

Some students did not learn to read well while in elementary school and may still have trouble with decoding, that is, they still may not have a large *sight vocabulary* (words they can recognize automatically when encountered in text), or they may not have a solid understanding of phonics so they are unable to read, let alone understand, anything beyond simple text. These students may also have avoided reading long enough to cause *low fluency* from a lack of practice, decoding skills, or general sight vocabulary. Fluent reading can be summarized as the accurate reading of connected text at a reasonable rate with appropriate intonation, pauses, and use of punctuation to make sense of the text. A lack of fluency means that a student's reading rate is too slow and laborious for the student to get much meaning out of longer or more difficult text. Such decoding and fluency problems cause some students simply not to be able to read the assigned texts. This picture describes a small but consistent percentage of students in middle and high schools (Curtis, 2002).

Torgesen and Hudson (2006) state that a fluent reader can maintain fluent reading for long periods of time, retains the skill after long periods of no practice, and can generalize across texts. They assert that a fluent reader is also not easily distracted and reads in an effortless, flowing manner. Some strategies to improve the fluency of adolescent readers include repeated readings of the same text, paired reading, listening to books on tape while reading, or making books on tape for younger readers related to the topic being studied. Torgesen and Hudson also stress the need for interventions to build sight vocabulary specifically through reading of words out of context to help older readers gain ground even more quickly. Improving students' reading fluency removes one barrier to reading comprehension.

A far greater number of students cannot effectively use the text to learn content, although they may have basic reading skills. This reflects a problem with *reading comprehension* and an inability to read critically, purposefully, or strategically. They may have difficulty comprehending the major points presented in the text or understanding how those points relate to each other or to their life experiences in general. Or, because of limited vocabulary and lack of reading strategies, they read all texts the same way, not getting beyond a level of literal comprehension. These students have difficulty making inferences, analyzing, or summarizing because their level of understanding of the assigned text is too partial. The strategies that are highlighted in this chapter can help these students develop as readers and writers.

Content-area literacy support should not be limited to struggling readers and writers; although their needs are most acute, the reality is that many students entering

9th grade reading on grade level lose ground through high school without consistent and purposeful content-area literacy support. Although above-average students headed for university classes may seem to be adequate readers and writers, many of these students end up taking remedial reading or writing classes at the postsecondary level (ACT, 2006b). One bright college freshman described her plight:

> I got good grades in high school and I took AP English, but no one ever taught me how to read these textbooks or to study for exams. I knew how to write a research paper, but I had no clue how to write an analytical essay or take good notes from a lecture. In high school I got by just fine, but I had no idea that I would need to read and write and study so much in college. It's hard.

Reading Between the Lines: What ACT Reveals About College Readiness in Reading (ACT, 2006a), makes a compelling argument that what matters most for students to enroll and be successful in college is being able to comprehend complex text. "Performance on complex texts is the clearest differentiator in reading between students who are likely to be ready for college and those who are not" (pp. 16–17). The six aspects of text complexity include the following:

- Relationships: Interactions among ideas or characters in the text are subtle, involved, or deeply embedded.
- Richness: The text possesses a sizable amount of highly sophisticated information conveyed through data or literacy devices.
- Structure: The text is organized in ways that are elaborate and sometimes unconventional.
- Style: The author's tone and use of language are often intricate.
- Vocabulary: The author's choice of words is demanding and highly context dependent.
- Purpose: The author's intent in writing the text is implicit and sometimes ambiguous.

These reading tasks are essential for all students, not only those that are college bound. Yet many students in middle and high school are not able to comprehend complex texts. Given proper guidance, support, and instruction, they can achieve higher-order thinking and comprehension of texts. Using both narrative and expository text, teachers must start with easier text and teach students to recognize the six aspects of text listed above while moving to increasingly more complex texts and tasks. So literacy support across the content areas is important for all students, regardless of their current abilities as readers and writers.

In the next section of this chapter, we outline the ways that content-area teachers can provide support for content-area literacy. To provide instructional guidance and support to teachers, school leaders need to know the basics of literacy learning and how to use reading and writing to learn in the content areas.

Ways That Content-Area Teachers Provide Literacy Support

Teachers want students to learn the content but also want them to become adept at reading and understanding the textbook. Teachers can help students do this through modeling, explicit instruction, and guided practice. The following vignette shows how the teacher from the earlier vignette expertly activates and builds on prior knowledge and engages students in metacognition. In addition, she scaffolds instruction for some students so that they can strengthen their literacy skills while learning the intended content.

Nancy Dean knows that Alesha is an avid reader with advanced language skills and will learn the basic concepts of the social studies curriculum without much assistance. But some of the other students in her class have not yet acquired a repertoire of productive skills and habits for reading and learning. As Nancy plans the lesson for the day, she knows that Cody and some of her other students will not have an understanding of early Roman times or of the geography of Italy. Reading about the significance of Pompeii could be a meaningless and disconnected activity for her students unless she helps them by building a knowledge base for the reading. She decides to begin the class session with a "predicting and confirming activity" (Irvin, Buehl, & Klemp, 2007). She presents students with the following word list and then asks them to work in groups to discuss why they think the city of Pompeii might be important to world history.

volcano	*summit*	*archaeologists*	*treasures*	*protect*
suffocated	*trade*	*port city*	*ships*	*Vesuvius*
ash	*killed*	*Pliny the Younger*	*tremors*	*wall paintings*
plaster casts	*forums*	*escape*	*preserve*	*eruption*

She then points to the map of the Bay of Naples in the textbook. She shows the class a time line and talks about why trade was important in this part of the world. Students then review their original predictions and confirm, reject, or revise them. Based on this, the class devises a description of life in early Roman times. The small groups generate three questions they have about the importance of Pompeii.

While Alesha and some of her classmates begin reading, Nancy works with Cody and a few other students to preview the chapter and discuss the important ideas and key concepts. She demonstrates how to take notes from the chapter using two-column notes in which the students write the three headings from the chapter in the left column. Students in Nancy's group read the text silently, stopping after each section to talk about what they thought were the important ideas. Each student "marks the text" by placing a red-arrow sticky note by an important point in the paragraph. Then students work toward reaching a consensus on the important points they wrote about in their notes. At the end of the reading, Ms. Dean asks the students to tell her the answer to the question "Why was Pompeii important to the study of world cultures?" As they talk, she constructs a concept map on the board. The students use this map to write their summary statement. At the end of the class session, Ms. Dean leads a class discussion to ensure that everyone understands the reading and the lesson and can summarize the major concepts. She concludes by describing how they will build on what they did today in class when they continue the study of early Roman times in their next class session.

To be able to support her students' reading and learning, Nancy had to learn about literacy—she read books, participated in study groups, attended professional development sessions, and observed in colleagues' classes. The literacy coach in her building often visited her classroom, offered suggestions, and modeled lessons. Her principal encouraged the entire faculty to incorporate literacy strategies into their teaching and often did classroom walk-throughs to see how many teachers were actually implementing them. Through conversations with the literacy coach and other colleagues, Nancy began to understand the importance of schema and connecting her social studies content to the lives and experiences of students. She accurately assessed that several students in her class would have no prior knowledge of early Roman times or a sense of what life was like in AD 79, much less the economic implications of the importance of trade in the area around the Bay of Naples. She wanted students to "think" while they read—generating questions, making inferences, visualizing, connecting to their prior knowledge, and organizing the information. She decided that the question "What was the significance of Pompeii?" should be the major idea that she wanted students to understand.

Thelen (1986) likens schema to file folders in a cabinet. Students benefit from being shown where and how new information fits in this filing cabinet. Because everyone has a unique way of organizing their schema, it is important that teachers help students make connections between new information and what they already know. Students come to school with bulging "file folders" on some topics and nonexistent "folders" on other topics. Sometimes acquiring new learning requires that teachers hand students a "file folder," put a label on it, and begin filling it with pieces of information to *build background knowledge*. When students know something about a topic, teachers need to help them by *activating background knowledge* or locating and opening their "file folders," reminding them of what they know and how they might build upon that information. Even when students know something about a topic, they do not always use that understanding unless they engage in a prereading activity to activate prior knowledge. When students know a great deal about a topic, teachers can assist them most by guiding them to review and *organize their knowledge* before reading. This activation and organization of schema is what good readers do while reading. This same tool can also be helpful to assist students in writing.

In the vignette, Nancy Dean used literacy support strategies such as the predicting and confirming activity to build background knowledge and get students thinking about what they already knew and did not know. As she learned more about how students learned, she moved away from lecturing and started using small-group discussion to help students generate predictions and questions; she found that students were more engaged and made better connections to their own knowledge and experiences if they worked in groups. Students who are English language learners had an opportunity to add to discussions and ask questions of classmates. Those with little prior knowledge about a topic built their background knowledge and increased their vocabularies. Students like Alesha had the opportunity to activate what they knew and organize it before reading. As a social studies teacher committed to improving students' academic literacy skills, Nancy's job was to understand her content, understand her students, and plan a strategy that engaged all students in active learning.

Scaffolding instruction means building a support structure for students so that they can tackle increasingly complex tasks. A scaffold is a temporary structure that is built to make a difficult task gradually doable. Ms. Dean scaffolded instruction three different ways for Cody and the other students with whom she worked: (1) she helped students identify the major ideas in the text by taking them through the previewing of text; (2) she explicitly taught and modeled how to construct two-column notes; and (3) she assisted them in writing summaries by developing a concept map on the board. Alesha already knew how to implement these strategies on her own; the students in Nancy's small group needed to learn these strategies. Nancy also correctly assessed her class and *differentiated instruction* by allowing some students to work on their own and pulling others into a small group for explicit instruction.

Differentiation and Literacy Learning

Students bring varying academic literacy habits and skills to the classroom. Supporting all students to grow as content-area readers, writers, and thinkers requires differentiation of process, product, and content depending on specific instructional goals. Differentiation of instruction gives teachers the opportunity to provide all students with strategies for accessing text, completing writing assignments, or learning new information. Teachers' assessments of students' literacy skills becomes especially important in planning for the progress of all students.

A *literacy support strategy* is an instructional strategy that supports weaker readers, writers, speakers, and thinkers to develop the skills and strategies that competent communicators use. Literacy support strategies break down literacy learning into smaller chunks so learners can understand and practice the components of literacy as they attempt to "put it all together." The goal is for students to learn and internalize these strategies so that they can use them as needed. Literacy support strategies include graphic organizers, prediction activities, column note taking, comprehension monitoring, vocabulary development strategies, and writing-to-learn strategies. Alesha demonstrated competence in using literacy strategies to help her engage with and comprehend her social studies text. The literature strongly supports the model of teachers gradually releasing responsibility with regard to teaching and learning of literacy support strategies (Pearson & Gallagher, 1983; Vygotsky, 1962; Wilhelm, Baker, & Dube, 2001). Teachers who explicitly teach and model strategies provide students with ample opportunities for guided practice followed by independent practice.

The need to differentiate instruction requires teachers to know and use literacy support strategies to attend to the literacy development of struggling, average, and strong content-area readers. In particular, teachers can use two main types of differentiation related to literacy learning: matching student needs to instruction and matching student needs to text. Knowing about both of these types of differentiation can help teachers and administrators recognize options for customizing literacy support.

Matching Student Needs to Instruction

Many middle and high school teachers complain about the number of students who cannot read the textbook. Literacy support through teaching, modeling, and the use of *before*, *during*, and *after* strategies for reading comprehension provides weaker readers with access to more challenging texts. Many struggling readers are able to gain meaning from texts above their independent reading "level" if they are sufficiently interested, have a purpose for reading, have sufficient background knowledge, or have some strategies with which to tackle texts that are more difficult.

Students at different levels can use the same strategies because the strategies focus on *process*, not product. It is often helpful for teachers to present and model the strategies using easier texts that are more accessible and then move to shorter excerpts of more difficult text. For more advanced readers, the teacher can use the same strategies but make them increasingly more complex, that is, from the beginning, the teacher can guide the more advanced readers to make connections to other texts, to use multiple and comparison texts, and to ask inferential and synthesis questions. These strategies will challenge them to use text to learn. This, in turn, will aid students' further development in writing to learn, speaking, and listening. Combining any of the reading, vocabulary development, and writing-to-learn strategies with interaction and collaborative learning strategies also increases their effectiveness.

Matching Student Needs to Text

At the same time that teachers provide students with strategies to read challenging texts, students need to build fluency, basic vocabulary, and content understanding through the reading of easier texts, particularly if the reading levels of some students are more than two to three years below grade level. When the same class contains widely divergent levels of readers, content-area teachers can use two approaches to ensure that students improve in their reading abilities but also learn the necessary content: use of leveled texts and use of multiple texts. Of course, content-area teachers must first determine the core concepts upon which instruction will focus. This identification of essential questions, key concepts, and learning objectives will drive the selection of texts and the nature of reading, writing, and discussion assignments used with either approach.

Use of leveled texts. Texts are written at different reading levels. The concept of "leveled texts" means that teachers can select a variety of books or readings on the same topic that match the reading levels of different students. Reading materials can be tagged with a reading level using a readability formula or a graded book list or by looking up the lexile score of the text. These identifiers can be useful to identify parallel curriculum materials so that students at different reading levels can access similar information using varied texts. The Lexile Framework for Reading is being increasingly linked to publishing companies, testing companies, state standards framework resources, and online databases. Using many widely known assessments, teachers can obtain approximate reading levels for students that can be correlated to the lexile framework. Although limited because readability formulas cannot account for content, interest, or text coherence, the approximate levels can help teachers find reading materials that vary in difficulty related to a unit of study. Media specialists and the Internet are two sources that teachers can use to find parallel curriculum materials. For example, several online databases provide lexile scores for many texts, and teachers can obtain the lexile score for an article or chapter using www.lexile.com.

Use of multiple texts. Because inquiry projects tend to engage students, even reluctant readers and writers are often willing to read and write to complete the project, and multiple texts can be used. The vignette in Chapter 1 about the Dream Team at Washington Middle School includes an example of an inquiry project. Inquiry projects are designed around a unit of study to encourage students individually, in pairs, or in small groups to carry out an investigation, answer questions of importance and interest to them about a particular topic, or generate a solution to a problematic situation. Teachers who design inquiry projects can ensure that students at various reading levels and language acquisition levels can work in small heterogeneous groups to investigate, synthesize, and present findings. Individual students can complete the research for these inquiry projects using varying levels of materials, and some students can include oral interviews or research from video sources. Vocabulary development, discussion, use of a variety of texts, and comparison of different types of text enrich the learning process and literacy learning of group members, regardless of students' reading levels.

As these approaches show, differentiated instruction can provide meaningful learning opportunities for students at all reading and language levels. Differentiated instruction using literacy support strategies is essential for meeting the needs of all students because students learn the content while simultaneously becoming more proficient at the process of learning (reading, writing, listening, speaking, and thinking). Planning for instruction in an environment where students have different levels of literacy, a variety of experiences, and different amounts of prior knowledge is a challenge. Ensuring that teachers plan for engaging curriculum and instruction across the content areas should be an important priority for school leaders. It is only through a concerted schoolwide effort in which students receive access to differentiated instruction across the content areas that students' academic literacy levels can be improved.

Writing Across the Content Areas

"Learning to write" involves the use of handwriting; spelling; knowledge of vocabulary; mastery of the conventions of punctuation, capitalization, word usage, and grammar; and strategies such as planning, evaluating, and revising text. "Writing to learn" acts as a tool for learning subject matter.

Writing is an integral part of learning in all content areas and has been referred to as "thinking on paper." Writing helps students clarify and solidify what they have learned and helps them respond to what they have read. Reading, writing, and learning are meaning-making processes that involve students in actively building connections between what they are learning and what they already know. Like reading, writing to learn depends upon an active rather than a passive approach to learning.

Using a meta-analysis, Graham and Perin (2007) identified 11 elements to improve writing achievement in grades 4 through 12. While not intended to constitute a curriculum, these 11 elements are intended to guide instruction as students move to more complex writing tasks as they move through the grades. These elements are

- Writing Strategies: Teaching adolescents strategies for planning, revising, and editing their compositions.
- Summarization: Teaching students explicitly and systematically how to construct summaries of texts they have read.
- Collaborative Writing: Developing instructional arrangements where adolescents work together to plan, draft, revise, and edit their compositions.
- Specific Product Goals: Assigning students specific, reachable goals for the writing they are to complete.
- Word Processing: Students working individually or collaboratively on writing assignments using computers producing neat and legible script.
- Sentence Combining: Teaching students to construct more complex and sophisticated sentences through exercises in which two or more basic sentences are combined into a single sentence.

- Pre-writing: Engaging students in activities designed to help them generate or organize ideas for their composition.
- Inquiry Activities: Engaging students in activities that help them develop ideas and content for a particular writing task by analyzing immediate, concrete data.
- Process Writing Approach: Involving a number of interwoven activities including such activities as creating extended opportunities for writing and emphasizing writing for real audiences.
- Study of Models: Providing students with good models for each type of writing that is the focus of instruction.
- Writing in the Content Areas: Enhancing students' learning of content material. (Graham & Perin, pp. 15–21)

All teachers can help students learn content and improve reading comprehension by incorporating writing-to-learn strategies into content-area instruction. Writing-to-learn strategies used across content areas can help students by helping them think critically about content information. The purpose of this type of writing in the content areas is to increase *learning*. Improvement of writing skills is not the primary goal, though it may ultimately be one outcome. Writing-to-learn exercises can serve as quick assessments of students' understanding of content, as well as help students to clarify their own ideas. Examples of writing-to-learn strategies that simultaneously increase content understanding and improve reading and writing skills include quick-writes, peer conferencing, rewriting text from other points of view, dialogue journals, learning logs, and connecting text with other media using a critical literacy perspective. The use of quick-writes and the think-write-pair-share strategy allows all students to participate in class discussions, not just the vocal few. Many students who are too shy to speak in class freeze up when asked to answer a question on the spot. A writing exercise allows these students to organize their thoughts so that they can reflect first and then be ready to discuss a concept. The literature suggests that before, during, and after writing-to-learn strategies should be linked to provide scaffolding for struggling and average readers as they work with advanced texts and concepts.

Classroom teachers across content areas can easily incorporate a number of short, discipline-specific writing tasks into their daily instruction. They may ask students to explain a concept; write a word problem; compare and contrast two concepts; write a caption for an illustration; give examples or make lists; describe or define; reflect; justify a solution; or write a review, critique, or summary. When teachers explain and model how to complete these tasks and provide exemplars of what is expected, this type of regular writing assignment can effectively connect reading and writing, facilitate learning, and improve thinking and communication skills.

To improve students' writing and thinking skills, teachers should also require students to do more formal types of writing in the content areas. Here the emphasis is on organizing and presenting thoughts within the conventions of a specific content or presentation format. Students should turn in first drafts of formal writing but should craft these pieces using steps of the writing process: brainstorm, draft, revise, edit, and publish. Effective writing instruction gives students frequent opportunities to write, accompanied with feedback and opportunities to edit and revise, along with guidance in how to do so (Williams, 2003). More formal papers will have different purposes depending on the discipline, the topic, and the teacher's instructional goals. The following types of writing represent the range of formats and genres that students should be fluent in upon graduating from high school:

- *expository writing*, in which students provide information or explain an idea;
- *persuasive writing or argumentation*, in which students persuade readers to take their point of view on certain topics;
- *analytical writing*, in which students analyze, compare and contrast, synthesize, and/or evaluate based on multiple sources of information;
- *research papers*, in which students generate a hypothesis, carry out an inquiry, and report on the process, the findings, and the implications;
- *creative writing*, in which students produce original pieces of art such as a poem, a play, or a short story; and
- *narrative writing*, in which students use expressive, autobiographical, reflective, or personal writing.

As noted in Chapter 1, many students are not motivated to write in school. It is helpful if assignments are designed to be written for an authentic audience, such as writing for the newspaper, writing a book for a younger audience about the topic of study, writing and performing a script, posting to a Web site or blog, exchanging writing with peers, writing letters to the editor, writing a grant proposal, or presenting report findings to a public board or expert panel. Writing in different genres can provide opportunities to teach students how to write for different audiences, an important life skill. Other ways to increase motivation to write include opportunities to discuss writing, peer editing (when one is trained to do so), and the use of computers to write and revise. Naturally, a safe and responsive classroom environment is essential if students are to develop the habit of sharing and discussing their writing.

Often teachers and administrators ask about the amount of reading and writing that middle and high school students should be doing. If students are to become fluent readers and writers of multiple genres, be able to read and write for various purposes, and independently use reading and writing to learn, they need daily opportunities to develop their skills. A hobby or skill takes time to develop to a high level of competence. Instructional leaders should encourage their teachers to incorporate reading and writing instruction, as well as multiple opportunities to read and write, into their lesson plans. When teachers make this kind of concerted effort, students benefit.

Ways That School Leaders Can Support Teachers

The principal is frequently the one who initiates and sustains a schoolwide literacy improvement effort. Other school leaders such as literacy coaches, literacy team members, media specialists, and middle-level leaders also play essential roles in a successful improvement initiative (see Chapter 8). All administrators must be able to recognize the basic elements of a literacy-rich classroom so they can support teachers as they provide literacy-rich instruction (see Chapter 6). Yet many administrators admit that this is not the case. Participating in book studies, attending professional development sessions and conferences, and observing the instruction of colleagues are ways for instructional leaders to learn about the processes and applications of literacy learning. School leaders lacking a background in literacy can learn about literacy alongside teachers. By exhibiting a commitment to lifelong learning, the principal sets the expectation that improving literacy expertise is a priority at the school and an important activity that requires the participation of all teachers and administrators. The following vignette describes how one principal took on the challenge of learning about literacy and leading the effort in her school.

Carmen Ramirez was a math teacher before she became an assistant principal and then a principal. She had to learn about literacy herself before she could expect her teachers to incorporate it into their content-area classrooms. She made it clear that she needed to understand the literacy learning process and know what a literacy-rich classroom looked like, and she invited teachers to join her on this journey. She bought multiple copies of I Read It, but I Don't Get It: Comprehension Strategies for Adolescent Readers *(Tovani, 2000) and started a discussion group over breakfast once a week. Teachers were asked to share some of the ideas from the book at faculty meetings and to report on how they used some of these ideas in their classrooms. This group eventually became known as "Ms. R's Literacy Breakfast Club." After the faculty seemed "ready" to learn more, she invited a literacy professor from a local university to speak to the entire faculty on the foundations of literacy learning and to demonstrate two learning strategies—KWL (What I Know, Want to Know, Learned) and semantic mapping. At the next faculty meeting, Carmen used a KWL to present information on the strategic use of grouping techniques to engage and motivate students; she deliberately used the words schema, metacognition, and scaffolding in her discussion. Teachers then "mapped" what they knew and wrote a short summary. Because the article that the teachers read was informational text, Carmen then asked teachers to discuss how the KWL and mapping activity would differ with narrative text and then to apply it to the text they used in their own classrooms. She announced that she wanted to see the strategies in teachers' lesson plans and that she, the literacy coach, and the assistant principal would be in classrooms over the next two weeks to assist teachers in implementing these strategies. Carmen also arranged times for teachers to observe in each other's classes as they tried out new strategies. The next month, she took her newly formed literacy team to the state reading conference. When they returned, team members presented what they learned to the faculty. Momentum in the use of content-area literacy strategies by teachers began to build.*

Carmen knew that it would take some time before all teachers felt comfortable integrating literacy strategies into their content areas, but she also wanted to give them the message that integrating literacy strategies into content-area instruction was not optional. She continued her Literacy Breakfast Club using books that deepened participants' knowledge of the literacy learning process and expanded their use of strategies.

Carmen knew her faculty. She understood how committed these teachers were to teaching their content to students. She expected some resistance to "every teacher being a literacy teacher," but the reading scores of the entire school had not improved over the past five years. How could she convince the faculty that their responsibility was to help *all* students read and write at higher levels? This would have to be a whole-school effort. Where should she begin, given that so few teachers had any training in reading? In fact, she did not know much herself.

Carmen wanted to send a clear message to the faculty that they would be working on improving literacy with all students. So she began with an invitation to join her over breakfast to learn more about literacy. She hoped that by admitting that she had a lot to learn, teachers and other administrators would feel less threatened. As Carmen herself learned more about the components of a literacy-rich classroom, she began to model various strategies at faculty meetings. She knew that teachers would need to experience the strategies themselves before they could use them in their classes. She also used the services of a consultant to help build conceptual and pedagogical knowledge about literacy. She created opportunities for teachers to discuss ways to help all students learn to read and write at higher levels.

As she moved from classroom to classroom, Carmen began to recognize how literacy looked in the different content areas. Having students read and discuss the math text was clearly different from asking students to read, discuss, and make a presentation on a novel. The writing assignments certainly varied among content areas as well. Science and social studies teachers certainly knew their content, but no one seemed to be teaching students to be more successful at reading for information found in the textbook and other texts. Carmen began to encourage conversations within departments about how to improve literacy in that particular content area with those particular texts. She informed teachers about what she expected to see, and then she and members of her leadership team systematically visited classrooms to give feedback. Strategic walk-throughs helped her collect data on the pervasiveness of the implementation. She shared this information with the literacy team, who then planned subsequent professional development opportunities.

In Chapter 6, we discuss how school leaders can use classroom observations, walk-throughs, teacher evaluations, and new teacher induction to create a school culture in which literacy is the focus. These strategies can only be used effectively when the administrators of the school possess basic conceptual knowledge about literacy learning and know what to look for in classrooms.

Key Messages

Supporting the literacy development of students requires that teachers and administrators are themselves learners about literacy—constantly developing and refining their own knowledge base. At a minimum, teachers and administrators need a basic understanding of the literacy learning process, how it connects to content learning, and how best to use strategies that involve students in literacy learning across the content areas. This chapter explained the literacy learning process and how to differentiate instruction. The key messages in this chapter are the following:

- All content-area teachers should support students to become effective readers, writers, and thinkers in their disciplines.
- Leaders need to understand literacy in order to lead a schoolwide literacy improvement effort, support teachers, and communicate with parents and the community about literacy.
- Two types of knowledge about literacy are important: conceptual knowledge (understanding the literacy learning process) and pedagogical knowledge (knowing how to implement content-area literacy instruction).
- Building background knowledge, activating prior knowledge, organizing information, and engaging in metacognition are essential elements for learning content.
- Differentiating instruction in the classroom can meet the learning and literacy needs of all students.
- Skilled teachers scaffold instruction to help struggling readers learn the skills and habits of strong readers.
- Writing helps students clarify and solidify what they have learned and helps them respond to what they have read.
- A strong, active, collective effort by all content-area teachers is the best way to ensure that students develop the literacy habits and skills they need.

The role of the school leader is crucial to integrating literacy and learning across the content areas. The first step for administrators is to understand the literacy learning process themselves and to encourage all teachers to become active learners about the process. Teachers need knowledge and support to provide instruction that develops literacy and learning in the content areas. School leaders can provide professional development so that teachers gain the knowledge and skills necessary to integrate literacy into their content instruction. Changing instructional practices across a school can be challenging, and it is natural that some teachers will resist changing the way they teach. Many school leaders recommend starting with volunteers; others begin with mandated changes. But however leaders proceed with the change process, leaders must communicate clearly that integrating literacy into content-area instruction *is not optional*. It takes time to learn anything new, but the time spent and the common focus on literacy can serve to bring educators in a school together to support student success.

3 Integrating Literacy and Learning
Interventions for Struggling Readers and Writers

Sustaining Literacy Development

Integrating Literacy & Learning

Implement a Literacy Action Plan

Allocate Resources

Support Teachers to Improve Instruction

Student Motivation, Engagement, & Achievement

Build Leadership Capacity

Use Data to Make Decisions

Across the Content Areas • Literacy Interventions • District

School Environment • Parents & Community

Why is this component important? Students who read and write below grade level need targeted intervention and support to avoid falling further and further behind. Students who struggle with basic literacy skills need the quality classroom instruction described in Chapter 2, but many will need additional help because they have to *accelerate* their literacy skills to succeed. Leaders can help struggling readers and writers by providing quality intervention classes, tutoring, and other types of assistance that provide explicit instruction and practice in how to read and write a variety of texts, and by ensuring that teachers provide increased support in their content-area classes.

Students are confronted with increasingly complex texts and tasks as they move through the grades, and content-area teachers must assume responsibility for integrating literacy and learning (the focus of Chapter 2). However, some students read and write at levels far below what teachers expect of students at their age or grade level. This is of great concern in middle and high schools, as content-area literacy expectations get harder and fewer years are left to ensure that these students develop the reading and writing skills they will need to successfully participate in college or career options. Even a year's worth of gain in each year would not be enough. To reach grade-level expectations, these students need to *accelerate* their literacy development through a targeted intervention.

An *intervention* is a program or a class or a session of some sort that is designed to address students' specific reading and writing challenges, thereby reversing a downward spiral of failure. Interventions provide students with the tools and strategies they need to make great strides in literacy development. Maintenance, remediation, or incremental progress is *not* the goal; instead, a successful literacy intervention helps students accelerate their skill development as readers and writers. Ideally, students performing below grade level should be able to make two to three years of gain for each year of participation in a quality intervention program.

Literacy interventions in middle and high schools take many forms. Some are built around a program that a school has adopted; some involve structured blocks of time and are taught by a reading specialist; and others are regularly scheduled classes in which students receive explicit instruction in reading and writing. Interventions may also include one-to-one tutoring, computer-mediated instruction, and after-school or summer programs focused on helping struggling readers and writers accelerate. The types of staff who teach intervention classes vary by school, but leaders should be cautioned that intervention teachers should have special training or they are unlikely to be able to provide the necessary instruction indicated by diagnostic assessment.[1]

Literacy Interventions for Struggling Readers and Writers makes up the second half of the component "Integrating Literacy and Learning" in the Leadership Model for Improving Adolescent Literacy, represented by the inner band on the graphic of the

---

[1] We are aware that pullout services and self-contained classes for special education or English language learner students are also considered interventions. We discuss the *literacy* needs of special education students and English language learners in this chapter but describing all the interventions these students receive is beyond the scope of this book. In this chapter, we are describing *literacy interventions* as those sessions, activities, or classes designed specifically to give support for developing literacy skills to students who are significantly below grade level in reading and writing.

model. It is important to remember that putting literacy interventions in place is just one piece of the larger picture. When schools put an intervention program in place hoping that it will meet the literacy needs of all students, many students do not get the help they need. One type of intervention is not likely to meet the needs of all of the struggling readers and writers in a school because students have difficulty for a variety of reasons. Further, without support across the content areas, struggling readers and writers often do not transfer and build their content-area literacy skills. School leaders need to assess student needs and implement a menu of interventions to address them.

As described in Chapters 1 and 2, all students require support across their school day in all subject areas. Programs for special education students and English language learners often operate separately from the "regular" program and sometimes do not include deliberate or adequate reading and writing instruction or opportunities to transfer and practice new skills with support. Students' literacy development must also be supported by the school environment and by parents, community members, and the school district. It is important to remember that a schoolwide literacy improvement effort is just that: it includes all learners, all teachers, all administrators, all stakeholders.

In this chapter, we discuss the needs of different types of struggling readers and writers, describe a variety of classroom contexts for intervention, and outline what is involved in meeting some of the literacy development needs of special education students, English language learners, and struggling readers and writers. We describe how one principal ensured that the needs of struggling readers and writers were met in her school. We then describe what exemplary instruction looks like in an intervention classroom and the difference it can make for students. The chapter concludes with key messages.

Struggling Readers in the Content-Area Classroom

Literacy-rich content-area instruction can improve the literacy habits and skills of most students, helping them make connections between content and the process of literacy learning. The strategic use of appropriate pieces of text can support content learning, give students opportunities to read extensively, and make connections between narrative and expository writing. But some students will need additional help to accelerate their literacy development. The following vignette describes the plight of struggling readers and writers in a science class where they do not receive specific literacy support.

Roger Duncan arrived early, organized his notes, and decided on the few concepts he wanted students to understand. He wrote the words fission, atoms, isotopes, *and* chain reaction *on the board. After he gave a short lecture on why basic nuclear fission is important to scientists today, he told the class to open their textbooks to Chapter 12, read the chapter, and answer the questions at the back. Then he walked around the room to monitor progress and helped individual students if they asked for assistance. All the students opened their books, and a few actually read the chapter and answered the questions; most engaged in "ping-pong reading," which consisted of "read the question—look for the answer; read the question—look for the answer." The majority of students finished the assignment before the end of the class period. Five students were pretty good at looking like they were completing the assignment, but they had nothing to turn in at the end of the class period.*

Jim flipped through the pages and looked at the pictures. Because his family talked about interesting topics at the dinner table and his father worked at a local power plant, he understood some of the pictures, charts, graphs, and diagrams in the chapter. He could struggle through the text, but never in one class period. Mr. Duncan said he could take textbook assignments home, and sometimes he did, but they took hours to get through. When it came to writing out the answers—that took forever, and he got most of the answers wrong mainly because he did not understand the questions. The special education teachers who helped him were more patient and seemed to know he needed extra time and help to understand a textbook.

Roy had no clue how to read the chapter. He had never heard about fission. He assumed it had to do with energy, but beyond that, terms such as chain reaction held no meaning for him. There was no way he could even attempt to answer the questions. He occasionally tried to read, but there were just too many words he did not know. His mother held two jobs, and many afternoons and evenings he was in charge of babysitting his younger brothers and sisters. He tried to help them with their homework, but it was easier to turn on the TV.

Maria stared at the book. She did not understand a lot of what Mr. Duncan said, but when the other students opened their books, she did too. Her family had moved to the United States three years ago, and she was struggling to learn enough English to talk to her English-speaking friends. Mostly she hung out with other Spanish-speaking kids because she could talk to them with ease. She was really trying to learn English, but it was hard. She had been a pretty good student in Mexico, but she understood very little of what her teachers said here. When the class period ended, she filed out.

Clarke did not care. He was on the soccer team, and there was a game on Friday night. He occasionally turned in an assignment because he had to remain eligible for sports. He figured he had enough points in this class that he did not need to do this one. So instead, he flipped through the book and visualized the winning goal.

Stephanie had been a straight-A student in elementary school. She was a phonics "star." She was good at reading words out loud. Her classmates were always impressed at how quickly and accurately she could pronounce the words. But when she had to read silently, she just could not make sense of it. Sometimes she whispered to herself, but the whispering distracted others and reading that way took a long time. She "read" the entire chapter but could not remember much of what she read. The questions did not make much sense to her either.

Roger Duncan missed the opportunity to provide literacy support to his students. He could have engaged them in interactive reading guides, pretaught vocabulary, assisted them in coding text to identify main ideas, or helped them construct graphic organizers for study. His above-average and average learners would have benefited from this type of literacy support. It is absolutely essential, however, for struggling readers and writers. When these students do not get the literacy support they need, they miss learning important concepts as well as ways to become better readers and writers.

It is important to remember that most middle and high school students struggle sometimes and will benefit from support as they tackle increasingly difficult texts in multiple genres. Balfanz, McPartland, and Shaw (2002) identified three different types of struggling readers entering 9th grade:

1. *Five to 10 percent of students need intensive and massive extra help* (nonreader through a 3rd grade reading level). These students may have trouble decoding even simple passages, lack fluency, may have a limited vocabulary, and have limited comprehension skills. *These students need* an intervention class or tutoring (or both), along with additional support in content-area classes. During intervention classes, these students need to master ways of figuring out words they do not know, engage in a great deal of vocabulary development, and be taught how to interact with and comprehend text while reading. In addition, they need explicit and frequent writing instruction and quality feedback on their writing.

2. *A larger group of students can decode but read with limited fluency* (5th or 6th grade level) and have limited content knowledge, usually learned in middle school. These students "get by" in content-area courses but find it difficult to learn from texts. *These students need* teachers to provide scaffolded instruction (see Chapter 2 for an explanation and example); build background information before reading; help them activate what they know and make connections to new knowledge; build fluency; and systematically introduce vocabulary. These students may also require tutoring or short-term intervention

classes to build reading comprehension skills and provide additional opportunities to develop fluency and expand their general vocabulary.

3. *Another group of students is not fully prepared to succeed* in standards-based courses in high school. They can read and comprehend, but not at high levels. They may not have mastered intermediate-level skills and knowledge and need the support of content-area teachers to master concept-dense high school texts. *These students need* the types of literacy-rich teaching and learning described in Chapter 2. As they attempt to tackle grade-level texts and tasks, they depend upon the support of their content-area teachers.

Balfanz and his colleagues concluded that all but those with the most limited skills (who require special intervention) can be helped to become significantly better readers through specific literacy support provided as part of the regular middle and high school curriculum. Their conclusion indicates the importance of middle and high school educators offering students strong and supportive content-area instruction integrated with literacy support strategies, as well as appropriate additional interventions for the lowest-achieving groups of students. The numbers may vary by school and district, but whatever the percentages in each group, school leaders can put together a combination of literacy-rich content learning and interventions to meet the literacy needs of all of their students.

Meeting the Needs for Additional Support and Intervention

Literacy interventions come in a variety of formats, but their intended purpose is to provide explicit instruction in comprehension, vocabulary, and fluency (and in some cases, phonics) and extended time for reading and writing. However, one size does not and cannot fit all. It is important that school leaders understand the variety of issues that struggling readers and writers confront on a daily basis. An intervention that works for students with a specific learning disability may not be appropriate for new English speakers. A program that focuses on decoding may not be what aliterate students need to improve their fluency skills. Teachers and administrators also benefit from understanding the affective consequences for students with poor academic literacy skills and how these can be addressed. When leaders understand the literacy issues these students face, they are much better able to ensure that appropriate interventions are put into place. Obviously, good diagnostic assessments are important when attempting to identify needs and establish criteria for participation in various programs. (In Chapter 7 we present information on using assessments to identify students who may need additional support.)

Struggling middle and high school readers have diverse abilities and needs. Figure 3.1 describes five prototypes of struggling readers and writers, as personified by the five students in the vignette. As the chart shows, some students have excellent fluency but limited comprehension; others appear to lack decoding skills when they read out loud but can manage to make sense of their reading when they read silently. Still others have language or attention deficiencies that need attention.

3.1 **Prototypes of Struggling Readers and Writers**		
Prototype	**Characteristics**	**Activities That Are Likely to Work**

Jim	• Long history of school failure
	• Lack of general knowledge
	• Poor decoding skills
	• Good listener; good speaker in specialized settings
	• Specialized knowledge
	• Special education designation for reading disability
	• Poor writer
		• Systematic phonics instruction
		• Ways of figuring out the meanings of unknown words (context, roots and affixes, conceptual redefinition)
		• Concept work and discussions
		• Preteaching of vocabulary
		• Prereading strategies
		   – Conceptual vocabulary activities
		   – Predicting activities
		   – Questioning activities
		   – Anticipation guides
		   – KWL and other charts
		• High-interest texts
		• Opportunities to write for authentic audiences using the writing process

Roy	• Long history of school failure • Poor reader, writer, listener, speaker • Limited general vocabulary • Lack of general knowledge and concepts	• Visualization activities • Concept work and discussions • Explicit instruction and feedback on writing • Vocabulary development activities • Tutoring • Systematic phonics and word-attack instruction • Discussion and group work • Language and vocabulary games • Listening to books on tape while following along with the text • Recording books on tape for younger students • Teacher read-alouds • Dramatization • Comprehension and listening strategies

3.1 **Prototypes of Struggling Readers and Writers** (*continued*)		
Prototype	Characteristics	Activities That Are Likely to Work

Maria	• New English speaker
	• Lack of vocabulary in English
	• Cultural differences that may interfere with learning
	• First language that may influence reading
	• Limited literacy in first language
	• Wide difference in skills between spoken and written English
		• Content delivered in native language
		• Cooperative learning activities
		  – Think-pair-share
		  – Jigsaw
		• Thematic units
		• Prereading activities
		• Comprehension strategies
		• Visuals that connect to life experience
		• Oral language practice and conversation
		• Graphic organizers
		• Wait time
		• Think-alouds
		• Dramatization
		• Group summarizing
		• Experiential writing

Clarke	• Lack of engagement in learning • Trouble in and out of school • Difficulty sitting still • Difficulty concentrating	• High-interest text • Discussion and oral language activities • Cross-age tutoring • Text interaction • Cooperative learning • Dramatization • Coding text • Writing for authentic reasons • Creating books on tape for younger readers

Stephanie	• Fluent decoding, little comprehension
	• No strategies to connect to text
	• Word calling
		• Emphasis on all parts of the reading process:
		  – Prereading
		  – Reading and comprehending
		    — Text interaction
		    — Visualization
		    — Prediction
		  – Rereading and responding
		    — Graphic organizers
		    — Writing about text
		    — Dramatization and oral interpretation
		• Comprehension strategies
		• Coding text
		• Writing using the writing process

Many students who struggle with reading also struggle with writing. "Researchers know that reading and writing often draw from the same pool of background knowledge —for example, a general understanding of the attributes of texts. At the same time, however, writing differs from reading. While readers form a mental representation of thoughts written by someone else, writers formulate their own thoughts, organize them, and create a written record of them using the conventions of spelling and grammar" (Graham & Perin, 2007, p. 8).

Like problems with reading, difficulties in writing can be damaging to an adolescent's learning and self-esteem. As students progress through school, they are frequently expected to express what they know or are learning through writing. Students may struggle to do so if they have limited vocabulary, limited organizational skills, lack of good models, limited understanding of text structures, or limited understanding of the grammar, language structures, or syntactics and semantics of English. Often teachers think that they are doing struggling students a favor by not assigning a lot of writing. Instead of necessary practice, these students end up with even less writing instruction and practice than their peers.

Improving writing is crucial to learning in all subject areas, not just during English classes, because writing is a vehicle for clarifying, analyzing, and synthesizing ideas. Writing assignments that are linked to content learning and prereading strategies encourage students to think about what they write, brainstorm, or discuss their writing and learning (National Writing Project, 2006). Simply increasing the amount of writing students are assigned is not enough. Most students require explicit instruction in content-area writing. Writing a lab report for biology requires a different set of writing skills than writing a poem for English. Teachers must model with students such skills as how to organize thoughts, develop ideas, and revise for clarity (National Writing Project & Nagin, 2003). Students need opportunities to create topics that matter to them, models to guide each of their different writing tasks, and the requirement to revise, edit, and improve. Providing rubrics for writing assignments is important because the structure, audience, and language used in writing should vary depending upon the purpose. The quality of writing depends on many elements, including substance, organization, clarity, voice, and tone. When writing tasks are authentic and connected to the content being read or discussed, students begin to understand that writing serves as a vehicle for communication and that writing can be done using a variety of genres and for a variety of reasons.

A general consensus in the field is that reading and writing should be taught in conjunction with one another. Cognitive activities such as schema activation and use, metacognition, and questioning (discussed in Chapters 1 and 2) are necessary for both reading and writing. As students grow in their ability to engage in this type of thinking, they can tackle more difficult reading and complete more complex writing. When students understand the text structure of a story, they can use that structure to write.

When students understand an author's purpose, they can more clearly set a purpose for their own writing and identify an appropriate audience. Writing, like reading, improves when students are taught to write across the curriculum by teachers who understand the reading and writing processes.

Strategies for Struggling Readers and Writers

Struggling students need smaller instructional groups and teachers who can provide instruction targeted at their individual needs and on their instructional level. Students are more likely to succeed if given clear, detailed explanations; systematic instructional sequences; and frequent opportunities for group and individual guided practice. Another important aspect is continuous, explicit, and consistent feedback with time for students to make corrections. Struggling readers and writers should not be allowed to practice mistakes but rather be given support to make the correct choices and to use strategies that help them self-monitor their comprehension.

Interventions for struggling readers and writers should include opportunities to develop vocabulary, increase fluency, enhance background knowledge, learn thinking/reasoning strategies, practice active comprehension strategies, and respond to reading through writing. For both struggling readers and writers, the use of graphic organizers can be very helpful. Graphic organizers can assist students with all parts of the reading process by asking them to interact with the text in various ways (anticipation guides, fishbone maps, KWLs, story maps); they can be used to build vocabulary (Frayer models, semantic feature analyses, triple-entry vocabulary journals) and as effective prewriting organizers (proposition-support outlines, history frames, concept maps, Venn diagrams). Each of these activities requires direct teacher explanation, modeling, guided practice, and independent practice to ensure that students can perform them on their own and apply them to new situations.

For both readers and writers who are struggling, it is critical to have hands-on experiences related to what they are reading and writing, as well as time to talk about it. Explicit word study and language study are also essential. Struggling readers and writers need explicit assistance to develop metacognitive skills through the use of strategies such as coding, quick-writes, revision protocols, editing checklists, written reflections, and other approaches to build awareness of their own processes as readers and writers.

In an intervention classroom, students can work in small, flexible groups that are determined by specific literacy needs. These groupings vary according to the instructional goals and student progress. Although each student has specific needs, most struggling learners share at least some common areas of challenge:

- *relatively weak vocabulary*, which may be the result of little reading during previous school years and limited background knowledge;
- *weak academic background*, including limited reading experience and limited vocabulary;
- *a view of themselves as poor readers and writers*, perhaps as a result of being labeled as such by educators in the early grades; and
- *few comprehension strategies* or less skill in using comprehension strategies, including little ability to monitor comprehension.

Although struggling readers and writers sometimes share characteristics, individual students do differ. For example, the literacy development needs of Clarke (see earlier vignette) are different in that he is a more capable student who is unengaged and unmotivated to complete academic literacy tasks. However, he is at risk for not maintaining grade-level reading and writing skills if he does not regularly apply his abilities to increasingly complex tasks and receive instruction in how to do this effectively. Close attention to the motivation and engagement issues raised in Chapter 1 could provide solutions to Clarke's literacy challenges. Improving Clarke's fluency and skill as a reader and writer might include providing him with books matched to his interests, instruction in a few powerful comprehension-monitoring strategies followed by time for monitored sustained silent reading and discussion as part of a community of readers, and authentic reasons to write. It would be helpful to engage him by asking him to write on topics he knows about in forms that benefit others (maintaining a Web site about soccer, creating a manual for the junior varsity team) or getting him involved in a research project about athletes and drug use, or injury and physical therapy issues for soccer players. In conjunction with these, Clarke will need strategies for interacting with text to maintain his engagement and attention, such as think-alouds, coding text, and column note taking. Placing Clarke in an intervention classroom would be a serious mistake.

Meeting the Literacy Needs of Special Education Students

Special education students like Jim need literacy support in the areas of decoding, fluency, vocabulary, and comprehension. Literacy intervention classes for students who have scored below the 30th percentile on a group-administered, standardized reading test will generally meet the needs of many special education students. In addition, these students may need extra support from a special education teacher during their content-area classes. Students with additional challenges such as learning disabilities, organizational issues, poor visual memory, or vision or hearing impairment might require even more specific types of interventions to help them succeed as readers and writers.

To address the decoding issues of readers who are struggling the most, the special education teacher can work collaboratively with the reading intervention teacher to ensure that students get consistent explicit instruction and practice with the building blocks of reading: phonemic awareness, phonics, and building a sight-word vocabulary. Addressing decoding issues requires teacher knowledge of these building blocks as well as knowledge of the reading process. Many struggling readers will also need explicit instruction in word analysis and ample guided practice to develop facility with language.

Fluency is a major issue for most students in the reading intervention class. Improving fluency means increasing word accuracy and reading speed. It is difficult for readers who misread a large number of words or read too slowly to make meaning of the text. Teachers charged with providing reading and writing instruction can help students develop fluency through activities such as paired reading, timed reading, poetry recitations, making books on tape, and oral interpretations. In addition, strategies to build sight-word vocabulary are often necessary to accelerate the reading proficiency of these students.

To address the general issues of vocabulary development and comprehension, special education and intervention teachers can build a classroom library of books that build conceptual knowledge but are written at a lower reading level. Teachers can use a general vocabulary program and teach a variety of vocabulary strategies. School leaders can support teachers' use of videos, films, guest speakers, demonstrations, and field trips to develop students' background knowledge before reading or composing related text. Teachers can provide explicit instruction, modeling, and guided practice with specific comprehension strategies for before, during, and after reading to help students build their comprehension skills. Students can then apply these strategies to increasingly complex texts.

Special education teachers and reading specialists can also serve as liaisons among content-area teachers, helping all teachers use a consistent and effective approach to literacy instruction. Special education teachers and reading specialists can coteach literacy intervention classes, ensuring that the reading needs of special education students are adequately addressed. Teaching paraprofessionals how to assist and prompt special education and other at-risk students to use the strategies and skills learned in the literacy intervention class and apply them to content-area instruction can also be helpful.

Meeting the Literacy Needs of English Language Learners

English language learners (ELLs) come to English-speaking schools with different degrees of literacy in their own language, which affects the acquisition of literacy skills in English. Some are highly literate in their native language and have much background knowledge in many areas of instruction. These students benefit from language support but rarely need a separate class to develop literacy skills. They know how to study, have academic experience in their first language, and can transfer many skills from first-language instruction to their second (or third or fourth) language. Other ELLs have little or no academic literacy skills in their first language. They may have come from an area of extreme poverty or an area of intense conflict, which prevented them from acquiring advanced literacy skills. "Literacy development is a particular problem for the ELLs who enter the educational system in later grades, especially in high school. Not only do these students have to master complex course content usually with little context or understanding of the way that American schools are structured and operate, but they have fewer years to master the English language. In addition, they are enrolling at an age beyond which literacy instruction is usually provided to students, and some have below-grade-level literacy in their native language" (Short & Fitzsimmons, 2007, p. 6). These students need basic reading and writing instruction along with language learning.

Because ELL students come with such varying background knowledge and experience with literacy in their home languages, these students require different types of support in the development of academic English. In addition to the assistance provided by content-area teachers, ELLs require the help of a specialized English-as-a-second-language (ESL) teacher who understands language acquisition and language development. The ESL teacher can help students make the transition from their home language to both conversational and academic English without confusing pronunciation errors for reading errors. ELLs also need language instructional materials that help establish the basic structure and conversational patterns of English. ELL students might receive this instruction in a pullout class or as part of an immersion program. It is important for school leaders to understand that spoken English generally becomes fluent before English used in reading and writing, and that when students "test out" of a literacy intervention class based in part on oral fluency tests, they probably will still require substantial literacy support in their content area classes.

Instructional leaders and teachers who work with ELLs need to be knowledgeable about effective practices for English language acquisition. This includes oral practice, demonstrations, group work, and thematic units with relevance to a variety of cultures. Another important support for ELLs is content-area text that is simplified in terms of language but not in terms of concepts. Lastly, school leaders need to be certain that reading assessments given to English language learners have valid norms for that population. There is often a difference between ELLs' reading proficiency in English versus their native-language reading proficiency. Planning for instruction based on assessment results requires an understanding of what the assessment results mean.

All teachers with ELL students in their classrooms can significantly help them as well as other students developing their literacy skills by establishing clear, predictable routines, by including explicit content-area literacy support as part of their teaching, and by writing directions and agendas clearly on the board each day. Instructional leaders, ESL teachers, tutors, and content-area teachers need to be knowledgeable about the stages of language development, the similarity and differences of languages to one another, and the basic structure of the English language so that ELLs experience literacy development across the content areas. In addition, these teachers need to work and plan together for the benefit of students.

ELL students like Maria (in the earlier vignette) also need teachers and instructional leaders who understand the relevance of cultural differences. Some cultures, for example, value class participation, questioning, and discussions; others do not. Teachers and instructional leaders ought to be aware of the cultural differences that can affect ELLs' perceived performance in the classroom. ELLs do not have to conform to all of the cultural components of U.S. schools, but they are more likely to succeed if they understand them. Part of the instructional program for ELLs and for the students they interact with can be the comparative analysis of culture. ELLs can master both English and content knowledge; it just takes time and support.

The Role of School Leaders in Providing Literacy Interventions

Students who struggle with reading and writing require extra attention and time. Finding additional personnel to provide literacy support sessions and finding the time needed in the school schedule can be a challenge, but failing to do so can doom students who arrive at middle and high school with limited literacy skills. The following vignette illustrates how one principal put together a plan to address the needs of the students with the most limited academic literacy skills at her school.

When Kathy Lowry first met with her newly formed literacy team, she presented data on student performance in the school. In 9th through 12th grade, 198 students had scored below the 30th percentile. Everyone at the meeting agreed that these students had to be in a regularly scheduled intervention class and that two reading specialists would each have to teach five classes of reading (each class would range in size from 15 to 25 students depending on the level of intensity required, based on the data provided by the reading assessment).

Kathy knew that the parents of these students would have to be contacted and their support enlisted. Parents often worry about the effect of placement in intervention classes on their child's self-image, as well as the effect on credits for graduation. After much discussion about who had the responsibility and the time to contact the parents, the team agreed on a compromise. The reading specialists would use the first two weeks of school to review data to ensure that students were properly placed, because scores on standardized reading tests do not always accurately reflect a student's ability. The reading specialists, along with two trained community volunteers, would administer an individual diagnostic reading test to each student selected for participation to confirm the appropriateness of placement and to determine an instructional plan for each student. The reading specialists would also contact parents, gather materials, and plan instruction during this initial period. The intervention classes would begin the third week of school.

The next problem was that 34 of the 198 students scored five or more grades below their actual grade level in reading. These students would require extra help in addition to the intervention class if they were to make progress and not fall even further behind. The literacy team members discussed stipends for faculty who would tutor students three times a week before or after school as well as an additional after-school class. They also discussed using America

Reads tutors and community mentors. When she was principal at the middle school, Kathy had had a bad experience with tutors because they had no training and were unable to help the students. Both students and tutors had been frustrated. One of the reading specialists, however, had success in her last position by preparing explicit lesson plans for each student, and she volunteered to do this again. Because the school budget was tight, the literacy team decided to try to enlist America Reads tutors from a local college. The reading specialist would train each tutor and monitor the tutors throughout the year.

All 198 of the students would require support from their content-area teachers. The literacy team knew that many of the faculty did not have the knowledge necessary to help the students. First, the faculty would receive a list of the students and their reading levels. Most content-area teachers did not realize that although their textbook may be on grade level, many students were reading two or more years below grade level. Second, the departments would plan professional development to show teachers a variety of content-area strategies for literacy support and to encourage teachers to use leveled and supplemental texts at the students' independent reading level at least once a week to build background knowledge. The media specialist and the technology resource teacher would help find materials. Third, the teachers could provide the reading specialists with a list of concepts for which the students needed to learn vocabulary and build background knowledge. The reading specialists would incorporate these concepts into the intervention classes and thus help the students learn the necessary vocabulary and gain background knowledge.

Like other principals, Kathy had hoped that the reading specialists would have time to work with teachers as well as teach the intervention classes. But the number of students needing intervention required the attention of two full-time teachers. However, the reading specialists' willingness to support both the tutors and the content-area teachers would augment the core program. Kathy began exploring her budget to add a new instructional role for the following year: literacy coach.

By forming a literacy team, Kathy enlisted the support of a group of teachers who were highly regarded by their peers and willing to become more knowledgeable about literacy. This group directed the literacy effort. Kathy knew that assessment must inform curriculum and instructional decisions and that the most immediate need was a literacy intervention for students in the lowest quartile. During intervention classes, the focus was on teaching students how to read and how to use reading to learn. A qualified reading specialist used the content assigned in other classes with a leveled text to teach both literacy skills and content. Ideally, instructional intervention is connected to the content-area instruction students receive the rest of the day. One goal of these sessions is to help students develop the skills to read a grade-level text independently.

Determining which students require which types of interventions is a placement issue that school leaders must address by putting into place structures and policies for assessment and using the resulting data to screen students, determine placements, and monitor program success. (In Chapter 7 we discuss how school leaders can use data to drive literacy teaching and learning.)

Types of Literacy Interventions

Sometimes schools investigate reading programs that tout large gains in student reading skills. Some of these programs do offer the advantage of sequenced instructional materials and teacher support. However, school leaders must carefully evaluate such programs and consider the following factors:

- the ability of the school to support the technology platforms required by many of these programs;
- the sufficiency of teacher professional development and ongoing technical assistance available and planned for as part of program implementation;
- the cost efficiency, which must make sense for the number of students whose needs match the program's target population; and
- the feasibility of the amount of time and consumable materials required to implement the program fully.

School leaders should recognize that it is highly unlikely that a single program will meet the needs of all or most struggling readers. Whether a specific reading program is used or not, school leaders have a number of options when deciding how to best provide additional support to students. Some of the formats leaders can use to provide literacy interventions are described in the following sections.

Pullout Programs or Additional Literacy Classes

This option pulls students out of one of their other classes daily or several times a week for instruction in literacy, or they attend a literacy class in place of another class. Such classes should not replace English class, but should supplement regular English/language arts instruction that provides embedded literacy support. Leaders need to ensure that an intervention class is not merely a second English class but is a class that focuses on explicit instruction in reading and writing. When a trained reading specialist is not available to teach this class, sometimes the assignment falls to an English/language arts teacher who may or may not be comfortable with teaching reading. It is important that English/language arts teachers who have inadequate preparation to teach reading and developmental writing receive additional training in specific reading comprehension strategies to use with struggling readers, basic phonics, how to teach basic composition, and approaches for developing fluency.

Pullout or additional classes for literacy are becoming more prevalent for struggling middle school readers and for 9th graders. These classes can take the form of reading and writing workshops, academic literacy classes, strategic reading classes, or study skills classes. Within each, students receive explicit instruction in reading and writing strategies, time for guided and independent practice, tools for assessing their own progress, time for sustained silent reading, and time for discussion of texts that students create and read. It is important that administrators expect teachers to set a clear goal, a predetermined time frame, and measurable outcomes.

These "extra" or pullout classes are sometimes problematic in middle and high schools because students who are lacking skills cannot afford to miss instructional time in their core content classes. Furthermore, these students often resent being pulled out of physical education or elective classes, where they frequently are succeeding. However, students may be willing to participate in these programs if the classes create a climate where it is okay to make mistakes and where the students perceive that the strategies being taught are applicable and practical.

Before- or After-School Programs

In these programs, students attend a class either before or after the regular school day. Although this option is desirable because it does not substitute for any other class, problems sometimes arise, such as unavailability of transportation and conflict with other school activities such as band practice, sports programs, and clubs. Coordination with all faculty members can help this type of program succeed. Practices and clubs can begin 45 minutes after school ends, or students can attend the intervention class before school. These programs should be taught by reading specialists or other qualified teachers.

Tutoring/Mentoring Programs

Tutors can provide an opportunity for the student to read aloud to an interested audience. This process gives the student a purpose for reading and a chance to ask questions and discuss ideas. If the tutors have received training, they can teach simple strategies such as asking students to make connections between self, the world, and other texts. However, tutoring generally cannot be substituted for an intervention class with systematic instruction designed for the student's specific needs.

In mentoring programs, an adult volunteer meets regularly with a student, giving encouragement and providing guidance. Although mentors do not usually help a student with reading and writing, the support of a responsible adult can help the student understand the importance of these literacy skills and thus motivate the student to engage more with learning. Tutors and mentors can provide the assistance that students often need to complete assignments and see the relevance in what they are learning in school.

Summer School Programs

Some schools hold a summer reading enrichment program to provide support and to ensure that students do not fall further behind. The goal of summer programs is to have students engage in activities that require reading in order to complete projects. Students can develop theme-based menus and prepare foods using recipes from multiple sources and serve them at a local homeless shelter, or read a short story and turn it into a play performed at the local library. Some programs collaborate with other organizations such as the local historical society to have students interview and then write up summaries of the lives of elderly residents in the community. Other programs have students examine a community issue of interest to the students with a cumulative presentation of results and recommendations. Note that these are not "skill and drill" remediation sessions but are designed to engage students in authentic reasons to read and write. Programs should include deliberate and purposeful instruction that embeds strong literacy support into meaningful content that builds strong prior knowledge. Preliminary research indicates that students who attend these summer enrichment programs maintain or improve their reading levels. However, these programs cannot replace the immediate needs for support during the school year.

To support the faculty in their literacy efforts, many schools are adding literacy coaches to their faculty. These master teachers offer essential leadership for the school's overall literacy program and oversee the reading program, mentor teachers, provide staff development, monitor assessment, purchase and review materials, and model lessons. (See Chapters 5 and 9 for additional information on literacy coaches.)

What an Intervention Classroom May Look Like

Students attending the same intervention class may have diverse and challenging reading difficulties. Imagine an intervention class that includes Jim, Roy, and Stephanie (see earlier vignette in this chapter). To address each student's needs, the reading specialist first needs to administer a diagnostic reading assessment and then plan instruction that

- addresses each student's reading challenges;
- strengthens students' abilities to transfer reading skills to the reading they do in their content-area classes; and
- where possible, connects the content and focus of vocabulary development and literacy strategies to what the students are doing in their content-area classes.

Middle and high school reading tasks require students to be fluent, strategic, critical readers. Helping struggling readers make efficient progress toward this goal is the job of the intervention teacher. The following vignette describes a reading intervention classroom where several of the students described earlier in this chapter might succeed.

Jim is still struggling to decode and expand his knowledge of sight words and learn ways of figuring out words he does not know. The reading specialist has decided that Jim would benefit most from use of a structured phonics and morphemic-analysis program on the computer. Jim uses the program for 20 minutes each day. The reading specialist has also paired Jim up with another student so they can do paired reading and can complete timed readings with easy, high-interest texts. They spend another 20 to 30 minutes daily on these activities. The last third of the reading intervention class is spent in a guided-reading group with the reading specialist in which they focus on before-reading strategies. Jim had almost given up as a reader, but he thinks his reading is improving and he has hope that the special education teacher that teams with his reading teacher can help him.

Roy still tunes out a lot, but he is learning to like some aspects of reading. The reading specialist is working with Roy, focusing on during-reading strategies with an emphasis on those that increase his interaction with the text so that his attention stays focused while reading. She provides daily guided-reading practice with feedback so Roy does not reinforce bad habits. She also gave Roy and several other students an online vocabulary-building program to use, which he likes because the words appear in a game format and he finds it easy to focus. He is amazed when he comes across these words when he is reading and he can remember what they mean. The reading specialist has taught Roy and three other students to do reciprocal teaching. The group works together on comprehending a text they choose from several offered by the reading specialist. Roy had never finished an entire book before this class, and he is feeling much better about himself as a reader since the class began.

Stephanie is learning that there is more to reading than calling words. Her reading intervention teacher began the year by teaching and modeling several reading comprehension strategies to Stephanie and others; the strategies are designed to scaffold all parts of the reading process. Their guided-practice group has focused on metacognitive strategies and questioning the text. Early in the year Stephanie completed a language-skills module on the computer that helped her understand cues when she reads. The cartoon format of the program made her laugh. Now she practices using those cues as she engages in prompted pair reading with another student. Stephanie also works daily with a reading comprehension software program that explicitly asks her questions about what she has read and provides direction if she asks for help. Stephanie likes the program because she can choose the reading selections based on her interests and because she does not feel "dumb" when she makes mistakes. All of these instructional approaches are helping Stephanie to learn to pay attention to all steps of the reading process, and she is beginning to connect reading with meaning.

The teacher in a reading intervention class has to be a master at multitasking. She knows her students' strengths and weaknesses and orchestrates the class to meet student needs. She is knowledgeable about all aspects of reading: phonemic awareness, phonics, fluency, vocabulary acquisition, and comprehension skills. She knows how to teach literacy skills and strategies explicitly, and she knows how to guide students as they learn to practice these skills independently. She plans instructional differentiation and skillfully matches students with books, and she sequences instruction in ways that move students forward. She understands and celebrates diversity, affirming students' strengths and expecting all students to learn. It is not an easy job, but when we asked one reading specialist why she worked with these students, she replied, surprised, "Because it is the most meaningful job in the world."

Key Messages

In this chapter, we discussed the needs of struggling readers and writers and what leaders can do to ensure these needs are addressed. All struggling readers and writers require extra literacy support during content-area instruction, and many would benefit from a separate intervention. Five prototypes of struggling readers were presented, including special education students and English language learners. Their characteristics as readers and writers and the particular skills they need to strengthen may vary. But all of their needs can be met with a combination of content area literacy support and targeted intervention classes. Program options for literacy interventions include pullout programs, after-school programs, mentoring/tutoring programs, and summer school classes. The key messages for this chapter are the following:

- Not all struggling readers and writers are alike.
- All struggling readers can benefit from literacy support strategies during content area instruction.
- Some struggling readers and writers need an intervention class taught by professionally prepared personnel (such as a reading specialist).
- School leaders are responsible for planning literacy interventions to ensure that all students receive the literacy support and development they need to become successful readers and writers.

The role of school leaders is to make sure that all students read, write, and think at high levels. This means that they make sure that addressing the needs of struggling readers and writers takes place all day and across the curriculum. In addition, some students may need a literacy intervention so that they can read and write on grade level. Literacy support ought not to be optional and offered only in classrooms where teachers are "willing." Instead, school leaders who initiate and sustain a schoolwide focus on literacy make sure that all students receive the literacy support they need.

4 Sustaining Literacy Development

School, Parent, Community, and District Support

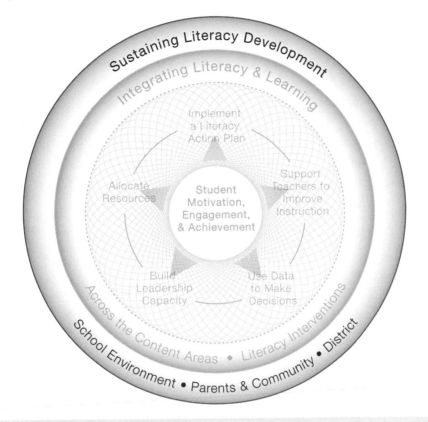

Sustaining Literacy Development

Integrating Literacy & Learning

Implement a Literacy Action Plan

Support Teachers to Improve Instruction

Student Motivation, Engagement, & Achievement

Allocate Resources

Build Leadership Capacity

Use Data to Make Decisions

Across the Content Areas • Literacy Interventions

School Environment • Parents & Community • District

Why is this component important? Literacy improvement efforts are strengthened or undermined by what goes on outside of each individual classroom. A literacy-rich school environment clearly communicates that the school is a place where reading, writing, speaking, listening, and thinking are priorities. Involving parents as partners in the literacy improvement effort is important as well. Beyond the school walls, school leaders must use community and district resources strategically to support and sustain a school-based focus on literacy improvement.

Young people attend schools as one part of their home, educational, work, social, and recreational lives. Although middle and high schools exist within a larger community and district context, too often schools are disconnected from the families and communities they serve. This disconnect represents a distinct challenge for a school-based literacy initiative because without home and community support and involvement, it is unlikely that the initiative will be highly successful.

Ideally, a middle or high school should function as an integral part of the community that it serves. *Community* can be defined as the school's students and their families, as well as the business and community resources in the geographic location of the school. It is important that schools define how they see the community, connections to the community, and resources in the community. A healthy school-community relationship, whether in a rural, a suburban, or an urban setting, is reciprocal and mutually supportive. It is the role of school leaders to involve the community in the school's literacy improvement efforts. Specifically, school leaders need to

- make certain that the school's literacy improvement effort embraces and celebrates the cultures of its students and the community it serves;
- explain how the school plans to recognize and build on the out-of-school literacies that students bring to the classroom; and
- include parents and community members in planning and implementing a literacy initiative and agree on ways that the school, the parents, and the community can collaboratively use resources to support students' development as readers, writers, and thinkers.

The more inclusive and adept teachers and leaders are at communicating clearly that students' home languages, cultures, and traditions are valued assets, the more willing students and parents will be to work together as partners with the school. The clearer the message is to everyone that literacy is a priority and that they have important roles to play in the school's literacy initiative, the more parent and community input and support the school is likely to receive.

A primary way to underscore this message is to create and sustain a literacy-rich school environment. Such a learning environment clearly demonstrates that the school is a place where all students engage in reading, writing, and thinking and that developing all students' academic literacy skills is truly a priority. A literacy-rich school environment provides the critical context within which the work of literacy improvement takes place. Elements of a literacy-rich school environment include

- having a publicly visible mission statement and course descriptions that describe the types of reading, writing, and thinking students are encouraged, supported, and expected to do;
- adequate and accessible literacy materials and resources including textbooks and works of fiction and nonfiction, computer software and hardware, reading programs, periodicals, paper, and supplies;
- the types of events it hosts and values, such as debates, plays, speech events, poetry jams, arts nights, book clubs, literacy tutoring, and ESL and computer classes for parents;
- the volume and quality of student work it displays;
- how teachers and leaders model and encourage reading, writing, and thinking and how literacy achievement is celebrated;
- the programs it provides for students for whom English is not a first language; and
- how it communicates with parents who may not understand how they can best support the school's literacy focus.

Ensuring that a literacy-rich environment exists is a responsibility of school leaders. Teachers and students know when they have the resources and tools they need to learn—and when they do not. Parents and students understand when they are valued as active partners whose voices are heard. Teachers are generally willing to provide the coaching necessary for literacy-rich cocurricular activities such as schoolwide sustained silent reading, debate clubs, literary magazines, book clubs, online and print newsletters and newspapers, and theater productions if leaders expect and support these activities. When resources, tools, and support are in place, everyone is willing and able to work together to improve students' academic literacy habits and skills. This includes the students, who must buy in to the goal of improving their reading, writing, and thinking skills and are much more likely to do so within an atmosphere of active and visible support. Thus, schools that publicly and explicitly provide a literacy-rich environment actively support the literacy improvement efforts of teachers, students, and leaders.

School districts are also a reflection of the homes and communities they serve. Some districts set a positive role model for schools through their efforts to value and appreciate literacy by

- establishing a districtwide literacy team;
- writing a literacy plan for the district with long- and short-term goals;
- working with parents and community members to foster student literacy;

- hiring and preparing school administrators to become literacy leaders;
- supporting schools through coaching, mentoring, and professional development for teachers;
- creating policies that require communication about students' reading and writing skills between schools to support appropriate placement decisions;
- providing curriculum focus and coordination so that literacy support is in place and sequenced as students go through the upper grades;
- maintaining a database of student performance that is readily available to school leaders; and
- channeling resources to schools for the purpose of improving literacy among students.

In districts that actively support student literacy, schools are expected to implement the various components of the model we suggest in this book. It is in these districts that a literacy improvement effort has a chance to become *sustainable* and literacy improvement becomes part of the culture of the school—part of "the way we do things around here."

Schools in districts that do not provide this level of leadership, guidance, and support have a tougher time implementing a schoolwide literacy improvement effort (Togneri & Anderson, 2003). But it can be done. These "beacons of success" in a district rally the resources in the community, creatively channel all available resources to literacy, and strategically hire and develop the most talented experts in literacy. School leaders need to understand what kinds of resources districts can provide and petition the district on behalf of their school's literacy improvement efforts. Conversely, when district requirements impede progress, school leaders who can communicate a clear rationale for what they are implementing are often in the best position to advocate for needed support.

Often these schools can act as resources for other schools in the district. Sometimes two or three schools in a district pool their resources to provide professional development for teachers or share a literacy coach. The concern in these pockets of excellence is that if the school leadership leaves for some reason, the progress toward literacy improvement will eventually fade away without district-level support.

In this chapter, we focus on the outer band of the graphic of the Leadership Model for Improving Adolescent Literacy. This component, "Sustaining Literacy Development," comprises three parts: *Creating and Sustaining a Literacy-Rich School Environment, Involving*

Parents and Community Members, and *District Support for School-based Literacy*. We describe how school leaders can work within the school, with parents and the larger community, and with the district to obtain necessary support for literacy improvement efforts. The first vignette in the chapter, illustrating a grassroots effort, is followed by some tips for building a literacy-rich school environment and learning culture that successfully involve the parents and community. A second vignette illustrates a top-down approach of a school district that initiated a focus on literacy. We then discuss some ways that districts can support schools to improve literacy. The chapter concludes with key messages.

Creating and Sustaining a Literacy-Rich Environment in the School

When Ralph Dearden became principal of Southwest Middle School, he brought his love for reading to the teachers and students. He had a poster-sized picture made of himself, feet propped on the desk while reading his favorite book. When he talked to students in the hall, it was always about books and reading. He asked parents and community members for donations of books and magazines to put out on tables in the front office. He had a sign made that read, "While you are waiting, please help yourself to a book or magazine. If you don't finish, feel free to take it with you." When students were lined up on picture-taking day, he wheeled a cart and handed them each a magazine to read while waiting.

He realized that teachers needed to be seen as readers if they were to be a positive role model for students. To that end, he started a book club for his teachers around different genres: one semester it was historical fiction, the next semester it was poetry, then mysteries, then essays. He encouraged teachers to start book clubs with students around different genres or topics. He also wanted to make sure that his parents were involved in the book clubs, so he offered copies of books so that they could read and talk about them with their children. A local Italian restaurant donated a spaghetti dinner once a month so that parents and students could come together to discuss the books. One of the teachers wrote a discussion guide, and the resulting conversations often branched off to other areas of concern for students and parents. The media specialist gave a short book talk on several new books so parents and students could vote on the next book to read. Once these book clubs got started, business partners contributed to the cost of the books.

Ralph also started a sustained silent reading (SSR) period every day after lunch despite some consternation among his teachers about "lost" instructional time. At a staff meeting he discussed the importance of student choice and how to help students choose a book that would increase their enjoyment of and engagement in reading. He stressed the importance of their modeling their own pleasure in reading and set his expectation that during SSR, everyone in the school would read—students, teachers, custodians, visitors. This was not a time for teachers to grade papers. Before reading, teachers led discussions on such topics as what students could do if they came to an unknown word and how to activate prior knowledge. At the closing of each SSR period, students were put in small groups to share what they read with other students. The mayor, a local football star, the superintendent, and anyone else who came to the school were all invited to read with students and talk about themselves as readers. Inspired by his principal, the soccer coach brought out his lawn chair and read a book in the middle of the quad during lunch period. Students gathered around to see what he was reading.

During Ralph's fifth year, the demographics of Southwest Middle School shifted dramatically from primarily African American and white students to include large numbers of limited-English-speaking immigrants from Mexico. Although the school had always been supportive of meeting diverse students' needs, this was a new challenge for many classroom teachers who could not speak Spanish and were not familiar with the students' native culture. Ralph was also personally perplexed as he saw that the new students did not attempt to read the magazines he handed out. Although they seemed to understand him when he spoke, their oral responses were short because their facility with English was limited. As he met the new students' parents, he realized that they had English language needs, too.

Ralph held a series of brainstorming sessions with his faculty and began asking questions in the district. He knew that meeting the needs of these new students would require district support. District curriculum specialists found other specialists who were experienced in working with English language learners and asked them to speak to teachers and administrators about the best methods of teaching and learning. A prominent person in the Mexican community was invited to help school district personnel understand the impact of immigration on families and children. Teachers began meeting after school to learn more Spanish and to adapt their instruction to accommodate these new students. The media specialist went online to find the best of adolescent literature in Spanish and English that might connect to the lives of the new Mexican immigrants, and she ordered both audio and print editions.

Ralph began a nightly program at the school in English as a second language and hired a bilingual staff to manage it. The staff offered English lessons for the parents, and the students received help with their homework and with English. Sometimes parents would bring food to share before their lessons. Ralph always made sure books in both Spanish and English were available for parents and students to take home. He also asked the local public library to supplement his efforts by offering materials and mentors for students and parents on weekends.

Ralph knew that developing fluency in English takes a long time, and he made it a priority for his school. Meanwhile, these district-supported activities quickly helped the new students feel at home at Southwest Middle School. Ralph often smiled during his walk-throughs when he saw his English-speaking students helping their new classmates.

Tools to create a literate environment include inclusive literacy-related clubs (book clubs, writing clubs, debate/speech teams, media clubs), highly visible literacy-based activities, authentic connections to the community, adult models of reading and writing, authentic reading and writing tasks, posted student work, and classroom libraries. Schoolwide initiatives such as sustained silent reading time, a read-aloud program, daily book commercials, or a community read can enhance efforts and give a clear message to students that literacy is important. The media center can play an important role as well. When the message about the importance of literacy is not clearly stated, supported, and sustained, students and teachers may not buy in.

By modeling his own love for reading and discussing books and igniting a passion for reading across the school, Ralph slowly changed the culture of Southwest Middle School to a place that visibly valued literacy. He used every opportunity to focus on reading and make it central to the mission of the school. He implemented school structures such as book clubs and SSR time to motivate increased student engagement in reading. He helped teachers understand how to make the most of SSR time. Most important, he involved the parents and community members in his efforts to make literacy central and obvious throughout the school.

Successful schools publicize their literacy vision and plan and actively recruit participation from the entire school community. This culture of literacy is evident throughout the school environment through written materials about literacy development; announcements about literacy-related events; posters that demonstrate student learning; publication of student writing in the school newsletter, on the school Web site, and in the local paper; and display of student writing on the school walls and in every classroom and office throughout the school building. A schoolwide culture of literacy encourages teachers to demonstrate their own enthusiasm for reading, writing, communicating, and thinking as part of all aspects of classroom learning. When every member of the school community takes responsibility for literacy efforts, a culture of literacy becomes pervasive.

Involving Parents and Community Members

Teachers who provide opportunities for students to incorporate their cultural heritage into curriculum and instruction help students make connections to their lives that engage them in learning. Many schools celebrate students' culture by displaying appropriate artwork and honoring cultural holidays and festivals. Treating all students with respect and dignity gives students the message that they, along with their cultural heritage, are valued. Recognizing and honoring literacy accomplishments by posting students' writing on the school's Web site, showing student performances on local cable stations, or having students respond to current events in the local newspapers are a few of the ways in which the culture of the community can be linked to a focus on literacy. Parents and community members can work hand in hand with the school to enhance literacy through collaborative ventures such as donations of books and magazines to classroom libraries, attendance at school literacy events such as poetry readings or student "open mike" events, or assistance with after-school tutoring for struggling readers and writers.

School leaders can do much to convey to parents and the community that literacy is an important focus for the school. It is the role of the principal, working with others, to establish and maintain a literacy-rich environment and learning culture at the school. Bringing parents and community members into the process of improving literacy makes critical connections for students and brings authenticity to the importance of reading and writing proficiently. Most parents want to understand how they can help with literacy efforts for their child and for the school. In addition, community members can help by providing positive adult role models, resources, and apprenticeship opportunities; mentoring students; and promoting the literacy effort. If parents and community members are not aware of and involved with the school's literacy improvement efforts, they may misunderstand, fail to support, or actively oppose new actions taken by the school.

To be partners with the school in the effort to improve literacy, parents and the community must be aware of the need and the roles that they can play. Parental roles can be placed on a continuum from simple recognition of literacy goals to full involvement in tutoring, mentoring, and organizing book clubs. It is the role of the school leadership to move the parents along the continuum in working with their own children and perhaps in helping others. Parents, like community representatives, need to receive training in how to best help students with their literacy skills. Many schools invite parents to attend their professional development sessions for teachers when literacy is the topic. Others hold special training workshops for parents and mentors who will work on reading skills with students. Some schools hold special classes for parents who need help with their own literacy skills and language development.

Another important aspect of parent communication is providing specific ways for parents to support their children at home when they are involved in reading, writing, speaking, and higher-order thinking about increasingly complex concepts. Many parents find it difficult to help their children entering middle and high school for two basic reasons. First, many adolescents are not interested in having their parents aware of what is going on in school, particularly if they are having problems. Poor grades are often the only clue that parents have about their student's struggles to learn. Second, the content is more difficult to understand as the students move through the grades, and many parents feel intimidated. Parents who struggled with reading and writing themselves, or who have language barriers, will not often seek help for their child from the school. If they do seek help, they may not be sure whom to talk to or what to ask for. Communication is essential to resolving these issues. Principals need to realize that if the community has large numbers of parents from a specific language group, providing information in that language is important in order to develop relationships. Often there are students, staff, community members, or teachers who might be able to provide skilled translation for newletters, cable broadcasts, or audiotape updates.

Accurate information for parents is essential to the entire literacy improvement effort because they will be the ones to encourage and support their child's hard work. (Figure 4.1 summarizes the kind of content that should be part of ongoing communication from the school.) Parents ought to be involved in the planning of the literacy improvement effort and the dissemination of the literacy action plan to other parents. School leaders can invite articulate and respected parents to be on the school's literacy team. Parent members on the team may include parents of current students as well as parents from sending schools. Although parents want to address the problems their students currently are having in school, they also want to prevent these problems from occurring in later years.

In addition to the strategies Ralph used in his school, leaders can use various other ways to have students see adults in the community as active readers, writers, thinkers, and communicators. Some large middle schools have developed grandparent programs in which local senior citizens are invited in one day a week to read with students and

---

4.1   Content of Ongoing and Frequent Communication with Parents

- The goals of the school's literacy improvement effort
- How parents can learn about their child's literacy progress
- Where parents can access literacy support within the school and community
- How parents can help the school help their child
- Homework and class projects with tips to help parents support their child's learning
- Text and online resources parents can access to learn literacy support strategies and study skills

---

to share stories about how the content relates to their lives. Others have used older students as reading role models. Eighth graders sharing their writing with 5th graders, high school students reading to 4th graders, and middle school students helping preschool students make a picture book or record a story are all ways to involve students in reading and writing together. Local libraries can provide weekend book clubs that connect adults and high school students. Retirees in the community can be asked to help struggling students read young-adult books of high interest that the students may not read on their own. Community organizations can host visual displays of students' work, sponsor writing contests, or provide incentives for students' achievements with summer reading lists. When schools invite parents and community members to participate in these and other literacy activities, often many step forward to volunteer.

The community can also support literacy through the media. The school Web site can feature literacy activities and opportunities in the school community and nearby towns or cities. Community members can help translate student writing, school newspapers, or the principal's letters to parents so those who speak other languages can access them easily. The school newspaper or local cable television station can run "commercials" of books or student-written documentaries of local events or multimedia presentations that are codeveloped by students and adult mentors in areas of interest. Churches, local businesses, and service clubs can further develop community awareness of literacy by posting information on reading materials and literacy skills. Local newspapers and radio and television stations can offer public service announcements on reading and writing that are written and performed by high school and middle school students.

Community organizations, service clubs, local businesses, and religious groups also can be helpful, but they need to first be informed and have the opportunity to contribute their ideas; then it is important to get feedback about how the school's literacy team responded to their ideas. Key stakeholders within the community include

- the director of the local public library,
- representatives of local businesses that employ students,
- religious leaders,
- local law enforcement and court officers,
- local government officials,
- newspaper and media representatives,
- service clubs such as Rotary or Masons, and
- local colleges and universities.

A key consideration is to have someone in the school building be the contact person for the parents, the community, and resource organizations. School leaders can select several community representatives to be a part of the initial planning for the literacy improvement effort. A communitywide literacy effort that is organized and coordinated with the school, using communication tools such as focus groups or surveys, provides an opportunity for community groups to determine how they can best help. Some groups may help by advertising the need for literacy development, while others may provide funds, mentors, resources, internships for students, and incentives. Community members can be encouraged to provide positive adult models of reading and writing. Some service clubs have made literacy improvement their top goal and provide grants and assistance to schools. If school leaders successfully communicate that a focus on literacy is an urgent priority and provide the structures and opportunities for the community to assist, it is likely that the community will respond.

District Support for School-Based Literacy Improvement Efforts

As mentioned earlier in this chapter, a school district can play an essential role in initiating or sustaining a literacy improvement effort. The success of any districtwide initiative, of course, ultimately lies in the quality of the implementation at each school. Sometimes individual schools begin efforts to improve literacy among students; most eventually need the support of the school district. School leaders who are able to garner resources and support from the district tend to lead more successful efforts. The following vignette shows how one superintendent took proactive steps to initiate and support literacy improvement efforts in all the middle and high schools in one medium-sized district.

It was obvious to Dr. Christine Quinn, the new superintendent of Westview School District, that the reading scores in the five middle schools and two high schools were not up to par. The elementary schools had received most of the district's resources during the past 20 years, and the secondary schools seemed to be just rolling along without much change or effort. Successful change would require a whole-district effort with support from the entire community. Parents who had stopped being involved in the schools after elementary school would have to become re-engaged if the literacy effort was to succeed. Community groups, businesses, and service organizations would all need to be a part of the planning, implementation, and provision of resources for the literacy improvement effort.

First, Christine assembled a cross-functional literacy team at the district level. This team included representatives of the administration, the professional development committee, the special education department, the English language learner department, the reading/language arts department, and all content curriculum areas—social studies, science, math, fine arts, and vocational programs. Additional members included four parents, two high school students, representatives from two community service organizations, and the director of the public library.

Christine distributed a copy of Reading Next: A Vision for Action and Research in Middle and High School Literacy *(Biancarosa & Snow, 2004) and asked members of the team to review it before the next week's meeting. The next week, they examined the school's student performance data to look at trends over the years, particularly the performance of selected subgroups. In addition, they compared the scores for each school with student performance statewide. A Middle School Literacy Action Team and a High School Literacy Action Team were formed, and over the course of the next year each team wrote a district proposal outlining goals, roles, and responsibilities of various people at the school and district levels, as well as strategies for meeting the goals.*

The principal, five school leaders, and three parents from each school were asked to review the draft proposals and give feedback to the respective literacy teams. After much discussion and input from the school groups, these recommendations were reviewed by each faculty and were adopted by all district middle and high schools. Christine then held regular meetings with the school principals, helping them understand how the proposed changes were directly based on the student performance data for their school and the demands of the state exam.

She helped principals evaluate current teacher assignments; the alignment of curriculum, instruction, and assessment; parent communication vehicles; and school schedules through the lens of literacy learning for students. In addition, the public library was asked to supplement the literacy improvement effort by offering after-school and weekend mentoring by members of the community. Churches and other community service groups brainstormed how they could help their local school's literacy efforts and offered their suggestions to the school leadership.

Principals led the members of the new school-based literacy teams through an analysis of the assessment data for their schools. Principals modeled their support by attending literacy conferences with their team members and began reading books about literacy. A week-long summer institute was held for all the middle and high school literacy team members, the superintendent, the cross-function district-level literacy team, and interested teachers. About 100 participants attended these all-day sessions, and they gained both conceptual knowledge (the literacy learning process) and pedagogical knowledge (best practices in the classroom). In addition, special sessions were organized for principals and literacy coaches to help them with issues of scheduling, classroom observations, and allocating resources toward the literacy effort. At the end of each day, they met by school literacy teams and began developing a literacy action plan for their school. A district-level administrator joined each school group to signal district support for literacy development and to take ideas requiring policy changes back to the district administration and the school board.

When school began the next year, each school enacted its literacy plan, and literacy team members implemented literacy support strategies in their classrooms. Literacy coaches and reading specialists helped other teachers learn to develop literacy-rich lessons, observed in classrooms, and gave feedback. Community groups provided mentors and reading coaches. Eventually, each school established model classrooms that others could visit. Christine's goal was for these literacy strategies to become pervasive throughout the district.

Westview was becoming a school district where literacy was the focus. The community was aware and supportive of the efforts of the schools. Schools displayed student work, held parent nights featuring oral presentations of student writings, and organized book clubs; business partners joined in by contributing guest readers, buying books, and providing giveaways for students and parents. Students and parents began to use the public library more frequently for after-school and weekend support. This systemic communitywide effort began with district leadership ensuring that all stakeholders had input and played key roles as the initiative progressed. This focus on literacy eventually became part of the culture of the district.

In this vignette, the essential component for success was the consistent, hands-on approach of the superintendent as she led and supported the literacy initiative. She understood that instigating and sustaining fundamental change requires a top-down and bottom-up approach that values and accommodates the views and expertise of all members of the community, not just those in schools. She also understood that each stakeholder had a point of view that could make a noteworthy contribution to her vision of literacy across the schools and in the community at large. Moreover, she systematically began planning a course of action that would ensure that the processes and products put in place would directly promote increased student achievement.

By forming clear relationships among the various planning teams during the school year, Christine established a clear line of authority and responsibilities from her office to each teacher and student in the school. For example, the district-level cross-functional team consisted of a broad array of constituents, including administrators, supervisors, school personnel, students, parents, and community members. Charged with examining student performance data across schools, this team had the courage to acknowledge the need to significantly improve academic performance. The superintendent's leadership style meant that they also had the support to investigate how best to design and implement a systemwide approach that would ensure success over time.

A second key ingredient illustrated in this vignette is the checks-and-balances system of feedback delivered among the various teams. Too often, reform efforts involve a group of district-level leaders who examine a specific problem and make recommendations for school personnel to implement, only to find later that implementation never occurred. Instead, teachers (and administrators) just waited it out until another set of recommendations was delivered to the school during the next school year—and ignored those as well. In many districts, the disconnect between the central office and the schools continues, despite the good intentions of all concerned.

In the vignette, the superintendent made sure that all of her teams had a process for communicating with each other to get clarification as well as to provide instructive feedback. Her initial district-level team communicated closely with the middle and high school literacy action teams. Similarly, those teams kept channels of communication open with the review team, which was charged with developing recommendations for all secondary schools. At the school level, principals formed cross-functional literacy teams that analyzed their school data and attended conferences to learn more about literacy instruction in their subject areas.

The week-long summer institute for school literacy team members, administrators, and other interested stakeholders was another component of Christine Quinn's vision. The content of the summer institute provided participants with both conceptual and pedagogical knowledge about literacy instruction. In addition, the recommendations adopted by all schools were woven among the sessions so that literacy efforts were consistent across the school as well as across the district.

To ensure classroom implementation during the school year, principals and their administrative staff provided hands-on support, both in the classroom and in seminars throughout the school year. The superintendent knew that teachers take their cues from their principal and other key administrators. Teachers notice when their administrators participate in professional development activities with them and when they do not. Christine knew that when teachers perceive that their administrators are not an integral part of their learning curve and support system, they may well not have the commitment and staying power to persist in the literacy initiative activities. Because the school leader sets the tone, Christine directed all school- and district-level administrators to sustain close working relationships with all stakeholders, including classroom teachers.

Many school districts, especially those in urban areas, face numerous challenges such as poor student achievement, low expectations and lack of demanding curricula for lower-income and minority students, student mobility, unsatisfactory business operations, and insufficient money to finance improvement efforts (Anderson, 2003). In the vignette, Christine Quinn did not let these challenges deter her from working toward her vision of literacy improvement in her middle and high schools. She and her colleagues worked steadily and successfully to overcome such obstacles and were rewarded by significant increases in student achievement because of the districtwide emphasis on literacy. Because of the superintendent's leadership, a districtwide sense of efficacy developed in which all participating stakeholders believed that they had the capacity to implement efforts to improve student performance.

The power of any literacy initiative is enhanced when it is structured to align with other district improvement initiatives. A study of three urban districts that advanced systemwide instructional reform showed four factors to be important in improvement efforts (Marsh et al., 2005):

• **Instructional leadership.** School districts that initiated successful improvement efforts helped principals set improvement goals and review relevant data. Some school districts actually rewrote job descriptions for principals to reflect a focus on learning improvement. Other school districts invested in preparation programs for new principals and reorganized supervisory structures so that principals got the help they needed. The method of principal supervision and job-embedded professional development for principals also seemed to make a difference.

• **School-based coaching.** Districts that led successful improvement efforts hired full-time coaches to offer job-embedded professional development to teachers. Often these coaches were recruited within the district and supervised by a coaching coordinator who developed and organized frequent professional development to help coaches acquire skills in working with teachers.

• **Curriculum specification.** Teachers are sometimes left to interpret state standards by themselves. All too often, the textbook becomes the curriculum. Districts that led successful improvement efforts wrote curriculum guides that aligned curriculum and assessment with state standards. When these guides are available from kindergarten through 12th grade, they provide a vehicle for smooth articulation between grade levels. They also promote consistency across grade levels and across schools in the district.

• **Use of data.** School district personnel can collect data that schools need for decision making. In addition, they can assist school leaders in knowing how to connect data to the school's literacy goals and objectives to help improve content-area learning and to make the important decisions of student placement in intervention classes. In the most successful districts, leaders knew how to interpret test results, evaluate student work, and translate those results into classroom practice.

Various chapters in this book describe these functions as they are enacted at the school level. When school districts support these efforts, however, the functions become more evenly implemented across the district. Honig and Hatch (2004) discuss the relationship between districts and schools as one of "crafting coherence," which is a process involving "schools and school district central offices working together to craft or continually negotiate the fit between external demands and schools' own goals and strategies" (p. 16). School leaders who succeed in setting goals and bridging or buffering them with the external demands of the district or the state can keep all stakeholders at the school level focused on the literacy effort.

School districts play important roles in making sure that the everyday managerial functions of schooling are performed. They mediate between the general public and the schools and, in the best districts, present a sense of efficacy and common good (Tyack, 2002). They act as mediators and interpreters of state and federal policy (Spillane et al., 2002). In turn, schools interpret state- and district-level policy for enactment at the school level. Effective district and school leaders are able to understand these policy requirements, interpret them, and implement school structures and policy requirements at the school level that best meet the literacy needs of students in the school. For example, one state mandated that all teachers with any responsibility for teaching reading in a middle or high school must acquire a reading endorsement consisting of six modules of 60 hours each. Although this endorsement was a hefty professional development requirement, some districts embraced the mandate to get as many of their teachers endorsed in reading as possible. These newly endorsed teachers brought their literacy knowledge to their content teaching and formed the nucleus of a schoolwide effort to improve literacy.

The vignette illustrates how districts can play an essential role in systemic, school-based literacy reform efforts beyond the everyday managerial running of schools. Although many schools have successfully improved literacy for their students, these efforts are usually not sustainable without support from the district. School districts also hold the purse strings. They generally allocate resources to schools. When these decisions are made with literacy improvement as a focus, a more coordinated and supported effort can ensue.

Key Messages

The school environment can support, lead, or hinder a literacy improvement effort. School leaders who proactively create a culture of literacy in the school send the important message to all stakeholders that literacy improvement for all students is important. In this chapter, we discussed several ways schools can create a literacy-rich environment.

Schools exist within a larger community and district context. Including parents and community members in the literacy effort is essential. It is important, first, that they understand the literacy goals of the school and their role in supporting it. The community can offer support by providing adult role models who value reading and writing through a variety of venues. In addition, the community holds many resources that schools can use to enhance their literacy efforts.

Districts that lead successful improvement efforts tend to focus on organized support for schools. Their approach to school improvement is systemic and coherent. For schools to improve the quality of literacy teaching and learning, they must make the effort and districts must support them. The following are the key messages in this chapter:

• Creating a literacy-rich environment in a school where reading, writing, and thinking are valued by students and adults is essential.

• Parents play an important role in the academic lives of students and can support literacy development in a wide variety of ways, especially for their own children.

• Ongoing and frequent communication to parents is important if they are to be informed about their children's education and able to provide encouragement and support.

• Parents and community members need to be a part of the literacy action planning process if they are to be effective contributors.

• Community groups often have funding and volunteers to assist the schools, but they need to be invited to participate.

• Districtwide initiatives can best support and sustain literacy improvement efforts in schools through a long-term focus on literacy as the core foundation of academic success.

• School leaders who lead successful efforts to improve literacy know how to work with the district to secure the resources and support they need.

Every task described in this chapter takes time and effort. Creating a culture of literacy in a school brings all stakeholders together for the benefit of improved student literacy. Bringing parents and the community on board to support the literacy improvement effort requires a great deal of coordination and planning. But getting the support of parents and the community can provide the resources required to lead a successful effort and sustain it over time.

Beyond the necessary role of school districts to manage employees, maintain safe schools, and coordinate resources, they can provide the leadership for districtwide school improvement efforts. In addition, they can lend support to schools engaged in creating a literacy-rich environment. Effective leadership at all levels is essential.

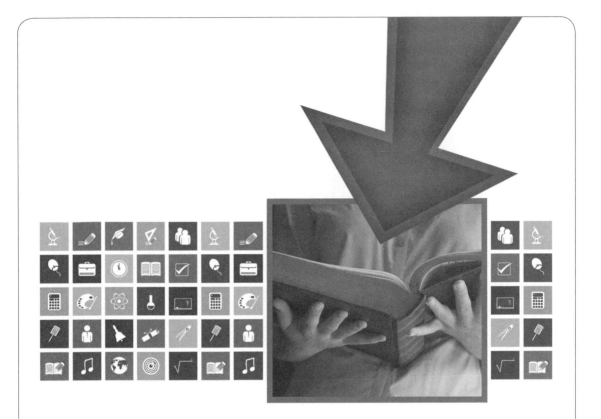

⭐ PART 2:
ACTION STEPS

5 Develop and Implement a Schoolwide Literacy Action Plan

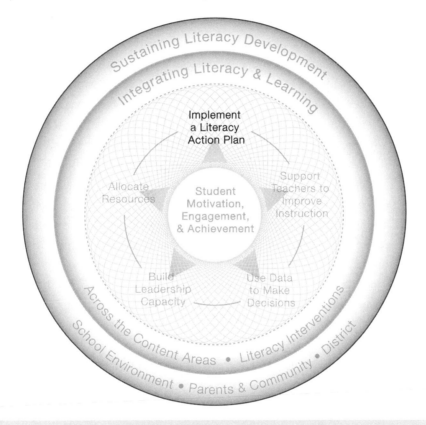

Why is this component important? A schoolwide literacy action plan is an essential blueprint for improving student achievement. An effective plan requires the skillful use of data about student performance, literacy needs and expectations in the school and community, school capacity to support literacy development, current teaching practices, and effectiveness of the literacy program. To generate change, leaders must actively use a literacy action plan to guide decision making around instruction, programming, and resource allocation.

Designing an effective literacy action plan to guide a schoolwide literacy improvement effort is not easy; however, such a plan is essential for school leaders who are serious about addressing the literacy and learning needs of students. In Chapter 7, we describe how school leaders can use student performance data to focus the school on improving students' literacy and learning and make appropriate decisions about student placement. Certainly, student performance data constitute the most critical information that drives planning for literacy improvement. A good plan specifically indicates what types of student performance data are being collected and how the data will be used. However, to ensure that improvement is sustained, additional types of data are important to consider when developing and implementing a comprehensive literacy action plan. After a plan has been developed and implemented, school leaders must then collect data to monitor its success, including the effectiveness of specific literacy interventions.

The biggest concern about developing a data-based literacy action plan is that it will not guide action. Too many times a plan is developed only to be "left on the shelf." Schmoker (2006) points out that most strategic planning in education is ineffective because the documents produced are fragmented, complicated, and convoluted, and often do not lead to improved student outcomes. In other words, the improvement plans are difficult to use, rarely used, or both. According to Schmoker, elaborate school improvement plans that do not focus exclusively and directly on curriculum implementation and improving instruction are not helpful to improving student achievement.

This does not mean that a literacy action plan is a bad idea. On the contrary, many schools we have worked with use their literacy action plan to focus their efforts and guide their work to improve student proficiency in reading and writing. However, school leaders must develop a data-based literacy action plan that they will actively use to guide ongoing decisions about instruction, programming, and resource allocation. School leaders need to obtain broad buy-in to the plan—it should not be developed by a small group of people and kept secret. It is important that the plan be measurable, coherent, concrete, and comprehensible to teachers and administrators. Last, it is important that the plan be seen as proactive, not as compliance to a mandate, even if a mandate is what prompted the plan's development. One principal told us that it was her school's literacy action plan that made the difference in how she was able to focus on instruction; now she thinks about how all decisions support or affect literacy development. Another credits her school's literacy action plan for their school's "staying the course" and making sure they are not distracted from the goal of improving literacy.

Implement a Literacy Action Plan is the top point in the graphic of the Leadership Model for Improving Adolescent Literacy and is the first *action step*. School leaders must work with their faculty to create a plan that brings together all of the other action steps discussed in the following chapters to ensure that every content area classroom and literacy intervention focuses on improving students' literacy habits and skills through emphasis on student motivation, engagement, and achievement.

In this chapter, we describe the key components of an effective literacy action plan and steps to develop this plan, along with approaches that leaders might use to collect and analyze relevant data. Then we describe a data-driven program-monitoring cycle that leaders can use to evaluate the effectiveness of the plan in action. Segments of a vignette describing how one middle school developed and used a literacy action plan are interspersed throughout the chapter. We conclude with key messages.

Essential Components of an Effective Literacy Action Plan

An effective schoolwide literacy plan guides action on many levels, focusing multiple activities toward increasing students' reading, writing, and thinking skills. A comprehensive literacy action plan has action steps related to five key areas:

- Strengthening Literacy Development Across the Content Areas;
- Literacy Interventions for Struggling Readers and Writers;
- School Policies, Structures, and Culture for Supporting Literacy;
- Building Leadership Capacity; and
- Supporting Teachers to Improve Instruction.

The key components of the literacy action plan mirror components of the Leadership Model for Improving Adolescent Literacy because the action plan acts as a blueprint for implementing a schoolwide literacy improvement effort. Determining appropriate overall goals for literacy improvement requires the gathering and analyzing of relevant data. Then, based on the data, leaders can define and implement action steps related to each component.

In the following section, we describe each of the essential components of a comprehensive literacy action plan in more detail and note the types of data that leaders can collect and analyze for each. Each action plan component also includes a mini-chart showing two related action steps that are part of a sample literacy action plan. Of course, the appropriate action steps a particular middle or high school should take will depend upon what that school's data indicate.

Strengthening Literacy Development Across the Content Areas

As described in Chapters 1 and 2, motivating and engaging students and developing their literacy skills are necessary outcomes for any literacy improvement effort. A schoolwide literacy action plan needs to include specific steps to set the expectation and provide the support so that all content-area teachers implement classroom instruction that is motivating, engaging, and strategy based. Figure 5.1 shows two examples of action plan goals that target literacy development across content areas.

5.1 Action Plan Goals for Literacy Development Across Content Areas					
Goal	Time Line	Action Steps	Person(s) Responsible	Resources	Evidence of Success
Activate subject area/ grade-level discussions on reading and writing strategies	School year	Schedule time for department meetings	Content area team leaders	Time on restructured days	Department minutes
		Share effective strategies in faculty meetings	Teachers, literacy team members	Planning time	Faculty agendas
		Include one strategy in each monthly faculty newsletter	Principal	Teacher suggestions and feedback	Monthly newsletters
Goal	Time Line	Action Steps	Person(s) Responsible	Resources	Evidence of Success
Locate and use a variety of texts in subject areas	Summer, School year	Assess and catalog available texts in subject areas	Media specialist and department chairs	Summer stipends, printing	List of texts
		Form a partnership with Newspapers in Education (NIE)	English chair	Time to make contacts	Agendas of meetings; NIE resources in classrooms
		Expand classroom libraries related to content	Principal and local school council	Time and budget for purchasing books	Number of libraries and books
		Explore options for subscribing to electronic text databases	Principal	Subscription fee	Purchase of database

Literacy Interventions for Struggling Readers and Writers

As we note in Chapters 3 and 7, setting up literacy interventions for struggling readers and writers is an important component of school improvement efforts. Deciding on the methods and types of programs to offer for these interventions will depend on data about student needs, school capacity, and teacher knowledge. Figure 5.2 shows two examples of action plan goals that target literacy interventions for struggling readers and writers.

5.2 **Action Plan Goals That Target Struggling Readers and Writers**					
Goal	**Time Line**	**Action Steps**	**Person(s) Responsible**	**Resources**	**Evidence of Success**
Purchase and implement reading program to meet the needs of students scoring in the lowest quartile on the reading assessment	Summer School year	Identify students in lowest quartile	District and school test coordinator	Test data	Student lists
		Research, identify, and purchase a validated reading programs for targeted students	Principal, reading specialist	Information on reading programs, funds	Research notes, meeting agendas
		Identify an intensive reading course in master schedule	Principal, assistant principal for master schedule	Flexible master schedule	Finished master schedule
		Assign qualified teachers to the reading course	Principal, human resources personnel	Qualified teachers	Teacher list with qualifications
		Place students in course and monitor progress	Principal, reading teachers	Course materials, professional development	Student grades, promotions, improvements on assessments
Goal	**Time Line**	**Action Steps**	**Person(s) Responsible**	**Resources**	**Evidence of Success**
Implement a schoolwide writing program	Summer School year	Research, identify, and purchase materials	Principal, assistant principals, teachers	Test data, grades, attendance data	Student reports sent to teachers
		Provide literacy professional development	Principal, district supervisors of subject areas	Outside professional development consultants	Teacher surveys, evaluations, sign-in sheets
		Provide time for cross-functional planning during the school day	Master schedule coordinator, department chairs	Flexible master schedule, instructional materials	Teacher surveys, minutes from planning meetings

School Policies, Structures, and Culture for Supporting Literacy

For many schools this is a "hidden" component not always articulated in a literacy action plan. Yet ignoring a school's policies, structures, and culture may mean that (1) there are aspects of these in place that will impede literacy improvement efforts if not addressed, and (2) action steps do not build on current school capacity in these areas, with the result that actions are not taken or sustained. For example, action steps that rely on a department structure for enactment may not be relevant if the school uses team-based instruction. Likewise, if a school faculty has had substantial training in a process for instructional planning or writing across the curriculum, it makes sense to build upon and connect the literacy effort to those areas of expertise instead of "replacing" earlier work. Figure 5.3 shows two examples of action plan goals that one middle school included in its literacy plan related to school policies, structures, and culture. Both goals focus on developing a school culture in which teachers coordinate their efforts to design and implement curriculum and instruction across subject areas, as well as to provide instruction based on a variety of assessment and performance options.

5.3 Action Plan Goals for School Policies, Structure, and Culture					
Goal	Time Line	Action Steps	Person(s) Responsible	Resources	Evidence of Success
Coordinate curriculum and instruction across subject areas	Summer School year	Form grade-level teams	Principal, assistant principals, curriculum chairs	Test data, grades, time to plan, summer stipends	Meeting agendas, formation of teams, assignment of students
		Form curriculum committees to develop instructional goals that encompass subject areas	Curriculum chairs, principal, assistant principals	Time during summer to plan for instruction, leveled instructional materials and texts, Internet access	Committee roster, planning minutes, agendas
		Develop themes and curriculum-integrated projects that support the themes	Curriculum chairs, department chairs	Instructional materials, planning time, summer stipends, district supervisors of subject areas	Teacher plan books, developed instructional materials
		Provide time for cross-functional planning during the school day	Master schedule coordinator, department chairs	Flexible master schedule, instructional materials, Internet access	Minutes of planning meetings, teacher surveys, evaluations

Goal	Time Line	Action Steps	Person(s) Responsible	Resources	Evidence of Success
Design and implement instruction that uses formal and informal assessment instruments	Summer School year	Form a cross-functional curriculum team to agree upon common assessment practice	Principal, assistant principals, teachers	Time to meet during the summer, stipends, assessment instruments	Meeting agendas, formation of teams
		Create common rubrics	Grade-level teams, department chairs	Time to plan, substitute coverage, sample rubrics, Internet access	Planning minutes, agendas, developed and field-tested rubrics, students' work
		Incorporate performance assessments in classroom instruction	Department chairs, teacher leaders	Sample performance assessments, planning time, summer stipends, district-level supervisors, support of testing director	Teacher plan books, developed performance tasks, student work and projects
		Provide time for cross-functional assessment review	Master schedule coordinator, department chairs	Flexible schedule, time before/after school, restructured days	Minutes of planning meetings, teacher surveys, evaluations

Building Leadership Capacity

As we make clear in Chapter 8, principals cannot lead a literacy improvement effort alone. They need to figure out how to augment staff expertise in literacy and distribute roles and responsibilities for literacy improvement across the school. A literacy action plan should specifically describe ways to build leadership capacity. For example, it can specify allocation of resources for new positions and time for new committees to meet and for teams and department chairs to discuss implications of the plan for their work, and for specialists to coteach, meet, or mentor others. The two examples of action plan goals in Figure 5.4 focus on strategies to build the leadership capacity of teachers by establishing demonstration classrooms and offering support for classroom-based research that examines student work.

5.4 Action Plan Goals for Building Leadership Capacity					
Goal	**Time Line**	**Action Steps**	**Person(s) Responsible**	**Resources**	**Evidence of Success**
Establish two literacy demonstration classrooms in each content area	Summer School year	Identify teacher leaders who can provide classroom demonstrations and modeling for their peers	Principal	Time to meet during the summer, stipends, assessment instruments	Meeting agendas, formation of teams
		Provide professional development to demonstration-classroom teachers	Principal	School literacy coach, outside professional development consultants	Classroom observations, teacher and student surveys, evaluations
		Create opportunities for classroom visits to observe demonstrations and modeling	Principal, department and/or curriculum chairs	Time to plan, substitute coverage	Observation rubrics, teacher surveys, notes
Goal	**Time Line**	**Action Steps**	**Person(s) Responsible**	**Resources**	**Evidence of Success**
Engage in classroom-based research by examining student work	Summer School year	Identify teachers and teacher teams to engage in classroom-based research	Curriculum and/or department chairs	Time to meet during the summer, stipends, assessment instruments	Meeting agendas, formation of teams
		Design tuning protocols for examining student work	Department and/or curriculum chairs	Time to plan, substitute coverage, professional materials	Sample protocols, examined student work, teacher and student surveys
		Provide common planning time	Principal	Substitutes; time for meeting outside of contract, if necessary; stipends; copying budget	Classroom observations, teacher and student surveys, evaluations
		Provide time for constructive feedback and follow-up activities	Master schedule coordinator, department chairs	Flexible schedule, time before/after school, restructured days	Minutes of planning meetings, teacher surveys, evaluations, presentations of results

Supporting Teachers to Improve Instruction

Middle and high school teachers cannot be expected to implement literacy support for students without targeted professional development and support. An important component of the overall literacy action plan is a plan for the types of support and professional development necessary to help teachers improve content-area literacy instruction and successfully implement literacy interventions with struggling readers. (We present information about formats and options for teacher professional development in Chapters 6 and 9.)

The two examples of action plan goals in Figure 5.5 focus on supporting teachers by providing coaching, peer observation, and collaboration, as well as by offering them opportunities to attend and present at local, state, and national professional conferences. Ultimately, of course, the measure of effectiveness for each of these action steps will be increased student achievement.

5.5 Action Plan Goals for Supporting Teachers to Improve Instruction					
Goal	Time Line	Action Steps	Person(s) Responsible	Resources	Evidence of Success
Engage in coaching, peer observation, and collaborative planning	Summer School year	Identify teacher leaders who can provide classroom demonstrations and modeling for their peers	Principal	Time to meet during the summer, stipends, assessment instruments	Meeting agendas, formation of teams
		Create opportunities for classroom visits to observe demonstrations and modeling	Principal, department and/or curriculum chairs	Time to plan, substitute coverage	Observation rubrics, teacher surveys, notes
		Provide professional development in coaching and mentoring	Principal	District supervisors of subject areas, outside professional development consultants	Classroom observations, teacher and student surveys, evaluations
		Provide time for constructive feedback and follow-up activities	Master schedule coordinator, department chairs	Flexible schedule, time before/ after school, restructured days	Minutes of planning meetings, teacher surveys, evaluations

5.5 **Action Plan Goals for Supporting Teachers to Improve Instruction** (continued)					
Goal	Time Line	Action Steps	Person(s) Responsible	Resources	Evidence of Success
Provide opportunities to attend and present at local, state, and national professional conferences	Summer School year	Provide department memberships in professional organizations	Principal	Funds for membership	Memberships and professional development materials
		Research local, state, and national conferences and submit proposals for attendance and presentations	Curriculum and/or department chairs	Research time, Internet access	Submitted proposals
		Send teachers and teacher teams to local, state, and national conferences	Principal	School and district funds	Teacher presentations to colleagues, conference evaluations
		Provide time for constructive feedback and follow-up activities	Master schedule coordinator, department chairs	Flexible schedule, time before/ after school, restructured days	Minutes of planning meetings, teacher surveys, evaluations

The Roles of School Leaders and the Literacy Team

As demonstrated in the charts associated with each component, leaders can apply sound action-planning principles to the context of literacy, setting data-driven goals, outlining action steps, delineating time lines and responsible parties, describing indicators of effectiveness, and allocating the necessary resources. Building this type of plan requires school leaders to have an understanding of issues related to student motivation and engagement, classroom contexts, and strategic interventions (see Chapters 1 through 3). Further, developing a schoolwide literacy action plan requires leaders to have an understanding of how to support teachers (Chapter 6), what types of student performance data are available to them (Chapter 7), and how to build leadership capacity (Chapter 8). In addition, it is important for leaders to have good information about school capacity, teacher knowledge and practice, and the literacy needs and expectations of the school and community.

The literacy team synthesizes the data on student performance, community input, teacher knowledge and use of literacy support strategies, and school support structures and policies to develop a clear picture of what currently exists and what is needed to improve literacy for all learners. Based on this review, school leaders set literacy goals that are data based, reasonable, and measurable. The team then develops a literacy action plan by assessing each goal and determining the action steps necessary to reach it. The action plan should include the person or persons responsible for each action step, the time line, and the measures of success.

Goal setting and action planning are the areas in which school leaders work with the literacy team to "put it all together." A data-driven process for goal setting and action planning is important to ensure that thoughtful actions take place and can be sustained. A literacy action plan that is grounded in student performance data and supported by additional data from assessments of school capacity, school and community expectations, and teacher practices is more likely to support student literacy and learning.

School leaders must play two additional roles to ensure that the plan that is developed is implemented. The first is to set forth a vision that stakeholders can support. One way to do this is through brainstorming as a faculty what the literacy improvement initiative would look like if it were successful. What would students be doing? What would teachers be doing? What would the environment be like? Then, an overarching vision statement must be developed that can set the tone for the initiative and be used to communicate to parents, students, and the community what the school is attempting to accomplish. Having this vision, actively referring to it, and using it to guide how teachers and students are supported are three ways that school leaders can ensure that the initiative will stay focused.

The second role is getting everyone on board. For a plan to succeed, collaborative implementation must occur. Teachers need to "buy in," or students will not receive equal access to quality reading and writing instruction and regular guided practice in content-area reading and writing. Having a common vision that is articulated, referenced, and used by school leaders will help, as will adequate and ongoing teacher professional development. (We provide ideas for how to work with reluctant teachers in Chapter 8.) The key point here is that it is the responsibility of school leaders to get everyone to be an active participant in enacting all the parts of the school's literacy action plan.

Leaders need to have and communicate a vision and secure the collaboration and effort of school staff. They also need to have a good plan, because without it, not much will change for students. This chapter focuses on the development of an effective literacy action plan. But we caution leaders to pay attention to the two issues of *vision* and *collaborative implementation* to ensure that the schoolwide literacy improvement effort is successful.

School leaders who have good data on students' reading and writing needs, measurable literacy goals, and specific action steps to address student needs can develop an effective literacy action plan. They can use this plan to guide the school's literacy improvement efforts over time. The next sections of this chapter outline how to gather and analyze this information and how this type of data can productively inform the processes of setting literacy improvement goals and creating a literacy action plan.

Using Multiple Data Sources to Develop a Literacy Action Plan

As we discuss in Chapter 7, student performance data are central to literacy improvement efforts in middle and high school. This type of data is critical when determining students' instructional needs as individuals and by grade-level cohort, determining the need for additional programming or types of intervention, and monitoring the success of support in the classroom.

Student performance data alone, however, are not sufficient for driving a literacy improvement effort because they do not take into account the school and community context within which learning and literacy development occur. Student performance data indicate *what* is needed but do not show *how* this can be put into place. Performance data also do not tell the specific actions required to ensure that the support structure is in place to sustain systemic improvement as opposed to something that will fade if key individuals retire or move to other schools. For example, in schools with high staff turnover, crafting a literacy action plan so that it incorporates new policies and support structures, grade-level or departmental agreements, and mentoring can make it more likely that changes will endure. Student performance data also do not inform school leaders about the level of support for literacy improvement that is already in place through school structures, policies, and resources and in terms of teachers' current knowledge and practice. For example, teachers may participate in professional development in content-area writing strategies that can be used to support reading comprehension. Professional learning communities may be in place that can provide a ready-made structure for a literacy improvement effort to build upon. Or the library collection may be outdated and limited, but the school may have available technology that can effectively support both reading and writing, as well as provide supplemental texts.

The goal of a literacy improvement effort is to create an organization that can sustain high levels of literacy and learning for current and future students. Few schools have unlimited resources to devote to literacy support; deciding how to use the available resources wisely requires gathering data about school and community priorities and expectations, current programs, structures and policies, and teacher professional development needs. Otherwise leaders may jump on bandwagons or select program options that do not maximize available resources, meet expectations, or address pressing needs. Figure 5.6 shows kinds of data in addition to student performance data that leaders can use as they develop a literacy action plan.

5.6 **Additional Key Data for Developing Literacy Action Plans**	
In Order to …	**Leaders Can Collect Data About …**
Set appropriate and measurable literacy goals	School and community needs and expectations about literacy
Assess resource allocation and adequacy of current policy and practices and determine what needs to be put into place or improved	The school's current capacity to support literacy
Determine current literacy expertise in the school, support teacher use of literacy support strategies, and develop a targeted professional development plan	Current teaching practices that provide literacy support across the content areas or as part of specific programs of study

In the following vignette, we present an example of how school leaders used multiple sources of data to develop a literacy action plan. To create their plan, in addition to looking at student performance data, school administrators carried out a needs assessment, determined the school's capacity to meet the needs of different types of learners, and determined the professional development and types of support teachers needed to improve content-area literacy development. The vignette is divided into sections that show how leaders at this school gathered and used each type of data to craft their literacy action plan. Each section of the vignette is followed by a description and additional examples of how leaders can collect and analyze data to create a literacy action plan.

DeWitt Middle School is a Title I school serving about 900 students in grades 6 through 8. The town where the school is located is in transition from a mill town to a town with a tourist-based economy. Several river guide companies are beginning to flourish, artist studios are being installed in the old factory by the dam, and new bed-and-breakfast inns and restaurants now occupy the handsome 19th-century homes that once housed company managers. Before the mills closed, it was quite possible to make a living with an 8th grade education.

When DeWitt Middle School recently conducted a survey of parents' expectations about student achievement, more than 80 percent of the parents stated their expectation that students should graduate ready for college, career, and citizenship. Yet 8th grade scores on the state assessment showed more than 50 percent of students were not meeting the standard in reading, and almost 80 percent were not meeting the standard in writing.

Tim Hancock, the school's energetic new principal, saw a focus on literacy across the content areas as a way to close this gap between parent expectations and student performance. Tim brought together his leadership team, which had representatives from all grade levels and content areas, and told them that the school had district support to conduct a literacy audit to determine how to proceed. The audit would help the team collect vital information about the school's capacity to support literacy improvement. An outside literacy consultant would analyze this information, together with student performance data and data on teacher knowledge and current practice; the consultant would make recommendations for what they should include in their literacy action plan.

School and Community Needs and Expectations About Literacy

In the vignette, it was necessary for Tim to understand the community's needs and expectations, as well as the expectations of the school's staff, as part of developing an effective plan. He made sure to understand the school board's priorities and the district's goals and to align the school's efforts with them. The parent survey indicated a gap between expectations and perceptions of what was occurring at the school for students. The faculty was polled to determine how their own knowledge and the literacy expectations of their students might be contributing to how instructional needs were being met.

It is important to decipher school and community needs and expectations concerning literacy so that the school can set measurable literacy goals that are responsive and appropriate. By conducting a literacy needs assessment, school leaders evaluate how the school is currently meeting students' literacy needs. The process can focus stakeholders' attention on literacy and can uncover missed opportunities and underused resources. Data sources that can contribute to the needs assessment include

- trends in state assessment results,
- teacher questionnaires,
- student surveys,
- literacy goals in school improvement plans, and
- focus groups and other discussions with teachers, students, and parents.

Based on the feedback received, school leaders can create or refine the school's plan for accomplishing its mission and identify areas of concern, thereby ensuring that its literacy goals match the expectations of students, teachers, parents, and the community.

The impact of this process will be different depending on the school and the community involved. Discovering the gap between assumptions and reality can be what enables one school to succeed with improving literacy where another fails to do so. Consider what would occur if the following community and school assumptions remained unchallenged:

• School leaders in an area with a large percentage of English language learners think they are meeting expectations with their current options for English-as-a-second-language and bilingual programs, yet parents and students strongly prefer a sheltered-instruction approach.

• Administrators assume that students have adequate access to computers, but due to scheduling, placement, and staffing issues, a majority of students are frustrated by their limited access.

• Some teachers assume that parents do not care because they do not attend school meetings and functions but low attendance may, in fact, be due to language barriers, work schedules, transportation issues, cultural differences, and low parent reading levels.

• Teachers' perceptions that a group of reluctant readers actually cannot read may be erroneous. It may be that these students will not or do not read what they see as irrelevant assigned reading but that they avidly read materials of interest outside of school. Thus, motivation instead of ability may emerge as an essential issue in addressing academic literacy development with certain students.

Examining assumptions such as these will provide key information school leaders can use when deciding what programs to put in place or what the school's literacy improvement goals should be. Setting literacy improvement goals without establishing baseline data to determine the starting point is not a productive way to proceed. Neither is setting a numerical improvement goal that does not address the differentiated needs of students with varying literacy abilities. For example, an arbitrary schoolwide goal of raising standardized test scores by a certain percent means little if disaggregation of the scores reveals that students in some programs are already scoring much higher than others. Thus, this arbitrary goal will allow the instructional needs of many students to remain unmet. By comparison, a goal of a 90 percent passing rate on the state reading test requires gathering current performance data about students at all levels of ability so that differential support can be put into place. In some cases, it might be necessary to set two goals to guide action—one for students on or above grade level and one for students whose reading level is below their current grade level.

Discovering the school and community expectations about literacy teaching and learning does not have to be an overwhelming task. Principals can work with their literacy team to determine what is known about

- specific programs to address the school's mission,
- students' reading and writing abilities,
- parents' concerns about literacy achievement,
- students' attitudes toward reading and writing, and
- teachers' beliefs about student literacy and learning.

For example, the literacy team might compare attendance, dropout, and graduation rates with literacy performance to determine if weak literacy skills are a strong contributing factor to students' motivation to complete school. Or leaders might survey student attitudes toward literacy and learning to assess the impact of social and emotional factors on academic success or failure. Figure 5.7 outlines a four-step process for conducting a literacy needs assessment.

5.7 Four Steps for Conducting a Literacy Needs Assessment

1. **Agree on questions.** The literacy team agrees upon a short list of important questions about literacy.
2. **Collect data.** Literacy team members make and carry out a data collection plan to ensure that they will have the information they need to answer pressing questions.
3. **Review and summarize data.** The literacy team reviews all of the information gathered and summarizes the data collected relative to each of the questions posed.
4. **Make recommendations and inform stakeholders.** Based on the information collected, the literacy team establishes a list of recommendations that define the expectations of school and community members around literacy and distributes a copy of these recommendations to all staff and community members who contributed data, so they know that their voices have been heard.

Assessing School and Teacher Capacity to Improve Literacy

The next step in developing a literacy action plan is for the literacy team to investigate the current capacity of the school and the teachers to respond to these recommendations.

Armed with those data, the literacy team can establish reasonable and measurable literacy goals. For each literacy goal, the team clarifies a rationale for its inclusion, develops action steps, and decides how the team will measure progress. This goal setting and action planning becomes the data-based blueprint for the school's literacy improvement effort.

The next part of the vignette describes how the DeWitt Middle School literacy team worked with a literacy consultant to conduct an inventory of school capacity and teacher knowledge and use of literacy strategies. To determine students' needs, the consultant analyzed student performance data. But to make recommendations to address these needs, the consultant relied on the additional data about school capacity and teacher practices.

The DeWitt Middle School literacy team worked with the literacy consultant to develop a school-capacity profile through several discussions about the school's current structures, policies, culture, and use of resources. All middle school teachers attended a presentation about adolescent literacy and then completed a comprehensive survey about their current teaching practices and knowledge about content-area literacy support. Tim also provided the consultant with the results from the diagnostic reading assessment administered individually to all 6th, 7th, and 8th graders.

The consultant analyzed the data and provided a report that documented the implications of the data as well as a detailed set of recommendations for action in the areas of school structures, policies and culture, content-area literacy support, strategic interventions, and teacher professional development. An examination of various types of data helped inform the recommendations.

Student performance data. *Teachers and administrators were aware that the percentage of students not meeting standards in reading was high. A closer look at the student performance data showed that although the vast majority of students tested "below grade level," most were only one or two grade levels behind. The issue was that students were not making a year's worth of literacy growth in a year's time. The majority of students were actually entering middle school on grade level, a tribute to the district's strong elementary literacy program. But without frequent, purposeful literacy support as part of content-area teaching and learning, these same students were losing ground while at the middle school. In addition, a small number of students had test results that indicated a need for more intensive intervention.*

Data on school capacity. *Data from the school-capacity profile revealed that some existing resources to support literacy were underused, such as the well-stocked library and the fact that 7th and 8th grade students had laptop computers. Other school capacities were* *haphazard, such as a lack of consistent policies about homework, lack of teacher access to reading assessment results, inconsistent use of writing rubrics, and a lack of common materials used to teach similar courses. Persistent themes included the lack of professional learning communities at the school and minimal expectations in many classes for critical thinking except for the "high achievers." In the opinion of the literacy team, the school did not have a strong culture of reading, writing, and thinking.*

*   **Teacher survey data.** Analysis of the results of the teacher survey showed that most teachers had very limited strategies for providing scaffolding before, during, and after reading; widely varying expectations for reading and writing even in the same grade level; and few strategies to teach vocabulary besides "assign, define, and test." Teachers said that students were not motivated to read and write but also said that they rarely allowed students to choose topics to read or write about.*

Investigating the School's Current Capacity to Support Literacy Development

Once recommendations are developed based on the needs assessment, a different type of data is required to answer the question: What is the school's current capacity for supporting literacy? To find out, school leaders can inventory resource use and the structures and policies in place that either support or limit literacy development. In the DeWitt Middle School vignette, school leaders hired an outside consultant. Often an outside perspective or use of an externally developed, structured protocol can provide the greatest insight and an efficient process for developing a picture of the school's capacity. Another approach is to ask the literacy team to work with educators throughout the school to develop an abbreviated type of capacity profile and then discuss *what is in place and working, what needs to be improved,* and *what needs to be put into place.* Figure 5.8 lists examples for how each area of capacity might contribute to literacy support.

        Based on these data, the team can figure out ways to improve capacities that exist but could be better used to support literacy development. Often these occur predominantly in five areas: time, technology, library, personnel, and schedule. Sometimes a brainstorming discussion is necessary to help transform what has typically been done into more effective support for literacy. (For more ideas about how to use resources effectively to support literacy improvement efforts, see Chapter 9.) Once the literacy team has created a school-capacity profile that outlines what capacities, structures, and policies can be put in place, the team will be well on its way to understanding the assets the school already has to contribute to the literacy effort.

5.8 How School Capacity Can Support Literacy Improvement	
Area of School Capacity	**Examples That Support Literacy Improvement**
School structures that support literacy	• Additional strategic reading classes or reading/writing workshop • Beginning all classes with reading relevant to the day's work • Portfolio assessment and student exhibitions • Scheduled, schoolwide sustained silent reading time (3 to 5 times per week) • Quarterly joint meetings of literacy teams from high school and feeder middle schools
School resources that support literacy	• Classroom libraries • Technology to support reading and writing instruction and assessment • Parallel curriculum materials at varying reading levels for units of study • Reading programs for learners with targeted literacy needs • Multilingual print resources and staff support • Literacy coach position • Teacher professional development
School policies that support literacy	• Regularly scheduled reading assessments as part of students' educational experiences • Transition teams that consider reading assessment information when determining student placement • Weekly common planning periods focused on collaborative examination of student work • Use of common writing rubrics to assess student work • Teacher agreement by department or grade level to use common set of literacy strategies • Expectation that ELLs use their first language when necessary to support literacy development in English and content area learning

Understanding Current Teaching Practices That Support Literacy

In the vignette about DeWitt Middle School, it was clear that data about teachers' current practices were central to developing the school's literacy action plan. Obtaining this information allowed school leaders to assess where there were gaps, plan the necessary time and content for teacher professional development, and focus the time of the newly hired literacy coach.

To determine how to best support teachers to improve literacy teaching and learning, leaders need data about current teacher practices, that is, what do teachers know and how do they currently develop literacy across the content areas? Answers to these questions will signal where teacher professional development and additional support are needed. They will also provide information about where strong instructional support exists for literacy development. To obtain good data about both, school leaders can survey, observe, and talk to teachers.

Survey teachers about the literacy strategies they know and use, the frequency with which they use them, and the areas in which they feel they need more information. A Teacher Knowledge Inventory (such as Figure A.1 in Appendix C) and questionnaires can be used to poll teachers about their knowledge and use of literacy support strategies. Principals might learn, for example, that teachers say that students have difficulty learning content-area vocabulary, but teachers do not know of vocabulary strategies they can use beyond "assign, define, and test." These data can be used to plan targeted professional development that addresses this need. Survey data might also inform leaders of what types of writing and reading are typically occurring in each content area, leading to data-based policymaking. For example, if very little writing is going on, setting a number of required writing-to-learn assignments each week might be an appropriate policy response.

Observe teachers during literacy walk-throughs and classroom observations (as described in Chapter 6) and assess how teachers provide literacy support and what types of issues they find challenging. For example, a principal might observe that teachers are able to use note-taking strategies introduced in a teacher workshop quite easily but find it more challenging to differentiate the use of reading comprehension strategies to meet the needs of readers at various levels. Again, these data can be used to promote schoolwide conversations or study groups about using multiple texts with the same unit of study or how to use literacy support strategies to help struggling readers engage with challenging texts.

Talk with teachers individually in goals conferences, in department or team meetings, or in focus groups targeted around specific literacy issues such as motivation and engagement. Listen for recurring themes around areas of frustration—these then become data upon which to base decisions for increasing certain types of resources and support. For example, the literacy team might decide that ordering content-area periodicals is a valuable way to ensure the availability of relevant reading material for each content area. Or instructional coaching could be made available for those teachers who do not understand how to set up reciprocal teaching in their classrooms. A continuation of the DeWitt Middle School vignette illustrates how these principles might be put into action.

The consultant worked with the middle school leadership team to develop a literacy action plan that would guide the school over the next three years. Because the team had data about school capacity and teacher knowledge, the plan was practical and built directly on the school's strengths. It established goals in each priority area. DeWitt Middle School leaders decided that the amount of content-area reading and writing would be increased by 50 percent in all classes, that more opportunities for free-choice reading would be provided, and that teachers would be expected to learn and use five common "power strategies" across the school. Another goal focused on increased teacher knowledge and use of literacy support strategies in all content areas. To support teacher development, the school would hire a literacy coach, administrators would focus professional goals on literacy improvement, and teacher professional development over the next three years would focus on literacy. In addition, school leaders recognized that literacy interventions for students who were reading more than two years below grade level needed to be put into place and teachers providing that instruction would need additional professional development, given that the school did not have a reading specialist.

Some action steps in each priority area were enacted immediately. For example, teachers at the school prided themselves on the quality of their teaching, and when multiple copies of selected texts were made available for teacher study groups, many voluntarily began to increase their literacy knowledge. Because all 7th and 8th grade students had access to laptop computers, ongoing sessions of professional development in technology began to include ways to use computers to support reading and writing. The schedule was changed to permit sustained silent reading twice a week beginning the following semester. Literacy interventions were explored, and the school purchased a reading program to meet the needs of those still struggling with decoding and basic fluency.

Tim hired a literacy coach, and together they developed a grant proposal to support the work. When DeWitt Middle School received the grant, the whole staff was informed that literacy improvement would be the school's primary focus for the next three years. A plan for teacher professional development was put into place that matched the data-driven recommendations of the audit report and incorporated the knowledge and strengths of the new literacy coach. Learning strategies, based on student needs, were introduced to all faculty, and Tim made it clear to teachers that he expected to see the strategies used when he did his walk-throughs. Having a plan made it easier to determine next steps and stay on track.

Monitoring Program Effectiveness

School leaders have to know whether implementing the literacy action plan is helping the school meet its literacy goals. Administrators and members of the literacy team should also determine if the plan needs to be changed or modified. To do this, the literacy team can create an inquiry-driven process for program monitoring by following these five steps (see Figure 5.9):

1. Determine what needs to be known. The literacy team begins the cycle by agreeing upon the questions to be answered; for example: Have we met this year's literacy goals? How will we know if a reading program is working? How will we know if our literacy action plan is successful and for whom? Are teachers in some departments using the literacy strategies more or differently than teachers in other departments? Do teachers who attend professional development provide more literacy support to students in the classroom versus teachers who do not attend?

2. Select appropriate data sources to answer each question. These might include reading logs, portfolios, and several measures taken before and after implementation of the literacy action plan, such as surveys of student attitudes, student test scores, individual reading inventories, and surveys or observations of teachers. Many of these sources are already in place from the data collection stage and can be easily reformatted for this purpose.

3. Describe evidence of success. In this step the literacy team articulates what success would look like for different groups of students. It is important that these measures be stated in data-based or observable terms and be reasonable to achieve.

4. Collect and analyze the data. During this step the team deepens and refines its inquiry. For example, if there is a difference in how boys versus girls are responding to a computer-based reading program, is it a significant issue? What needs to occur for the students who are not being helped by the program? Or, if there is a difference in how teachers implement literacy support as a result of attending professional development, is there evidence that the difference is harmful? Are there specific groups of students who are not making a year's worth of literacy growth per academic year as a result?

5. Decide what actions to take. If the literacy team sees that programs are working for some students but not others, what modifications or alternatives can be put in place? If some teachers are providing stellar literacy support but others show no changes in their classroom practice and evidence shows that students are missing out, how can this situation be remedied?

Figure 5.9 shows the cyclical nature of this kind of five-step, data-driven process for program monitoring.

At DeWitt Middle School, implementation of the literacy action plan continued. But school leaders were concerned that they would not know if the plan was succeeding. They met and

5.9 Inquiry Cycle for Program Monitoring

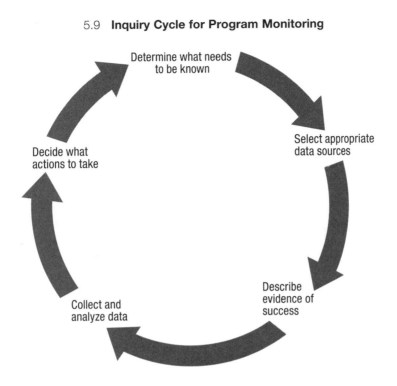

Determine what needs
to be known

Select appropriate
data sources

Decide what
actions to take

Describe
evidence of
success

Collect and
analyze data

Source: From *Inquiry Cycle for Program Monitoring,* by J. Meltzer, 2006, Portsmouth, NH: Center for Resource Management, Inc. Reprinted with permission.

developed a set of indicators that would tell them if teachers and students were meeting the literacy improvement goals they had set, and they designed a set of data collection activities so they would be able to tell what was working.

School leaders observed that teachers who were initially reluctant were now on board as they saw success with the use of literacy support strategies in their classrooms. At weekly team meetings, formerly a time when teachers focused on logistics and issues with individual students, the literacy coach and principal were updated about how teachers were using various literacy support strategies. A math teacher reported that she was "asking the students to do QARs [Question-Answer Relationships] all the time, and their answers have really improved." A science teacher said that he "used knowledge rating guides and Frayer models with the vocabulary words and retention went up a lot." The social studies teacher reported that she "modeled all of the roles for reciprocal teaching and the students practiced them, and now the students seem to be engaging more with the reading."

Despite these encouraging signs, a repeat of the reading assessment showed only slight progress for the majority of students, although the group of students who were further behind made gains. The literacy team reviewed the data and decided to recommend a number of refinements to their original literacy action plan to ensure that students were reading and writing more and receiving more reading and writing instruction. Time for the schoolwide sustained silent reading program was increased from twice a week to four times a week. The literacy consultant provided tips for improving the culture of reading during SSR, and the literacy coach shared them at team meetings. Teaching teams developed common agreements around what strategies would be used to support student learning across content areas. The principal explicitly indicated that he expected a specified amount of content-area reading and writing accompanied by instruction and modeling in every content area two to three times per week. In addition, the principal and assistant principal increased the number of walk-throughs they did each month from one to four. As a result of all these measures, more reading and writing instruction began taking place. The current reading assessment was not providing the information teachers needed and was requiring too many resources to administer, so school leaders researched options for a new reading assessment that provided more diagnostic information for every test taker. The literacy team made plans to repeat the audit in two years to assess the overall impact of interventions over time.

The district literacy goal is to have continuous improvement of at least 10 percent more students each year meeting and exceeding the standard on the state assessment in 4th grade and 8th grade, with a 10 percent drop each year in the percentage of students failing to meet the standard over the next five years. The district feels this will be possible through a focus on content-area literacy support and literacy interventions. Early results show that DeWitt Middle School is certainly doing its part to meet or exceed that goal.

If literacy goals are not being met, it is time to get some additional information as to why this is the case. When literacy goals have been met, then the literacy team can set new goals that further scaffold literacy learning for all students. These may include directly involving all teachers in the use of data to improve literacy and learning, and broadening the schoolwide use of data, as we describe in Chapter 7.

Sometimes data seem to show progress or lack of progress when the real issue is how the data are being analyzed. For the purposes of program monitoring, data disaggregation is essential. Figure 5.10 describes two typical mistakes in monitoring progress and the kinds of data analysis that can remedy the problem.

5.10 Mistakes in Monitoring Progress and How to Remedy Them

• *Total progress or progress of structural groups is presented without an understanding of the composition of learners in those groups.* Use data to ensure that students are equally distributed (by gender, ability levels, ethnicity, economic levels) across academies or teams or are strategically clustered within/across small learning communities, teaching teams, or academies (e.g., clustering of ELLs or special education students to provide more intensive support through coteaching with ELL/bilingual or special education teachers on a particular team).

• *Year-to-year cohort comparison does not show "progress."* When monitoring the success of a literacy action plan, use trend-analysis strategies that look beyond year-to-year comparisons to determine if the program is truly making a difference or if what looks like positive results are only reflections of cohort differences. As a leader, ensure that the reported data are credible.

As the DeWitt Middle School vignette indicates, a solid blueprint for improving literacy schoolwide can be put into place through a literacy action plan that incorporates the features described in this chapter. Although other schools' demographics, priorities, school capacity, teachers' practices, and student assessment results may be different from those at DeWitt Middle School, adapting sound action-planning principles and using data wisely can help school leaders develop, implement, and monitor an effective plan.

Key Messages

In this chapter, we described how school leaders can use data to develop, implement, and monitor schoolwide literacy action plans that ensure that students have the academic literacy skills necessary to be successful at school, at work, and in citizenship. Equally important, by generating a culture of continuous improvement in which individuals ask questions, collect and analyze data, take actions, and then collect more data to examine the impact of what was done, leaders become fluent in the strategies needed to be data-based decision makers. Focusing this data-driven inquiry process allows the principal and other school leaders to be in the driver's seat to improve literacy support and development for all students. Key messages in this chapter include the following:

• An effective literacy action plan designed to meet the needs of all students in the school is essential to leading a comprehensive and coordinated literacy improvement effort. A literacy action plan allows all members of the school community to understand the school's current status, goals for the future, the actions to be taken to reach the goals, who is responsible, and how success will be measured.

• Effective use of data is the key to a successful schoolwide literacy initiative. Data on student performance, school and community needs, school capacity, and teacher practices are helpful in developing an effective literacy action plan.

• The leader of a school has many sources of data that can be used to clarify and articulate the vision for literacy and learning in the school, to develop a literacy action plan, and to monitor the plan's effectiveness.

• A literacy action plan has five key components:

1. Strengthening Literacy Development Across the Content Areas
2. Strategic Interventions for Struggling Readers and Writers
3. School Policies, Structures, and Culture for Supporting Literacy
4. Building Leadership Capacity
5. Teacher Professional Development

Using a data-driven plan to monitor the program is important to ensure that the literacy action plan is effective.

As school leaders know, having a plan does not guarantee the availability of resources to implement the plan. The data may indicate a need for clear actions that school resources do not appear to permit. For committed school leaders, this situation often makes it difficult to develop, implement, and monitor a data-driven literacy action plan. However, two points are important to keep in mind. With a data-driven plan in hand, it is often easier to obtain district, grant, and community resources to support the school's efforts. Second, sometimes the ways that resources have been used in the past constrict people's ideas of how they might be used differently. School leaders need to think creatively about how resources might be reallocated to support literacy improvement. (In Chapter 9 we discuss possible solutions to these and other issues related to resource use and limitations.)

A data-driven literacy action plan brings together all of the components of the Leadership Model for Improving Adolescent Literacy. Using this plan to chart the way forward, leaders will be able to keep their school on course for sustained improvement of literacy and learning for all of their students.

> Appendix C provides a Teacher Knowledge Inventory that leaders can use as they develop a schoolwide, data-driven literacy action plan.

6 Support Teachers to Improve Instruction

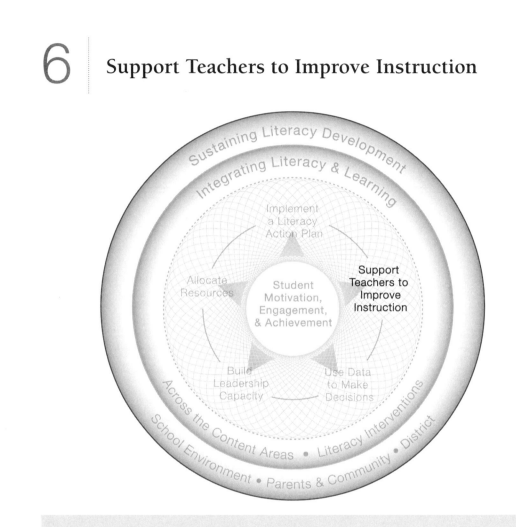

Why is this component important? Effective instruction in content-area literacy is essential to improving student achievement. The role of school leaders is to ensure that all teachers have the support and guidance they need to improve students' literacy development. School structures and a school culture that encourage collaboration, collegiality, and coaching can help teachers and administrators to successfully play their part in the literacy improvement effort.

The single most important factor in determining student performance is the teacher (Alliance for Excellent Education, 2005). School leaders face the challenge of motivating, guiding, and supporting teachers to reach higher levels of performance. Most of today's middle and high school teachers are still on their own, teaching in isolation behind closed doors and following schedules that often do not support collaborative planning, collective examination of student work, or peer coaching. Leaders can put in place a variety of strategies to generate and sustain a culture of change and improvement. This is imperative if a schoolwide literacy improvement effort is to be successful.

Support Teachers to Improve Instruction is the upper-right point of the star in the graphic of the Leadership Model for Improving Adolescent Literacy and the second *action step*. School leaders focused on the process of improving teaching make it a priority to create a school culture of development and change—a school culture in which *learning for all* is paramount. Teachers who continually learn new strategies for teaching reading, writing, and thinking in their classrooms provide motivating opportunities for students to engage and apply these strategies in reading and writing text throughout the content areas. Making this the norm, not the exception, is critical in order to make literacy and learning a priority throughout the school.

To improve literacy teaching, and ultimately learning, the structure and culture of schools must embrace opportunities for collaboration, collegiality, and support. Establishing mechanisms for infusing literacy development into every classroom, monitoring teachers' use of these mechanisms, and providing appropriate support encourages collaborative ownership and progress toward implementation of a shared vision of the school as a place where everyone engages in high-level reading, writing, and thinking.

Four structures are widely acknowledged to support teacher development of literacy knowledge and expertise:

- professional learning communities,
- making the work public,
- literacy coaching, and
- teacher professional development.

In addition, leaders have the responsibility to make sure that effective instruction is occurring in the classroom. They do this by means of

- classroom observations,
- literacy walk-throughs,

- teacher evaluation, and
- new faculty induction.

Supporting teacher development and monitoring of classroom instruction are activities that take place regularly in every school. We discuss each, however, within the context of literacy improvement. The chapter closes with key messages.

Supporting Teacher Development

Mike Dennis was nearing the end of his first year of teaching when a university in a neighboring state accepted his wife into graduate school. Mike applied to teach in a school in this university town and then received an invitation for an interview. The principal, Martha Rundel, explained that as a new teacher he would be assigned a mentor and that literacy learning as well as content learning was important at the school. She asked if Mike was willing to contribute to the literacy learning effort as he taught music and explained that various people would be observing his teaching to help him with this effort. This was certainly different from his old school, where no one seemed to care what he did as a music teacher and the only observation he had was from the principal for his end-of-year evaluation.

When Mike explained that he did not really know much about how to teach reading, Ms. Rundel said that she would expect him to attend workshops for new teachers in the district, and his mentor would help him plan lessons that were "literacy rich." He wasn't quite sure what he was in for, but he accepted the position when it was offered to him.

Before the first day of school, Mike received a telephone call from his mentor. The mentor introduced himself as the department chair for the fine arts department and asked if Mike had a copy of the state standards for music instruction. He offered to review Mike's first month of lesson plans and asked if Mike had received his copy of Classroom Strategies for Interactive Learning *(Buehl, 2001) in the mail. He mentioned that Mike would become a part of the fine arts literacy learning community that met for lunch each Wednesday to discuss new strategies to use. He also said that he would be observing in Mike's classroom throughout the first month. In addition, the literacy coach and the assistant principal would each carry out a classroom observation before January to give him feedback on his teaching.*

Mike was amazed at how many offers of support he received from colleagues, and he welcomed feedback on his teaching. He realized, though, that the standards were high, and his teaching was on display. He was a little nervous about this challenge to teach reading because he didn't really feel prepared. Ms. Rundel said that at this school the "work was public." What did that mean?

Ms. Rundel gave a clear message to her new teachers that she expected every teacher to integrate reading and writing into content-area teaching. The stakes were high, but Mike would receive the support he needed through being a member of a professional learning community, through making the work public, through literacy coaching, and through professional development.

Professional Learning Communities

A professional learning community exists in a school when educators form a supportive group and commit themselves to continuous learning. In a learning community, professional development is integrated with the day-to-day work of teachers through their interactions, dialogue, and reflections (Eaker, DuFour, & Burnette, 2002). When teachers form a professional learning community around literacy, they overcome the isolation of their classrooms and create a support group of peers who are learning about literacy, trying new literacy strategies, and solving problems together. More specifically, members of a professional learning community for literacy

- interact with one another to clarify the purpose of a literacy strategy,
- share ideas for incorporating literacy strategies into their content area,
- model literacy strategies for one another,
- share new literacy skills or knowledge,
- collect and analyze information on how students are responding to new literacy materials or instructional practices,
- collaboratively plan literacy lessons,
- encourage one another to make literacy a priority, and
- inspire one another to continue learning and improving.

The collaboration and collegiality inherent in professional learning communities can provide significant benefits to teachers as they embark on the challenges of incorporating literacy instruction into their content-area teaching. Improved teaching effectiveness can result from teachers trying out new literacy strategies or having access to a greater variety of literacy strategies and approaches through sharing with peers. Teachers are more likely to reflect upon their own literacy instructional practices if they are involved in collaborative dialogue about literacy teaching. Further, this collaboration can create a culture that incorporates planned literacy improvement as an expectation of the professional staff and promotes a norm of continuous improvement.

Making the Work Public

Making the work public means that teachers can no longer work behind closed doors. When teachers have the opportunity to observe one another's classes and discuss which strategies work best with which students, they open their doors to innovative teaching techniques and soliciting support from colleagues. Strategies for making the work public include peer coaching and creating demonstration classrooms that enable teachers to learn from one another's pedagogy and to share instructional practice. Teachers who are known to integrate literacy and learning in their classroom instruction can establish demonstration classrooms and publish a schedule of when they will use particular strategies with the content they are teaching. Or teachers might attend professional development together and also receive instruction in how to serve one another as peer coaches. In both cases, the expectation is that teachers will be observing in colleagues' classrooms during their planning period or during a regular teaching period with substitute support. Literacy coaches can coordinate these visits and provide the mentoring and debriefing for teachers who visit the demonstration classrooms. Ideally, one demonstration classroom or peer coaching team will be established in each of the content areas. This "open door policy" helps to create a culture of collaboration, collegiality, and continuous improvement. Leaders can support this concept by providing release time for teachers, establishing an expectation that teachers can learn from one another, and making professional development available for coaches and mentors.

Looking collaboratively at student work to determine individual student progress is another part of making the work of the school public. Teachers can examine a selection of student work ranging across content areas and grade levels to provide a full picture of student learning. Student work is also a good focal point when literacy coaches and teachers discuss what is happening relative to literacy in a classroom. When students struggle to complete assignments in content-area classes, it is tempting to assign easier work that students can "do." But when a literacy team or a department compares the level of work students are asked to complete in class against standardized state tests, they often notice a discrepancy. Teachers can also collaboratively develop rubrics for writing, research, and presentations to ensure that common and high standards are being held across classes; establish agreements about the types and frequency of use of literacy strategies; or analyze the literacy demands of the standards and discuss which strategies might work best to help students succeed in addressing them. Such a process of inquiry encourages professional collaboration, shapes classroom instruction and further opportunities for student learning, provides concrete examples of student development, and informs teachers of students' challenges and successes.

Literacy Coaching

A school's literacy improvement effort can be more effective if led by a professional literacy coach. A well-trained literacy coach offers invaluable feedback to teachers, providing a clearer picture of their strengths and weaknesses. Because most teachers of content classes lack training and experience with activities that build reading and writing skills, they may need support and guidance in learning how literacy strategies can enhance learning in their classrooms. A literacy coach can assist in identifying appropriate texts to use with students, collaborate in devising lessons that help students learn effectively from content texts, and model activities that engage students in reading and writing while they learn new content. In these ways, the literacy coach becomes a support and guide for teachers as they learn and change their practices throughout the school year. All of the literacy coach's roles require teaching skills, depth of knowledge, and the ability to work well with peers.

Standards for Middle and High School Literacy Coaches (International Reading Association, 2006) was written with the collaboration of the International Reading Association, the National Council for the Social Studies, the National Council of Teachers of English, the National Science Teachers Association, and the National Council of Teachers of Mathematics. Representatives from these professional organizations stated that qualified literacy coaches must have dual skill sets. First, they must have leadership skills to collaborate effectively with other teachers, to provide instructional coaching, and to evaluate the literacy needs of the school, teachers, and individual students. Second, they have to be "skillful instructional strategists," or able to implement strategies to improve the academic literacy of students. The International Reading Association endorses the hiring of a professional literacy coach in secondary schools, but without administrative support, the coach has little credibility or authority. Administrators can model the importance of developing literacy in the school and provide both encouragement and practical support such as books, materials, meeting places, and release time for study groups.

When a school has no full-time, trained literacy coach, other coaching options include peer coaching from colleagues from the same department or team. In smaller schools, the curriculum coordinator can fill the role of literacy coach. Or a literacy coach can teach a few classes and use other class periods to work with teachers. Leaders should explore how to obtain the resources to provide one or more on site literacy coaches, as they are a valuable asset to any schoolwide literacy initiative.

Teacher Professional Development

All of the suggested strategies involve teacher professional development in one form or another. Although teachers can proactively learn about literacy and best instructional practices for their content area, they cannot teach what they themselves do not know. It is critical to provide ongoing options for teachers to increase their knowledge about literacy instruction. Some of the professional development will involve entire departments, grade-level teams, or the entire faculty. Mandatory professional development will help teachers develop a common knowledge base about literacy support strategies, or it can be structured around a literacy topic of great interest, such as expository text strategies, differentiating instruction, vocabulary development, or improving writing. It is important that the focus remain on literacy and that all teachers be asked to share how they plan to use the available options to increase literacy expertise.

Quality professional development on the topic of content-area literacy occurs over time and includes an introduction to literacy support strategies, modeling, practice, content-area examples, and planning for and discussion of applications in the classroom (Putnam & Borko, 2000). It can be offered through a variety of in-person and online formats. In both cases, the impact of teacher professional development is likely to be greater if teachers participate in teams, cohorts, or pairs. Figure 6.1 lists various formats for professional development activities.

When employing outside consultants for on-site professional development, principals will need to make sure that the consultants understand the school's literacy goals and specific concerns. School leaders should review proposed course syllabi and communicate priorities when working with university faculty to provide professional development. Often a variety of formats will be necessary to meet teacher needs for professional learning because teachers, like students, have different learning styles and preferences.

Monitoring Implementation

Professional development and other structures for teacher support are misused if nothing changes in the classroom. It is the responsibility of school leaders to make sure that teachers use what they learn and apply it effectively in the classroom. The four structures

---

6.1 **Possible Professional Development Formats**

- After-school or evening classes held once a week or twice a month
- A professional development period scheduled during the school day
- Summer institutes with in-person or online follow-up throughout the year
- Friday/Saturday classes once a month
- A series of day-long workshops addressing before-, during-, and after-reading strategies; vocabulary development strategies; and writing-to-learn strategies, held on Saturdays or during workshop days
- Peer-led workshops conducted on site during early release days
- Online classes
- Targeted conference attendance followed by peer-led workshops on selected topics
- Strategy demonstrations at every faculty meeting
- Monthly events for sharing literacy strategies
- Literacy and learning study groups

(classroom observations, literacy walk-throughs, teacher evaluation, and new teacher induction) discussed in the second part of the following vignette illustrate how leaders can help teachers implement what they have learned.

Mike learned a lot while discussing the Buehl book with his colleagues. He tried out some strategies, observed in a colleague's classroom, asked the literacy coach for help, and asked for feedback from his mentor. He thought about ways of teaching literacy using the "William Tell Overture." As Mike and his mentor talked, they recounted all of the times this overture was used as a theme song in advertising and in television shows. So Mike began his lesson by writing on the board, "What do the Flintstones and Pizza Hut have in common?" After a lively discussion, he showed an opening clip from The Lone Ranger *and asked what the music conveyed to the students. He used the students' comments to discuss the opera, the life and times of composer Gioacchino Rossini, and the significance of the story of William Tell. He then related it back to why the Flintstones, Pizza Hut advertisements, and* The Lone Ranger *would adopt this overture as their theme song.*

As his mentor observed the lesson during first period, he noticed that Mike missed opportunities to teach vocabulary. During their post-teaching discussion, the mentor suggested spending time with the libretto, or text, of the opera, expanding students' vocabulary to other words with the Latin root libr-, such as "library." Also, the mentor noted how the overture of an opera sets the tone much like an introduction to an essay, something that Mike had not thought about.

The mentor asked Mike if he thought the students knew that an opera is a dramatic representation of a story set to music. He suggested that Mike might have students read a short story of William Tell's heroic defiance of an evil tyrant and dramatic rescue at sea. Then students would discuss how this story inspired the music Rossini wrote. Mike readily incorporated this instruction into the next day's class. Mike was beginning to see connections between the music he wanted students to study and appreciate and their development as readers and writers.

Mike wanted students to "speak" the language of music. For example, he intentionally said that "the libretto of the opera was the story of William Tell." What he was now learning from his colleagues and from his professional development sessions was that he could combine students' speaking about and understanding of music with their literacy development. Reading the libretto of an opera was different than reading other genres such as a story or a passage in a science book. Classroom observations, walk-throughs, and his annual evaluation helped Mike set and reach his goal to become an effective teacher of music *and* literacy.

Classroom Observations

Classroom observations are essential tools for instructional leaders. It is important to note, however, that for classroom observations to improve instruction in reading and writing, the observer must provide meaningful feedback in a timely and sensitive manner. A literacy coach, a fellow teacher (maybe a member of the teacher's professional learning community), a department chair, or a member of the school literacy team may conduct these observations. Observations directed at improving literacy instruction can help to create and sustain professional dialogue about the teaching of reading and writing that is occurring in the individual classroom. The focus of the observation is an aspect of instructional practice that is agreed upon beforehand, such as a literacy strategy for teaching comprehension or vocabulary. The role of the observer is to describe what is happening in relation to the agreed-upon focus of the observation. Therefore, it is essential that the school leader conducting the observation be informed about effective literacy instruction and able to recognize effective reading and writing strategies when they are incorporated into a content-area lesson.

Following the observation, a professional dialogue occurs about the lesson with the expectation that both colleagues can learn from the experience. The dialogue focuses on the effectiveness of the literacy strategy that was incorporated and reflects on how the students were better able to comprehend the content as a result. An essential outcome of the discussion is to decide what happens next with regard to literacy instruction for this group of students. What are the appropriate next steps to support the teacher after the observation and dialogue? What assistance might the observer be able to offer?

The observation ought not to occur for evaluative purposes. As Metcalfe (1999) points out, "For many schools the challenge is still to move towards the kind of culture in which observation is accepted as a normal part of the way in which colleagues work together and where it is seen as one of a number of ways of improving professional practice" (p. 449). Teachers will not be receptive to having others observe and support their initial efforts if the purpose is to document competence, thus undermining the entire premise of collegial support and collaborative improvement of practice.

Literacy Walk-Throughs

Literacy walk-throughs provide school leaders with an opportunity to collect real-time data that reveal the literacy instructional practices used throughout the school building. The walk-through is an important element in influencing change in a school because it allows school leaders to enter each classroom and provide instructional feedback (Downey, Steffy, English, Frase, & Poston, 2004). Walk-through classroom visits are meant to be brief, allowing leaders to get a glimpse into the everyday instructional practices in the school. Although visits are spontaneous in order to see the normal behavior of teachers and students, they can also be planned and specifically targeted to identify aspects of literacy instruction. The purpose is to collect evidence of the literacy practices that are being used throughout the school. Some things to look for during a literacy walk-through include

- word walls with content-area vocabulary,
- instruction in literacy strategies,
- student work exhibiting thinking about texts,
- student writing about content-area learning,
- a display of the school's literacy vision,
- students reading a variety of texts at multiple levels, and
- evidence of differentiated literacy instruction.

The data gathered during literacy walk-throughs form the basis for professional conversations with faculty or individual teachers for the purpose of informing and improving instructional decisions, strengthening teachers' abilities to deliver effective literacy lessons, and improving the literacy success of all students. Through this structured walk-through process, school leaders maintain and deepen their understanding of the literacy teaching and learning practices taking place in the school as well as the literacy needs of teachers and students. The results can be summarized for discussion with staff, professional development planning, or conversation with individual teachers.

Teacher Evaluation

Teacher evaluations can offer important feedback as well as provide teachers with an understanding of the need for professional growth and improvement. Unfortunately, the most common practices in evaluation are limited in their capacity to improve teaching and chiefly serve as monitors of minimal competency for retention (Loup, Garland, Ellett, & Rugutt, 1996). Teachers are sometimes uncomfortable with the evaluation process, especially if it occurs only once a year.

School leaders who emphasize the function of teacher evaluations as a means to seek out, document, and acknowledge good literacy teaching practices give a clear message that literacy is central to the mission of the school. Although the evaluation instrument is often dictated by a union contract, a teacher evaluation system to improve literacy should give teachers useful feedback about instructional practices and the opportunity to set and evaluate goals to improve their practices; it should also provide guidance about how to make changes to improve literacy development in their classrooms. The teachers can then consider their professional goals around literacy, as well as the roles, responsibilities, contributions, and outcomes that directly guide the evaluation. For example, at the beginning of the year, teachers may be asked to write professional goals, aligned with the school's literacy vision and plan, for improving their instructional practices in literacy. Included should be a statement on how the teachers intend to reach their goals through professional development, participation in professional learning communities, coaching, and integrating specific strategies into classroom practice. Subsequently teachers can explain how they will demonstrate that they have met these goals. Finally, the results of teacher evaluation can be used to encourage teachers' professional growth around literacy instruction and to contribute to their personal and professional goals. Evaluations should include multiple and varied sources of information, including student and parent surveys, logs of professional activity, student outcome data, walk-through and observation data, evidence of progress on literacy goals, and self-evaluations.

New Faculty Induction

After a school has created a literacy vision and an action plan to improve learning, developed a culture of improvement and change, and established norms of teacher behavior that ensure continued growth in literacy knowledge and expertise, it is important to maintain this focus by carefully inducting new faculty. New faculty members must be *brought on board* to accept the school's literacy vision and have a clear understanding of the goals and expectations. New teachers face difficult challenges every day, such as classroom management and discipline, adjusting to the physical demands of teaching, managing instructional tasks, and sacrificing leisure time—not to mention the need to incorporate literacy instruction into their content and differentiate learning for the various levels of student ability. New teachers can benefit from a comprehensive induction program that includes quality mentoring, professional development with follow-up support, collaboration with others, and formal assessments (Smith & Ingersoll, 2004). Comprehensive induction programs provide new teachers with the necessary models and tools for integrating literacy strategies into their content-area, as well as mentors and support groups to guide them through curriculum planning, establishing literacy goals, and meeting the school's instructional priorities. Figure 6.2 lists suggestions for various ways to support new faculty.

Mentoring is the most important factor in the success of new teachers. New teachers working with a mentor are more likely to produce positive gains in student achievement (Strong, Fletcher, & Villar, 2004). Mentor teachers can combat the isolation often felt by new teachers while providing feedback and support on their literacy instructional practices. Mentors can help new teachers reflect on the effectiveness of their literacy lessons and redirect their efforts for the following day. In addition, mentor teachers can transmit instructional, planning, and management skills critical to good literacy instruction that novice teachers may lack. The mentoring system helps new teachers grow professionally as they adjust to the realities of teaching reading and writing within their content area.

In the vignette, Ms. Rundel immediately introduced Mike to the culture of collaboration and collegiality in the school. Although expectations for excellent teaching were high and his work more public, he received the support he needed to be successful in integrating literacy development into his teaching of music. Many formal and informal

---

6.2 Suggestions for Supporting New Faculty

- Foster an interest in and positive attitudes toward beginning teachers and their development as literacy teachers.
- Give beginning teachers excellent mentors who support growth in instructional practices for literacy.
- Plan a thorough orientation at the start of the year for beginning teachers (and do a few refresher courses throughout the year) to reinforce the school's literacy vision and plan.
- Assign beginning teachers a limited number of preparations per day so that they have time to effectively integrate literacy strategies into each lesson.
- Place a limited number of exceptional or difficult children in the classes of beginning teachers so they can learn to differentiate literacy instruction.
- Expect all teachers to reflect on their literacy instructional practices and to model quality reflections of literacy practices for beginning teachers.
- Create a safe haven for beginning teachers that is perpetuated not only by educational leaders, but also by the administrative staff and veteran teachers.
- Provide varied opportunities for professional growth in literacy.

---

structures were present in this school to keep the focus on improving student literacy and learning. School leaders who effectively implement these structures as a key part of their role as instructional leader will be much more likely to successfully support teachers in improving their literacy knowledge and expertise—and in putting that knowledge and expertise to work in the classroom, where it will make a difference for students.

Key Messages

Effective instruction is the key to student learning. For a school faculty to improve the literacy learning of their students, an essential first step is to provide teachers with the knowledge and support they need to deliver literacy-rich instruction. Then teachers need to know that school leaders are aware of their efforts and that they are expecting literacy development to occur in all classrooms.

This chapter suggests eight strategies that school leaders can use to support and monitor teacher development and implementation of effective literacy practices. While improving literacy instruction, ultimately these strategies will also help create a literacy-centered culture focused on improvement and change. Key messages in this chapter include the following:

- Improving student learning through excellence in teaching is at the heart of improving literacy and learning.
- School leaders should encourage and expect excellent literacy instruction and be able to support teachers in developing the skills and strategies necessary to ensure schoolwide implementation of the literacy improvement effort.
- School leaders support teacher development for literacy instruction by developing professional learning communities, making the work public, coaching, and providing professional development.
- School leaders monitor teacher implementation of effective literacy practice by conducting classroom observations and literacy walk-throughs and connecting teacher evaluations and new teacher induction to the school's literacy goals.

School leaders are responsible for linking teacher development and improved classroom practice. Savvy principals find ways to carve out time for teachers to participate in professional learning communities and study groups, to meet with mentors, and to attend various types of professional development activities. Leaders need to support professional learning communities and participate in professional development with teachers to ensure consistency in expectations, support, and follow-through. Use of tools and strategies such as literacy walk-throughs and observation and evaluation protocols can assist teachers and provide ways to monitor classroom practice. The school leader's role as instructional leader is critical to the success of a schoolwide literacy improvement effort.

> Appendix C provides a Classroom Observation Guide that leaders can use as an instrument for monitoring teachers' implementation of effective literacy practices.

7 | Use Data to Make Decisions About Literacy Teaching and Learning

Why is this component important? Too many decisions about classroom practices are based on preference, tradition, intuition, or unsubstantiated beliefs. Collecting and analyzing data on student performance in the areas of reading and writing provides school leaders with the information they need to make appropriate decisions about students' placement in literacy intervention classes and the level of literacy support they need.

The idea of using data to drive school improvement initiatives is not new, and the efficacy of making decisions based on data instead of tradition, impression, or anecdote is well documented (Lachat & Smith, 2004). It is important for school leaders to understand the types of data they have available to them about students' abilities to read and write so that they and others can make the best decisions about instruction, programming, resource allocation, and placement. In discussing what leaders need to do to support students at risk, Lachat and Smith (2005) found that effective use of data requires a systems approach that includes ensuring quality and accuracy of available data, staff access to timely data, the capacity for data disaggregation, the collaborative use of data organized around a clear set of questions, and leadership structures that support schoolwide use of data. It is critical, therefore, that leaders

- recognize their responsibility to set up a culture of continuous improvement based on use of data,
  - model how to analyze and use data to make instructional decisions,
  - work to ensure that teachers and administrators have the data they need in the forms required to inform instruction, and
  - understand multiple ways that data about student performance can be used to inform support for literacy in the content areas and placement of students in literacy interventions.

Use Data to Make Decisions is the lower-right point of the star in the graphic of the Leadership Model for Improving Adolescent Literacy and the third *action step* for school leaders. In this chapter, we focus on how leaders and teachers can use various types of student performance data to address the literacy and learning needs of students. Student performance data are the heart of any schoolwide literacy improvement effort. It is vital that school leaders understand the types of data that can be collected about students' reading and writing and how analysis and strategic use of the data can help ensure that students get the assistance they need. Analysis and understanding of student performance data also help focus the schoolwide literacy action plan on addressing student needs. The chapter concludes with key messages.

Using Student Performance Data to Improve Literacy and Learning

The following vignette describes how school leaders at one high school used data in multiple ways to drive their literacy improvement efforts. Their focus was on obtaining data that would enable them to spotlight the literacy and learning needs of their students. The vignette illustrates how having the data enabled teachers to rally behind a schoolwide effort to improve student achievement through a focus on literacy.

The administration and the literacy team at Washington High School were concerned that as many as a third of their students were unable to read on grade level. State assessment results seemed to support this conclusion. Community employers and parents had expressed their concern as well. Many teachers were disbelieving, insisting that the issue was one of student motivation, not ability. Some of the teachers' comments reflected this attitude: "They could do it if they wanted to." "The issue is too much TV and video games, not ability." "They just have no work ethic!" Undeterred, the literacy team asked their consultant to recommend a quick assessment they could use to determine students' reading levels. After reviewing several options using the Literacy Assessment Review Tool (Figure A.3 in Appendix C), the team chose the Scholastic Reading Inventory (SRI) because of its reasonable cost and the ability to administer it on the computer.

Students took the online assessment during their English classes, and teachers met during the next professional development day to review the results. They noted how low Sally M. scored despite being an A/B student. One teacher said, "She has been complaining about how much stress she feels and how long it takes her to do all of her homework!" Then they read Bryan C.'s score. He scored above grade level. His teachers were surprised because many did not even think he could read, given that he rarely completed any work in his classes. They concluded that he should be doing more challenging work if he could read this well. The comments went on. One group of 11th grade male students' scores seemed absurdly low given teachers' perceptions of those students as avid and able readers, and teachers agreed that some students may not have taken the test seriously, something they would emphasize and monitor more closely next time. True to the prediction of the literacy team, about a third of the students were reading two to three years below grade level. This was the case for more than 40 percent of the 9th graders. Contrary to findings in other schools, the number of boys and girls in this group of struggling readers was about the same.

Based on the results of the SRI and student performance on the state assessment, the literacy team made two recommendations to the faculty and the school board:

- *Retest students scoring at the Basic 1 and 2 levels on the* Scholastic Reading Inventory *using an individual diagnostic reading test to establish reading profiles, and communicate the results to teachers who had these students in their classes.*
- *Establish a strategic reading and writing class for all incoming 9th grade students who scored below grade level on the SRI. This class would be in addition to their English class.*

Teachers completed a survey regarding their knowledge and use of literacy support strategies in the classroom. Based on the survey results, the literacy team worked with the professional development committee to set up a series of workshops on literacy support strategies that would help students develop reading comprehension skills in the content areas if used regularly. These strategies were designed to support both struggling and average readers. In addition, the literacy team members and the professional development committee wanted to make sure that students scoring above average were challenged with advanced reading materials and tasks. Teachers who already used literacy support strategies as part of their teaching were asked to share their use of those strategies at department and faculty meetings and to invite colleagues into their classrooms to observe the strategies in action.

The school literacy team also decided to repeat the SRI testing annually to determine which students needed assistance and to monitor the success of the literacy interventions. When the diagnostic reading profiles showed weak vocabulary to be an issue for most students scoring poorly on the SRI, the school instituted a schoolwide program to build vocabulary across grade levels and content areas.

The percentages of students who met or exceeded the standard on the 11th grade state reading and writing assessment went up steadily over the next three years. When teachers saw increased student success, they began to endorse the schoolwide literacy improvement goal: each student at or above grade level will make at least one year's worth of progress in reading in one year's time, and each student below grade level will make a minimum of two years' progress in reading each academic year. At Washington High School, increasing numbers of students are now meeting this goal.

Many middle and high school leaders face a similar scenario with regard to literacy: scores are low on standardized reading tests, teachers say students cannot read the textbook, and discipline referrals go up whenever reading is assigned. Students have a variety of excuses: "I'm not good at all that book stuff." "Reading is hard." "I don't like to read." But to do something about this, school leaders need to know and respond to the facts. This means using various types of data to make decisions to ensure that teachers and the school as a whole support students with all levels of academic literacy skills. As shown in the Washington High School vignette, a schoolwide, data-based approach to a focus on literacy can lead to significant student progress.

Data sources are not independent of one another. Good data about one area will inform the questions generated about another. In the vignette, parents and the community were concerned, which led school leaders to assess student reading levels. Answering questions about student performance led the literacy team at Washington High School to put additional literacy assessments and support programs into place. Finding out more about student literacy needs prompted the literacy team to wonder what literacy strategies teachers currently knew and used so that appropriate professional development opportunities could be planned. As the vignette makes evident, and as described in Chapter 5, a systems approach to reviewing assessment data is essential for data-driven decision making.

Being able to disaggregate student performance data is important, both to ensure that one group of students is not failing to make progress and to make appropriate decisions about resource allocation and programming. In the Washington High School vignette, there were no data that indicated specialized interventions were needed for at-risk students based on gender. But many other middle and high schools have found that boys are much more likely—sometimes by as much as three to one—to score significantly below grade level in reading. When this is the case, programming that takes into account many of the instructional approaches mentioned in Smith and Wilhelm's (2002) *Reading Don't Fix No Chevys* may be in order. These approaches include ensuring student access to the types of classroom environments described in Chapter 1, with special attention to literacy tasks completed as part of problem solving; hands-on experiences and inquiry projects; frequent use of technology to support literacy development; clear directions and frequent feedback; opportunities to address interests, pursue ideas, and work collaboratively; and completion of reading and writing for authentic purposes.

Improved programming, teacher professional development, and resource allocation occur when school leaders have access to students' performance data and use the data wisely. As discussed in the vignette, Washington High School used the *Scholastic Reading Inventory* to look at what needed to occur as part of content area instruction for all students, prompting a schoolwide focus on vocabulary development and on literacy strategies to address content-specific reading and writing skills. The literacy team recommended a policy be put in place so the *Scholastic Reading Inventory* could also be used as a screening tool to identify students with additional needs. (The SRI was featured in the vignette, but any other reading assessment that met school needs and reported results in terms of grade-level referencing would be suitable.) Based on the general test results, students scoring below a certain level were assessed using a more diagnostic assessment to determine specific needs. School leaders could then use this data to set up programs to address the needs of these students.

Understanding Data Related to Literacy

Reading and writing are the cornerstones of academic literacy development and content area-learning. Therefore, it is important that school leaders have good information on what students know and can do in the areas of reading and writing.

Why Collect Standardized Assessment Data?

In the high-stakes environment in which schools operate, standardized test data are the type of student performance data most people focus on. Standardized test data are one important measure of how well schools are supporting students' literacy development throughout middle and high schools. Typically, standardized data will show performance relative to grade-level peers or to standards and will provide a scale that allows schools to monitor individual student and cohort growth.

Having a way to measure progress is an essential factor in a schoolwide literacy improvement effort. The measure may not bring good news at the beginning, but it is critical to know where student performance is *now* so school leaders can begin to address unmet needs, maximize successful approaches, and improve current instructional programming where necessary.

But the real reason to collect standardized data about students' reading and writing proficiency is not to compare performance with other schools or to compare the scores of one cohort to the next. The reason to collect standardized student performance data is to ensure that all students make at least a year's worth of growth in reading and writing each academic year and that students who are behind in reading and writing make more than one year's growth each year. When this is not happening, school leaders need to know—and to *take action.*

Why Disaggregating Data Is Important

When student performance data on standardized reading and writing tests are disaggregated, school leaders can become aware of which students are succeeding and which students may need additional assistance to meet the growth target. A focus on student progress as a whole is not helpful for ensuring that individual students' literacy needs are being met and could mask the fact that specific groups of students may require changes in instructional support to be successful. For example, students who enter 9th grade reading at grade level may be losing ground, something many schools are finding to be true when consistent content-area literacy support is not in place. Or it may turn out that significantly larger numbers of socioeconomically disadvantaged students are reading two or three years behind their grade-level peers, or that the assumption that special education students account for almost all of the struggling readers is patently not the case.

Student performance data are especially important to disaggregate when monitoring the success of literacy interventions. For example, some students participating in an intervention classroom may be improving their reading skills, but others may show few gains. Skillful use of student data will tell school leaders if the distinguishing variable is gender, initial reading level when entering the program, attendance, proficiency in English, or length of time in the program. Where the target level of growth is not occurring, it is the responsibility of school leaders to work with all educators in the school to make sure that programs are adjusted as necessary.

Monitoring Literacy Development

Monitoring literacy development is a complex process, and we strongly recommend that school leaders put effective structures in place that certainly include, but are not limited to, the use of standardized or state assessment data. Teachers need more than an annual snapshot of information to meet the instructional needs of students.

How to best use literacy assessment data is highly dependent on the type of assessment and when it takes place in the learning process. For example, a *formative assessment*, such as a classroom test, can inform instruction by showing what students can and cannot do at that point in the semester. A *diagnostic assessment* provides information on subcomponents of the reading or writing process to indicate where instruction should be focused. A *summative assessment* provides comparison scores for the level of proficiency of students as a result of instruction or at a given point in time (such as at the end of a semester or a unit of study). A unit test or course final exam is a summative assessment, as is a state assessment test if the curriculum is aligned with state standards. All three types of assessment can provide important information to guide or revise instruction.

An additional assessment issue is this: What do the data that are reported tell educators? Do scores indicate how students performed against an expected level of competence, as is the case with a state assessment, which is *criterion referenced*? Or do scores tell how students in the school compared with other students at the same grade level nationwide, as is the case with a standardized assessment, which is *norm referenced*? School leaders who understand assessment terms as they relate to literacy can evaluate the options they have regarding data about student performance. Figure 7.1 defines several key assessment terms that leaders should know.

Types of Reading and Writing Assessments

Many school leaders are not aware of the types of assessment options they have and the types of information provided by each. Depending on the choices of the school or district, educators have seven basic sources of data about the reading and writing abilities of middle and high school students: (1) state reading and writing assessments, (2) standardized reading and writing assessments, (3) leveled reading assessments, (4) diagnostic reading assessments, (5) school or district writing prompts, (6) content-based course/grade-level common assessments that require reading and writing, and (7) classroom assessments that require reading and writing. As shown in Figure 7.2, each has advantages and disadvantages and provides different types of information.

Setting Up Structures, Policies, and Systems for Using Data

Sometimes data are collected but no system is in place to make the data available to teachers and administrators. In many middle and high schools, no reading assessments are in place. These situations need to be remedied if literacy improvement efforts are to succeed. The school literacy team is a good place to start to determine what data are currently being collected about students' literacy skills and how the data are currently being used by administrators, department chairs or team leaders, and classroom teachers.

To determine the adequacy of how data are currently being used, school leaders can discuss the following questions with members of the literacy team:

7.1 Assessment Terms as They Relate to Literacy

Alternative assessment—Assessing the literacy skills of students through alternative methods such as systematic review of samples of student work or documented observation of students' reading behaviors.

Diagnostic assessment—Assessing the literacy skills of students in a variety of areas against a set of criteria in each area to determine the difference between students' demonstration of skills in that area and the expected skills for their grade/ability level. For example, diagnostic reading assessment might test word-attack skills, vocabulary knowledge, oral-reading fluency, and silent-reading comprehension to determine which of these may be causing difficulty for a particular student.

Formative assessment—Assessing the literacy skills of students as a part of instruction so that the results can inform what additional types of instruction—review, reteaching, additional guided practice, enrichment—may be helpful for each individual or cohort of students to develop fluency with the targeted reading or writing skills. For example, classroom assessments that require students to respond to text in some way or to complete a writing assignment can be used to indicate students' current reading and writing skills.

Summative assessment—Assessing the literacy skills of students at a particular point in time, at the end of a unit of study or annually at the same time of year, to determine what reading and writing skills they demonstrate relative to their peers. It is typically used to evaluate student progress or to provide information related to program effectiveness.

Criterion referenced—An assessment designed to measure student performance in reference to established performance or content standards related to reading and writing.

Norm referenced—An assessment designed to measure student performance in reference to the performance normative curve of a peer group on the same assessment of reading and writing. It is important that literacy assessments be normed on a similar population in terms of age, demographics, language, or other delineator.

• What questions does the team want to answer about students' abilities to read and write to ensure that current programming is meeting student needs?

• What types of student performance data does the school currently collect?

• Do the data provide the information the team feels are necessary to support the literacy improvement effort?

• What additional data does the team feel are needed and what recommendations does the team want to make regarding additional assessment?

7.2 Seven Data Sources About Students' Reading and Writing Performance

Data Source	Examples	Type of Scoring/ Assessment	What It Measures	What It Reports	Advantages	Disadvantages
State assessments	NY Regents Exam; MCAS; FCAT	Criterion/ summative assessment	Meeting of state standards	Categories—e.g., does not meet, partially meets, meets, or exceeds	Free to districts; aligned with state curriculum frameworks; common measure across state; all students who do well, score well; can be used as program evaluation tool	Reporting is too late to use for instruction; not diagnostic for individual students; to be used effectively as a diagnostic for program strengths and weaknesses, need to do individual item/strand analysis
Standardized assessments	Stanford 10; Terra Nova; Gates-MacGinitie	Norm-referenced; scale scores or stanine scores or percentiles/ summative assessment	Reading proficiency; vocabulary	Ranked performance against others in that grade	Can be administered to a group; some breakout of subskills; can be used as a program evaluation tool; norms are current, and off-grade norms are available	Limited diagnostic capability; often the reporting is too late to use to inform instruction; often hard to interpret; norms do not indicate "actual level" but report relative to how students in that grade level typically perform; skillful interpretation requires statistical knowledge
Leveled reading assessments	SRI*; DRP*; STAR Reading Assessment	Reading level; lexile score or DRP level/ formative or summative	Reading comprehension	A score that corresponds to a reading "level"	Easy to interpret; options are increasingly online, providing instant scoring/ results; results typically linked to book lists at student's "reading" level; tends to be less expensive	These measure the construct of "reading" differently; some question about reliability/validity for middle and high school because interest/ motivation play a role in some students' scores; not diagnostic

7.2   Seven Data Sources About Students' Reading and Writing Performance (continued)

Data Source	Examples	Type of Scoring/ Assessment	What It Measures	What It Reports	Advantages	Disadvantages
Diagnostic reading tests	DRA*; GRADE*; DAR*; NWEA* Reading Test	Profile of subtest scores/formative, summative, or diagnostic	A variety of components of reading proficiency, vocabulary, and comprehension	Subtest scores with grade-level referencing	Can provide a more in-depth "reader profile"; can be linked more easily to instruction; typically easier to get reporting in a timely manner	Most need to be administered individually, in whole or in part; each defines and measures aspects of reading somewhat differently; understanding and using measures can be challenging; other than NWEA, parallel forms/ reading passages for pre-post are limited
School or district writing prompts	On-demand writing to a standard prompt	Rubric scoring by one or more readers/summative or diagnostic	Ability to use traits of good writing in a specific piece	Holistic or trait scoring of writing ability	Rubrics can be developed that capture traits of writing valued by the district; progress of students over time can be tracked; co-scoring by teachers is helpful to increase understanding of writing challenges students face and to inform instruction; can be used both diagnostically and summatively	Reliability of scoring is questionable if only one person scores each piece; takes a lot of time to score; student interest in prompt may vary, affecting validity of scores as a measure of progress; good parallel prompts require piloting to develop, a step often not taken

7.2 Seven Data Sources About Students' Reading and Writing Performance (continued)

Data Source	Examples	Type of Scoring/ Assessment	What It Measures	What It Reports	Advantages	Disadvantages
Course/grade-level assessments that require reading/ writing	Common assessments; exhibition or research project	Rubrics; checklists; grades portfolio/ summative	Content knowledge; reading and writing ability	Multiteacher assessment of student knowledge and literacy skills	Allows for common expectations and standards for performance to be set across classes; rubric development can help instruction target specific academic literacy habits and skills; collaborative review allows teachers to review and modify instruction	Takes time to score; need for inter-rater reliability to be established; instructional preparation and support often varies among teachers so validity of assessment needs to be monitored and clear parameters for support and instruction need to be adhered to
Classroom assessments/ projects that require reading/ writing	Essay test; term paper; lab report; I-search project	Rubrics; checklists; grades portfolio/ formative or summative	Content knowledge; reading and writing ability	Individual teacher assessment of student knowledge and literacy skills	Assessment most directly matches instruction and can provide direct, timely feedback about student literacy and learning; rubric scoring combined with checklists and scoring guideline can direct student attention to important aspects of the assignment	Grading or scoring relies on the judgment of a single teacher; assignment has greater chance of being poorly constructed to actually assess content and literacy learning because many teachers have weak backgrounds in assessment development

*Key to Abbreviations: DRA—Diagnostic Reading Assessment; DRP—Degrees of Reading Power; GRADE—Group Reading Assessment and Diagnostic Evaluation; NWEA—Northwest Evaluation Association; SRI—Scholastic Reading Inventory

Source: From Seven Data Sources About Students' Reading and Writing Performance, by J. Meltzer, 2006, Portsmouth, NH: Center for Resource Management, Inc.

Adapted with permission from Public Consulting Group, Inc.

• How could the school improve the use of data to inform instruction and placement decisions?

As seen in the vignette earlier in this chapter, it may be necessary to use more than one type of literacy assessment to understand what programs and approaches are needed to address various student needs. If a school needs additional assessment data beyond what currently exist, the Literacy Assessment Review Tool (Figure A.3 in Appendix C) provides a set of questions to ask when considering a reading assessment.

Examining data is important when planning both literacy support across the content areas and strategic interventions for struggling readers and writers who need additional support. School leaders are responsible for setting up the structures, roles, expectations, and policies to ensure that data are used effectively. Leaders should consider taking the following four actions:

• develop a literacy assessment calendar and map for all teachers that indicates what reading and writing assessments will be given, when and by whom they will be administered, and what each assessment will tell the school about student performance;

• establish a policy and procedure for how and when assessment results will be disseminated, when teachers will have time to examine the results, and how teachers are expected to use the results;

• establish a policy and procedure for the literacy team to review all literacy assessment data on an annual basis and provide a summary analysis and recommendations to the school; and

• develop a system and policies for communication with parents about assessment timing and results, with students about the reason for assessments, and with sending schools so that assessment information can be used for placement decisions and program review.

School leaders should also evaluate the technology infrastructure at their school and consider carefully the capacity of technology to support test administration, dissemination of results to teachers, and communication with parents and sending schools.

In the following sections we discuss in more detail specific policies, structures, and procedures relative to data use in conjunction with content-area literacy support and literacy interventions.

Using Data to Inform Instruction Across the Content Areas

Classroom teachers' effective use of data for literacy improvement does not happen automatically. When school leaders create data-analysis templates and protocols and set up the conditions and expectations to facilitate teachers' use of assessment data, teachers' instruction becomes more targeted to the literacy needs of students. When principals approve schedules that provide common planning or release time, it becomes possible for groups of teachers by grade level, teaching team, academy, or department to study data collaboratively, question the data, and make plans to respond to what the data say about the needs and progress of individual students. Ensuring that teachers have this time and establishing the expectation that the time be used to examine data to improve instruction is the role of the principal.

Teachers might use this time productively in a number of ways. For example, teams of teachers might spend common planning time or release time looking at the results of diagnostic reading assessments, using a protocol to analyze student work, or co-scoring student writing prompts. Using the data, teachers can make adjustments in grouping, pace, and materials and put into place needed support. Figure 7.3 shows more about how these forms of data can affect content-area literacy instruction. Thus, in a very real way, student assessment data have the power to drive instruction for individuals and groups of students when teachers get timely access to quality information about their own students' reading and writing skills.

Using Assessment Data to Make Placement Decisions

Assessment is the first step in providing help for struggling readers and writers. The data can help identify the type of program needed, specific weaknesses, ways to group, skills to emphasize, and student progress. Although other academic literacy skills may also be weak, it is essential that specific interventions occur for reading and writing.

The types of data needed to make effective placement decisions may include standardized assessment data, teacher perceptions, and diagnostic reading or writing assessment. Assessment results can also be helpful in evaluating the effectiveness of the overall literacy program. (Chapter 5 includes information about how to set up a program-monitoring cycle.)

As discussed in Chapter 3, one size does not fit all when it comes to providing effective educational programming for struggling readers and writers. Setting up a tiered system of interventions for struggling readers is the key to matching students with

7.3 How Various Forms of Data Can Inform Instruction	
Type of Data	**How It Can Inform Instruction**
Diagnostic reading assessments	Teachers can alter grouping of students to ensure extra modeling and guided practice, use parallel texts for struggling readers, and differentiate use of reading comprehension strategies.
Collaborative examination of student work	Teachers can get specific suggestions from colleagues about how to meet students' literacy needs based on an evaluation of strengths and challenges in written work.
Scoring of writing prompts	Teachers can assess students' writing strengths and challenges, create targeted mini-lessons, and provide modeling, exemplars, and guided practice as needed.
Analysis of classroom assessment results	Teachers can develop a picture of the class that indicates where reteaching is necessary and what literacy and learning skills need strengthening through additional instruction and practice.
Individual item analysis of performance on standardized test by a cohort of students	Current teachers can gain an understanding of students' collective needs, and former teachers can gain program feedback.
Team or departmental examination of common assessment results	Teachers can get feedback on the success of teaching approaches and determine where curriculum adjustments are needed.

interventions that will address their needs. When examining student performance data to make placement decisions, educators can consider the information in Figure 7.4 as a general guide for decision making. The ranges in level of performance (the first column in the figure) should not be rigid. That is, all tests have a margin of error that must be considered, and student performance may vary somewhat from one test administration to another. Percentile ratings are based on peer performance, not level of required literacy skills to meet college, career, or citizenship demands. So although it may not seem necessary to provide support to students scoring just below "average," consider two points: (1) ratings are based on how students at that grade level typically perform; and (2) students in this range in middle and high school do not automatically make one year's gain in literacy development each year without purposeful support in content-area literacy.

In some schools, the majority of students may read at levels significantly below grade level and need extra literacy support. In this case, it will take strong leadership to change structures, such as the creation of an extended literacy block, and supports, such as high-quality instructional materials and teacher professional development, to ensure that students accelerate their literacy development.

7.4 Guide for Using Standardized Test Data for Placement Decisions		
Performance Level	Additional Monitoring or Assessment Needed	Placement Decision (Where Student Will Get Literacy Support)
51st percentile or above	General monitoring	Content-area classroom with good literacy instruction
41st–50th percentile (1–2 years below grade level)	Close monitoring	Content-area classroom with good literacy instruction and specific attention to literacy needs
26th–40th percentile (2–3 years below grade level)	Additional assessment	Intervention class and content-area classroom with specific attention to literacy needs
Lowest quartile (more than 3 years below grade level)	Additional assessment and close monitoring	Additional intervention/tutoring and intervention class, and content-area classroom with specific attention to literacy needs

Note: These percentiles are guidelines only, as student performance on a particular assessment can be due to a number of variables. Decisions about placement in a literacy intervention should be made on the basis of more than one piece of data.

What about students scoring on or above grade level on a screening test, such as a state assessment test, a standardized reading test, or a general reading test designed to provide a "reading level" (see Figure 7.2)? These students will require classroom-based content-area literacy support as they read and write increasingly complex text. But they are unlikely to need additional intervention outside of the content-area classroom to maintain grade-level status.

Determining the Nature of Students' Reading and Writing Challenges

For students who appear to require substantial intervention in class or additional intervention outside of class, additional diagnostic assessment is necessary. Setting up a policy and procedure to ensure that this occurs is important. A reading specialist can administer an individualized assessment to determine the individual student's specific reading challenges and establish the student's reading level as well as the level of development of reading and writing subskills. These subskills might include vocabulary, word-attack skills, types of comprehension (literal, interpretive), oral reading, syntax use, sentence semantics, editing skills, and spelling. Understanding what is contributing to the students' reading and writing difficulties is important for developing an appropriate instructional response. Accurately determining the instructional reading level of the student is also critical. As noted in Chapter 3, most struggling readers and writers require explicit instruction, extensive modeling and guided practice, use of targeted instructional materials, and repeated opportunities for independent practice and feedback in the areas where they have difficulty. It is the role of school leaders to ensure that appropriate interventions are available, staffed with highly trained teachers, and monitored for effectiveness.

Establishing a Culture of Continuous Improvement Through the Use of Data

Establishing a culture of continuous literacy improvement through the use of data does not happen automatically. Savvy school leaders understand the power of student performance data as an ally in educational improvement efforts. But, as described earlier in this chapter, embedding effective use of data by literacy team members and teachers requires targeted effort. In the vignette at the beginning of the chapter, teachers "bought in" to data-driven goals only after some progress could be demonstrated. The progress was evident only because of new consistent structures and policies that were put into place. In the vignette, regular testing cycles, policies for additional testing, structures for communicating results to teachers, and procedures to address concerns about the validity of test results for certain groups of students were put into place. Beyond that, school leaders who ensure the appropriate allocation of resources—time, personnel, materials, and technology—make it possible to sustain a data-driven culture of continuous improvement and programming. At Washington High School this included

- resources for assessments;
- use of technology;
- scheduling and personnel to administer the assessments;
- time for examination, analysis, and reporting of data by the literacy team and the teachers;
- professional development for teachers to respond to students' needs; and
- resources to put the schoolwide vocabulary program and the literacy intervention class in place for struggling 9th grade students.

Effective use of student performance data can lead to actions by teachers and administrators to implement instructional improvements, make placement decisions, allocate resources, guide program selection and implementation, and instigate professional development. Knowing the types of information various kinds of data can provide is important. Figure 7.5 provides three additional examples of how leaders can encourage the use of student performance data in their schools to improve literacy teaching and learning.

7.5 **How to Use Data to Improve Literacy and Learning**

1. **Analyze subskill and individual test item reports from standardized tests.**

• Lead teachers through a structured investigation that helps them to identify weaknesses and strengths across a whole grade or within a team or individual class.

• Facilitate teacher agreements to use common literacy support strategies that address patterns in the data.

2. **Administer and examine the results of a leveled reading assessment.**

• Expect teachers to use results to plan appropriate use of parallel curriculum resources and explicit instruction in literacy support strategies.

• Use pre- and post-tests with the same cohort of students to inform teachers of student progress.

3. **Establish a policy in which administration of a general reading assessment is immediately followed by additional testing for students performing three or more years below grade level.**

• Make a map by grade level, gender, and assessment information to determine the "picture" of required literacy support at the school level.

• Work with the literacy team and the reading specialist to ensure that students have access to appropriate programs that meet their literacy development needs.

Caveats

Although data use is essential to a schoolwide literacy improvement effort, school leaders should be aware of the following caveats:

• Overreliance on one measure can be a mistake. Tracking literacy development is complex and should be accomplished using multiple types of measures.

• Getting accurate assessment data about adolescents requires that they do their best on the assessment. This means that students have to know why the test is being given and how the information will be used. If students perceive that a test is irrelevant, many will not take it seriously, and leaders may make inappropriate decisions based on invalid data.

• It is important to review unexpected results, whether they are atypically high or low, for specific students. In some cases, retesting will be the best way to make sure that the students' level of proficiency has been accurately captured. Then appropriate instructional response can be determined.

• Pre- and post-testing of the same cohort of students to determine growth and value added is recommended. Comparing the performance of this year's 9th grade with last year's can produce erroneous assumptions of progress or lack thereof because the cohorts are made up of different students. However, longitudinal trends are important to track to monitor program improvement. Leaders should make sure that growth, or lack thereof, is real—not within the margin of error—so that small losses and gains are not misinterpreted as significant for either individual students or cohorts.

• When setting up a pre- and post-testing schedule, two or three parallel forms of the test should be available so that students do not become overly familiar with the passages used. When possible, schools should administer a midyear assessment to provide information that can guide decisions about midyear adjustments in program and placement.

• Tracking growth using classroom or course assessments (such as rubric scores received from two different writing prompts or the difference in performance on this year's and last year's presentation) can provide unreliable information about literacy skills because topic, motivation, scoring reliability, and differences in preparation for the task can strongly influence results. However, these measures can be a good way to inform instruction and to monitor program effectiveness.

Key Messages

Good student performance data are essential to school leaders in charge of a schoolwide effort to improve literacy and learning. The seven primary types of student performance data provide insight into students' abilities as readers and writers. It is important for school leaders to discuss with members of the literacy team (1) what questions they want to answer about students' abilities to read and write in order to ensure that current programming is meeting student needs; (2) what types of student performance data they currently have access to; (3) whether the types of data they have provide the information they want; and (4) how they could improve their use of current data to inform instruction and placement decisions.

Using data in the ways described in this chapter, school leaders can choose, develop, and sustain instructional and programmatic responses that will develop the academic reading and writing abilities of all students. The key messages in this chapter are the following:

• To improve literacy and learning, school leaders need good sources of data about student performance as readers and writers.

• Different types and uses of student performance data are needed for literacy support across the content areas and for placement of students into appropriate intervention programs.

• Data quality, access, procedures, policies, and use are systemic issues that leaders should consider.

• School leaders create a culture of data-based decision making by modeling productive ways to ask questions, analyzing appropriate data to answer these questions, and establishing structures so that teachers can use data to provide targeted instructional support and get feedback on the effectiveness of programs.

As many school leaders are aware, even when the necessity for data-driven decision making is clear, obtaining good student performance data or timely access to it is not always easy. Resource challenges sometimes prevent them from taking action steps even when the data strongly support those decisions. (Chapter 9 discusses some ways that school leaders can meet some of these resource challenges.) Meeting students' literacy needs in middle and high schools may require a complete review and modification of how literacy programming currently takes place and how resources are typically used. School leaders who are ready and willing to collect and analyze data—and to act on what the data tell them about student literacy and learning needs—have the best chance of ensuring that students will be prepared to meet the literacy challenges of the 21st-century workplace, higher education programs, and productive citizenship.

> Appendix C provides a Literacy Assessment Review Tool that leaders can use as an instrument to systematically review reading and writing assessments.

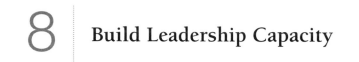

8 | Build Leadership Capacity

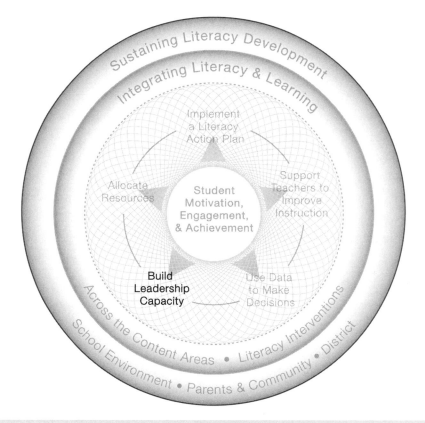

Why is this component important? Individual principals or district leaders cannot improve students' literacy habits and skills by themselves. Therefore, building the literacy leadership capacity of other administrators, literacy coaches, reading and media specialists, team leaders, department chairs, curriculum coordinators, and teachers must be a priority. It is only with the collaborative effort of people in all of these roles that a schoolwide literacy improvement effort can be successfully launched and maintained.

The role of *instructional leader* is essential for any middle or high school principal who is serious about supporting students' academic success. Principals are increasingly focused on the priority of helping teachers improve classroom teaching and learning. As the school's instructional leader, the principal greatly affects the quality of individual teacher instruction, the height of student achievement, and the degree of efficiency in school functioning (Leithwood, Louis, Anderson, & Wahlstrom, 2004).

Although there are certain administrative tasks the principal must do to ensure an efficient and safe school, the primary task of the principal is to focus the school toward activities that lead to higher levels of literacy, critical thinking, and content area learning for all students. Instructional leadership may involve planning how literacy learning will be scaffolded across grade levels and departments so that students will be able to read increasingly complex texts within all content areas. Or it may include evaluating the literacy demands of state and classroom assessments and supporting teachers to develop instructional plans that prepare students to meet those demands. This type of instructional leadership is systemic, focusing on how the educational program *as a whole* can support student learning.

"Schools operated by principals who were perceived by their teachers to be strong instructional leaders exhibited significantly greater gain scores in achievement in reading and mathematics than did schools operated by average and weak instructional leaders" (Fullan, 2001, p. 156). Many principals do not have the expertise or feel that they have the time to provide the necessary instructional guidance and support that teachers need to improve literacy and learning. Yet instructional leadership is essential in order to initiate and sustain a schoolwide literacy improvement effort.

Literacy improvement is a large undertaking; one person cannot do it alone. The role of the principal in a literacy improvement effort is similar to that of a general contractor on a building project. Just as general contractors do not have the expertise to complete all of the necessary building tasks and, in any case, would not be able to build an entire structure by themselves, school principals must see their job as that of coordinator of the literacy improvement effort and must enlist others to ensure success. Assuming this role means getting the input and full participation of literacy coaches, reading specialists, department chairs or team leaders, other administrators, and the literacy team and working with them to define everyone's roles and responsibilities regarding the literacy improvement effort. The undertaking also means that teachers participate by following the recommendations of literacy leaders in the school and working to make their instruction literacy rich.

Build Leadership Capacity is the lower-left point of the star on the graphic of the Leadership Model for Improving Adolescent Literacy and the fourth *action step*. It is an essential strategy for achieving schoolwide literacy improvement goals. In this chapter, we describe how principals can build others' leadership capacity and the roles that others must assume to support the development of students' reading and writing skills. The chapter includes three vignettes that help readers see what this might look like in action. At the end of the chapter we discuss how principals can work with resistant teachers. The chapter concludes with key messages.

Distributing School Leadership

Principals can empower teachers to become literacy leaders, involving them in school decisions regarding literacy instruction. By forming a literacy team, principals can get necessary assistance to carry out the critical functions of curriculum and instructional support, coordination, and supervision. Sharing leadership allows the principal to incorporate the talents and energy of other administrators, literacy coaches, reading specialists, curriculum coordinators, and teachers. The following vignette illustrates how a school can strengthen its schoolwide literacy improvement efforts through deployment of a literacy leadership team and collaborative effort.

The literacy team at Madison High School has been together for five years. Team members have presented their work at three national conferences. Although Madison has many other committees (such as technology, student advising, and cross-curricular connections), the literacy team is the most active in the school, and other teachers consider team members as literacy resources. It wasn't always that way, though.

The school district mandated that every school form a literacy team of at least six people, one of whom had to be the principal. The Madison literacy team, along with teams from other schools in the district, was invited to a two-week professional development opportunity during the summer at which they learned basic literacy support strategies and how to examine student work and teacher-made assessments. Teams received time and guidance to examine student performance data for their schools and were asked to set goals for their school. Each team was also told that they had to deliver 10 hours of professional development for their entire faculty each quarter. Madison High School is a large and ethnically diverse school with more than 200 faculty members. The Madison team wondered how they could ever accomplish this goal.

Through innovative scheduling, the principal created a professional development period for each teacher. As part of the school day every Monday, each teacher participated in professional development in literacy. Outside consultants were sometimes used for these sessions, but most of the presentations were conducted by the literacy team members, including the principal. Each week featured a single literacy support strategy across the entire school. All administrators, curriculum coordinators, resource teachers, and classroom teachers were expected to attend the Monday sessions. When administrators, the literacy coach, or department chairs conducted observations in classrooms that week, they expected to see the strategy used and to have the opportunity to help teachers with implementation.

The literacy team members met with much resistance and the predicable attitude of TTSP (This Too Shall Pass), but they persevered. Over time, more and more teachers began to use literacy support strategies in their content-area teaching; eventually, scaffolding instruction and professional discussions about teaching and learning became part of the culture of the school. During the past two years, along with reinforcing the use of the various strategies, the literacy team concentrated on strong and effective implementation of one schoolwide strategy. Last year, every teacher learned and incorporated QARs (Question-Answer Relationships) into their instruction. This year, they learned and began to use writing-to-learn strategies and introduced reciprocal teaching.

The test scores at Madison have steadily increased. Last year the school posted an 8 percent increase in reading scores. Teachers say things like, "The juniors this year already know how to take two-column notes, so I can concentrate on critical-thinking tasks." The literacy team now has 14 members. Team members recently went through a process to reassess the status of student literacy achievement and to set and prioritize new goals. They presented these proposed goals to each department for input and wrote a new literacy action plan to carry them through the next three years. The plan included long- and short-term goals, strategies to implement the goals, and the materials and resources necessary for implementation.

Madison High School is meeting its goals through schoolwide collaboration and a focus on building the capacity of many of the teachers. Madison's effective and respected principal has been described as low-key but persuasive, always trying to find ways to help teachers improve student learning. The principal learned about literacy along with her teachers and used creative and innovative ways to make sure that strategies introduced during professional development were implemented into classroom instruction through classroom observations, demonstrations at faculty meetings, and mentoring opportunities. With a faculty of more than 200 and at least 20 new teachers hired each year, the principal knew that she could not lead the effort to improve schoolwide literacy alone. Through her continual focus on literacy, the principal, with the help of others, slowly changed the culture of the school to one in which teachers took seriously their role in improving students' reading and writing skills.

"Leadership involves mobilizing school personnel and clients to notice, face, and take on the tasks of changing instruction as well as harnessing and mobilizing the resources needed to support the transformation of teaching and learning" (Spillane, Halverson, & Diamond, 2004, pp. 11–12). When empowered by the principal, teacher leaders can exercise decision making for literacy, take ownership of these decisions, and value themselves and others as capable literacy professionals. Administrative leaders such as assistant principals and curriculum coordinators can provide support through feedback from classroom observations and literacy walk-throughs, model the use of literacy strategies, and share instructional resources such as journal articles or book lists. Support personnel such as special education teachers and reading specialists can partner with classroom teachers to coteach literacy skills or work with differentiated small groups to provide literacy support. Distributing instructional leadership can strengthen the literacy capacity of the school as a whole by equipping the organization with a better structure for good decision making. Distributed leadership involves joining together people with differing specializations and competencies in networks rather than hierarchies (Elmore, 2002). Networks that focus on literacy improvement often find ways of working together in effective ways. Spillane (2006) discusses the relationship between the situation (literacy improvement), leaders, and followers over time as "leadership practice." This leadership practice, effectively distributed and focused on literacy, is what can lead to improvement in literacy among students.

Effective literacy decision making depends on a continual focus on the teaching and learning of reading, writing, thinking, listening, and speaking/presenting. Teacher leaders for literacy, such as the members of the school's literacy team, should continually increase their knowledge and expertise through independent reading, sharing classroom literacy activities, and attending literacy workshops and conferences. Once teacher leaders become knowledgeable in literacy, they "can help other teachers to embrace goals, to understand the changes that are needed to strengthen teaching and learning and to work towards improvement" (Leithwood & Riehl, 2003, p. 3). This collective knowledge around literacy then becomes an invaluable resource in directing and supporting the literacy improvement initiative and distributes the knowledge and responsibility for successful implementation throughout the school community.

Some degree of distributed leadership already exists in every school; however, this distribution may not be the most efficient for building instructional leadership capacity for improving literacy. For example, department chairs may exhibit leadership when reviewing curricula or facilitating decisions about textbook adoption, but this leadership may not be focused on literacy improvement. Principals should consider the leadership structures that already exist in their schools and how they can modify or improve these to direct them toward schoolwide literacy improvement. Figure 8.1 provides a list of questions that can guide a discussion about this issue.

8.1 Questions to Consider for Distributing Leadership for Literacy Improvement

• What formal and informal structures and processes do we have in place for making literacy decisions?
• How are our decision-making structures and processes directed toward improving literacy teaching and learning?
• What literacy decisions are teachers and principals empowered to make? Will their voices be heard at the school and district levels?
• Do teachers and principals believe they have the opportunity to make meaningful literacy decisions?
• Do teachers and principals believe they have the needed skills and knowledge to make meaningful literacy decisions? What specific skills and knowledge do they lack?
• What steps have been taken to build trust among the staff and administration?
• What steps have been taken to build the skills and knowledge needed to use distributed leadership?
• Do teachers want to be involved in school-level decisions around literacy, or do they perceive such involvement as extra work without much corresponding incentive or impact? What steps have been taken to facilitate their consideration of a shared decision-making structure?
• What steps have been taken to institutionalize our decision-making structures around literacy so that they exist beyond the departure of any particular person?

Principals can take several actions to distribute leadership for literacy throughout their school communities. They can

• create a strong school literacy team to guide literacy improvement efforts and provide teachers with the support and resources they need;
• offer professional development to build the leadership capacity of teachers in the area of literacy;
• increase their knowledge and skills in identifying successful school improvement strategies and other strategies that the literacy team believes are needed to make meaningful decisions built on research findings and best practices;

- take steps to increase teachers' involvement in the decision-making process; and
- connect incentives to teacher participation and show the impact of teachers' participation and decisions.

When principals are dedicated to building a school's leadership capacity for literacy, teachers receive the support, encouragement, and direction they need to improve literacy teaching and learning in their own classrooms—and they develop important leadership skills that benefit their colleagues and students throughout the school.

The School Literacy Team

The school literacy team is responsible for developing goals, strategies, and measures to implement cross-curricular literacy development. The goal of their efforts is to improve the achievement of all students, with a focus on the needs of students at risk. The literacy team should include representatives from across subjects, grades, and special areas, and it can benefit from the additional voices of parents, students, and community partners. Although there is no one model for the composition of a literacy leadership team, essential members include the principal, reading and library/media specialists, literacy coach, counselor, content-area teachers representing different departments, and resource teachers (bilingual or special education) who work with students across multiple grade levels. In smaller schools it sometimes makes sense for the existing school improvement team, leadership team, or design team to function as the literacy team. When this is the case, it is important to ensure that the current team commits to taking on literacy improvement as a high-priority vehicle for their school improvement focus and amends its membership, if necessary, to include people in all of the desired roles.

The literacy team members can extend their own knowledge and expertise about adolescent literacy for at-risk students, including effective programs and resources. With this expertise, they can develop a schoolwide plan that includes professional development for teachers, training for volunteers, processes for identifying and monitoring students at risk, and a clear list of program goals. Figure 8.2 outlines the key roles of the literacy team.

The Literacy Coach

Coaching is an essential component for improving literacy instruction in middle and high schools and is a powerful intervention with great potential (International Reading Association, 2004). In schools where teachers regularly work with literacy coaches, the teachers as well as the coaches experience "increased willingness and ability to

---

8.2 Key Roles for the Literacy Team

- Share knowledge with all teachers.
- Review the school timetable to ensure that it supports student literacy.
- Review and recommend professional and classroom resources to support literacy.
- Develop, implement, and monitor a schoolwide literacy action plan.
- Develop a professional development plan for teachers.
- Establish community links that support literacy growth for at-risk students.
- Build relationships with neighboring elementary and secondary schools to ease the transition for students and to share successful practices.
- Review student achievement data and other relevant information in order to identify and track the progress of at-risk students.
- Monitor the effectiveness of programs, interventions, and resources.
- Communicate with the other teachers in the building.

---

collaborate, peer accountability, individual teacher knowledge about other teachers' classrooms, increased levels and quality of implementation of new instructional strategies, and support for new teachers" (Symonds, 2003, p. 4). In essence, coaching helps build a culture of improvement and change around literacy within the school.

Literacy coaching facilitates the development of professional relationships based on a shared language and a school culture that promotes continuous improvement in instructional practices for teaching reading and writing. Coaching reduces the isolation experienced by many teachers in middle and high schools and encourages teachers to explore important literacy issues together in an atmosphere of openness. The following vignette describes how one literacy coach worked with colleagues.

When Brandon Browning finished his master's degree in reading education at the local university, his principal asked him to teach the literacy intervention classes at Mountainview Middle School. Brandon taught the classes for several years, enjoying the contact with the students and refining strategies for supporting their growth as readers and writers. He also facilitated an annual workshop for content-area teachers so that they could teach students the strategies necessary to become more successful in negotiating their textbooks. Brandon suggested that colleagues consider the use of leveled texts on the topics that were covered in science, social studies, music, art, and language arts to build students' background knowledge so that struggling readers could be more successful in their content-area classes. He talked to some of the other teachers about the literacy support strategies he was using in hopes that they would reinforce them in the content-area classes.

During his fifth year of teaching the reading classes, the school district decided to hire literacy coaches for each middle and high school. Brandon decided this would be an interesting challenge for him. His principal agreed. The school had a literacy team, but it lacked vitality, so Brandon received permission to add a couple of members, collected and analyzed the data on student achievement, and (with the support of his principal) called a meeting. The literacy team was now representative of the entire school community, and Brandon now had allies to support his work of mentoring teachers.

Because Mountainview had never had a literacy action plan (LAP), Brandon thought a "literacy status report" was in order. He led the literacy team through a series of conversations to formulate goals for the upcoming year. After several sessions, the LAP was ready for feedback from the rest of the faculty. He presented the plan to each teaching team for feedback and discussion and took those suggestions back to the literacy team, who revised the plan accordingly. He knew that he would need buy-in from all content-area teachers if he was to be successful in helping teachers integrate literacy support strategies into their content-area instruction.

Brandon began his work with teachers by meeting with each department to listen to their perceptions of the literacy needs of students. Predictably, "students who could not read the textbook" were mentioned as a common problem across all departments. Brandon showed each team the student achievement data and helped them brainstorm ways to help students who were struggling to keep up in their classes. Working with the reading intervention teachers, he volunteered to administer individual diagnostic tests to determine how best to help these students. Brandon carefully chose strategies that lent themselves to a particular academic discourse and then asked for volunteers from the literacy team to help plan lessons, model instruction, and provide coaching and mentoring. He wanted to develop the teaching skills of this group of teachers first.

After a semester of working in classrooms, Brandon decided it was time for making the work of literacy improvement more public. After the holiday break, on a professional development day, he began by talking about how literacy support strategies can help students become more independent readers and learn more content. He spent the rest of the morning explaining the idea of scaffolding and providing examples of how literacy support strategies could be linked to support readers before, during, and after reading. During the afternoon session, literacy team members each presented a strategy to their department that they had used successfully in their classrooms. Brandon asked them to share the data they collected on student performance before and after the strategy use and any anecdotal comments about how they

thought the strategy had helped with student learning. Administrators sat in on these sessions
and strongly encouraged teachers to try out these strategies for themselves.

Brandon's wife, Heather, asked what he did all day since he did not have a classroom
assignment. As he explained his roles and responsibilities to her, he realized that some of the
teachers might also wonder how he was using his time. As the year progressed, he clarified
his duties with the rest of the faculty and asked how he could be of more help to them. He
particularly asked for feedback from his principal and the literacy team. It became clear that
he needed to focus on his role as facilitator (working with the literacy team, departments,
and grade-level teams), coach (working with individual teachers in the different content-area
classrooms), and evaluator of literacy needs (collecting, analyzing, sharing, and discussing
student achievement and other types of data). It was a busy school year for Brandon, but as it
drew to a close, he had big plans to involve more teachers, to concentrate on specific strategies
across the content areas, and to meet the goals set by the literacy team.

As demonstrated in the vignette, a school's literacy improvement efforts can be greatly
enhanced when led by a professional literacy coach. Brandon was able to lead and coordinate the efforts of the school literacy team. He offered invaluable feedback to teachers, providing a clearer picture of their own teaching performance and how they could improve it.
Most teachers of content-area classes at Mountainview lacked training and experience with
activities that build reading and writing skills. They needed support and guidance in learning how literacy strategies could enhance learning in their classrooms. They needed an
expert who could help identify appropriate texts to use with their students, collaborate in
devising lessons that would help students learn effectively from content texts, and model
activities that would engage students in reading and writing while they learned new content. Brandon provided this support to the teachers in his school.

Further, Brandon and the literacy team became a foundational support and guide for
teachers as they learned and changed their practices throughout the school year. His roles
as the literacy coach required teaching skill, depth of knowledge, and the ability to work
well with his peers. In addition to these responsibilities, Brandon coordinated his efforts
with school administrators and developed a networking system with the literacy team.
Without administrative support, Brandon would have had little credibility or authority.

It is also the responsibility of literacy coaches to make sure that the literacy
improvement effort is not totally dependent on them. If the literacy coach leaves the
school for some reason, the literacy effort must go on. The job of a literacy coach is to
initiate the effort and also make sure that it can be sustained. Having this responsibility
means that the coach needs to engage a core group of supportive faculty to help

infuse literacy skills across the curriculum. In addition, literacy teams provide specific, accomplishable school literacy goals that literacy coaches are responsible for addressing in all of their activities with teachers. As leader of the school literacy team, the literacy coach establishes credibility and guides the literacy activities of the school, including data analysis, literacy enhancement activities for students, and professional development.

Teacher professional development that focuses on showing teachers how to infuse literacy development within each content area is essential. It is one of the literacy coach's responsibilities to plan and implement professional development. The coach, with help from the literacy team, identifies topics, presenters (in some cases the coach may be the presenter), and formats (whole faculty, team meetings, department meetings, planning-period meetings) for professional development. In addition, the literacy coach can monitor the effectiveness of professional development and continually assess the changing needs of the faculty.

Professional development should accompany ongoing follow-through mentoring and support. Specifically, literacy coaches should be attentive to the use of good literacy practices (or lack of these practices) in the classroom, offer specific and collaborative support, and mentor teachers as they improve their practice. In short, the literacy coach becomes a guide for teachers as they learn and change their practices throughout the school year. According to the International Reading Association (2006), the key roles for literacy coaches are the following:

- Work with the literacy team and school staff to improve reading instruction.
- Assist teachers in assessing the literacy needs of students (and determining the most appropriate tools making these assessments).
- Provide professional development to teachers and demonstrate how to improve literacy instruction in the content areas.

Other Members of the School Staff

It takes dedicated teamwork to ensure that all students have the literacy skills they need for success. This section describes the key roles and responsibilities of other school staff to make literacy a priority and focus in all classrooms.

School Administrators

Principals lead successful literacy improvement efforts by functioning as instructional leaders who make literacy a school priority. Such leaders work collaboratively with school staff to build a professional learning community focused on literacy. They ensure that the school literacy plan includes provisions for students at risk. These principals pay special attention to finding and developing school leaders, providing opportunities for shared learning, and building support for the school literacy plan. As the main instructional leader of the school, the principal sets the tone of the school and establishes and maintains a literacy-rich school environment (see Chapter 4).

But all administrators who evaluate teachers and have responsibility for any aspect of the instructional program should participate in a schoolwide effort. This includes assistant principals, deans, special education or bilingual education directors, guidance counselors, and program directors. These administrators should know and communicate to others the school's progress on the literacy action plan; contribute to making the school clearly communicate that reading, writing, and thinking are priorities; and know how to assess literacy support during walk-throughs and classroom evaluations. They should participate in faculty book talks, student-faculty book clubs, and sustained silent reading time, and they should attend literacy events taking place at the school, such as author's visits, plays, poetry slams, and speech events. It is important that all administrators provide this type of knowledgeable support. Figure 8.3 lists the key roles of school administrators.

8.3 Key Roles for School Administrators

- Collect and analyze data to guide instruction.
- Set high standards of achievement for teachers, students, and staff.
- Develop and support a literacy plan that promotes increased student achievement in literacy.
- Allocate adequate funds to support the school's literacy plan.
- Provide time for professional development on literacy strategies and for literacy team meetings.
- Require all content area teachers to use literacy strategies and tie use to evaluation.
- Monitor student progress in reading.
- Encourage schoolwide literacy projects and model the importance of reading.
- Involve parents in students' literacy growth.
- Actively participate in professional development sessions.

Curriculum Coordinators

As the decision maker about curriculum and instruction in the district, the curriculum coordinator plays a pivotal role in the success of a school's literacy plan. It is the curriculum coordinator's role to evaluate curriculum and instruction using a literacy lens and to ensure that curriculum materials provide appropriate opportunities and support for content-area literacy development. It is also the curriculum coordinator's role to evaluate the appropriateness and content of reading programs and their associated materials and resources. When a school has a literacy coach, the coach and the curriculum coordinator work collaboratively to ensure that curriculum, instruction, and assessment are aligned and that the literacy demands of each are supported and understood. Figure 8.4 summarizes the key roles of the curriculum coordinator.

8.4 Key Roles for Curriculum Coordinators

- Collect and analyze data to guide instruction.
- Assist the principal in coordinating the school's literacy plan.
- Serve on the school literacy team.
- Remain current with research on literacy.
- Recommend literacy materials.
- Conduct professional training and follow-up activities in literacy.
- Assist in facilitating school literacy programs.
- Encourage parental involvement in student literacy growth.
- Attend district-level staff development workshops and share the information with faculty and staff.
- Alert staff to literacy-related professional development activities.

Reading Specialists

All educators need some expertise in literacy development. But teachers who work primarily with struggling readers and writers need specific expertise. These reading specialists typically have reading certification and are essential to successfully meeting the literacy development needs of struggling readers. An effective reading specialist at the middle or high school level has

- high expectations for the literacy achievement of all students,
- expertise in literacy instruction for adolescents,
- skill in using data to support student literacy achievement,
- understanding of the literacy demands of various subjects and grades,

- demonstrated success with students at risk, and
- knowledge of current research in adolescent learning and literacy for students at risk.

Figure 8.5 lists the key roles of reading specialists.

8.5 Key Roles for Reading Specialists

- Model the use of a variety of literacy strategies to support the learning of struggling readers.
- Administer diagnostic assessments and use the results to develop instructional plans that meet students' literacy needs.
- Teach intervention classes.
- Communicate with parents about students' literacy needs.
- Promote cross-curricular literacy by encouraging the integration of literacy in all subject areas and supporting the school literacy team.
- Work with teachers to support students at risk.
- Train and supervise tutors and paraprofessionals.
- Share literacy resources and recent research and inform school administrators about ongoing professional development opportunities.
- Share effective strategies and practices and serve as a resource.

Library/Media Specialists

The school library/media specialist is in a unique position to support the literacy action plan through multiple venues. A library media specialist can work with teachers to provide online resources to support the use of texts at varying reading levels, provide instruction in research strategies, facilitate a student reading club, sponsor speakers and programs, participate on the literacy team, and order resources for professional development. Figure 8.6 lists the key roles of library/media specialists.

ESL/Special Education Teachers

ESL teachers and special education teachers are capacity builders who can lead colleagues to a deep and rich understanding of the barriers to achievement for students at risk. These teachers are dedicated to developing and implementing strategies and programs to ensure that students graduate with the literacy and numeracy skills they need for a seamless transition to the workplace, college, or university. They often have substantive background and experience in language-related instruction, including reading. Figure 8.7 lists the key roles of ESL/special education teachers.

8.6 Key Roles for Library/Media Specialists

- Use student data to order appropriate reading materials.
- Serve on the literacy team.
- Promote the literacy plan by collaborating with teachers to provide suitable resources for topic units.
- Design or participate in schoolwide celebrations of independent reading.
- Arrange for special library programs that promote literacy.
- Provide online literacy resources and serve as liaison to technology-based literacy instruction.
- Enhance creativity in literacy instruction through such vehicles as reader's theater, poetry coffeehouse, storytelling.
- Collaborate with the reading specialist and literacy coach on literacy initiatives.

8.7 Key Roles for ESL/Special Education Teachers

- Use, model, and share research-based instructional practices that build the literacy and language skills of English language learners and special education students.
- Review existing achievement data and practices to make appropriate student placements and to identify successes and needs across the school.
- Draw on information from teachers across the school to build a broader, clearer picture of what works in support of students at risk.
- Support teachers who have innovative ideas to help students who are at risk.
- Develop a schoolwide plan that builds on successes and closes gaps for students at risk and that includes priorities, time lines, actions, resource requirements, communication strategies, and benchmarks for success.

Department Chairs or Team Leaders

The department chair or team leader serves as the instructional leader for all other teachers in the department. In a literacy improvement effort, the involvement, modeling, and enthusiasm of these teachers can be what differentiates success from failure. Figure 8.8 lists the key roles of department chairs or team leaders.

8.8 Key Roles for Department Chairs or Team Leaders

- Collect and analyze data to guide instruction.
- Establish high expectations for all teachers in the department.
- Develop goals and plans for the department that include literacy.
- Evaluate appropriateness of materials to support the school's literacy plan.
- Serve as a liaison between the department and the literacy team.
- Coordinate departmentwide literacy activities.
- Attend district meetings and share pertinent information with the department members.
- Lead and monitor literacy professional development tied to their content area.

Content-Area Teachers

Students have different learning needs, strengths, and interests, and the right to achieve the highest possible level of literacy. Teachers who support students' literacy development base their classroom practices on research, regularly assess achievement, diagnose gaps, and provide instruction that meets the specific learning needs of their students. Such teachers create organized, responsive, and stimulating learning environments. They do not work alone but see themselves as part of a team committed to supporting every student's achievement. Teachers need the support of school and system leaders who can help them acquire the knowledge, skills, and resources they need and can help them develop innovative, effective solutions for their students who are at risk. Teachers also need the support of families and community agencies.

Teacher leaders understand the value of working collaboratively with other teachers and the principal to ensure that students' learning is improved through coordinated, complementary approaches to literacy instruction. This collaboration includes

- meeting regularly with colleagues to engage in professional dialogue and share resources that promote best practices;
- participating in cross-grade/cross-subject discussions about student achievement, student learning needs, and instructional and assessment practices;
- helping to establish school literacy goals, strategies, and measures; and
- engaging in professional development related to improving literacy skills for students at risk.

Figure 8.9 lists the key roles of content-area teachers in the literacy improvement effort.

8.9 Key Roles for Content-Area Teachers

- Plan and organize instruction to meet individual literacy and learning needs of students and groups.
- Motivate students to learn.
- Teach literacy habits and skills within the context of content area teaching and learning.
- Assess student achievement.
- Work collaboratively with colleagues.
- Use assessment to improve instruction.
- Make connections with families and the community.
- Teach content-specific standards regardless of the literacy levels of students.

Dealing with Resisters

Principals will inevitably have to deal with resistant teachers who may not want to take on new challenges, who perceive literacy development as being someone else's job, who feel that explicit literacy instruction will spoil the pleasure of reading for students, or who express negative behind-the-scenes resistance that can sabotage the literacy initiative. It is important to help these teachers understand that the goal of the school is to consistently improve learning for all students and that achieving this goal requires improved literacy teaching and learning by all teachers on staff. The following vignette describes how one principal dealt with resisters in her school.

When Jalma Baker walked into the superintendent's office, she knew she was going to be asked to take over the principalship at Valley High School (VHS). She also thought she knew why. She had succeeded in creating a literacy-rich and supportive environment at the middle school over the past eight years—and the test scores had slowly but steadily risen. It was a long haul, and it took constant effort, but finally, the teachers were all focused on literacy learning in every classroom. Could she really start all over again at the high school?

Valley, home of the Eagles, is known for its International Baccalaureate (IB) program. Traditionally, the district's highest-achieving students attend VHS and are generally accepted into prestigious colleges and universities. The teachers in this program are scholars themselves in their respective content areas. But Jalma knew exactly why she was pegged to fill the spot. Almost 18 percent of the students, none of whom were in the IB program, were performing poorly on state tests in reading and writing. Accountability measures in the state had made it increasingly more uncomfortable for districts to ignore these underperforming high school students. Jalma also knew that VHS had a group of students who currently read on grade level but would likely need continued literacy support in the content areas to maintain that status. The superintendent asked her to take the position but stressed that Valley High School needed to meet the literacy needs of all of the students and that the responsibility for this would be in her hands. "I have no doubt that you are the person who can do this!" the superintendent said encouragingly.

Jalma accepted the position and spent the summer thinking about how best to approach this very talented, but possibly resistant faculty. She could hear them now:

"I teach physics, not reading."
"Why didn't they teach them to read in the elementary grades?"
"I wasn't trained to teach reading."
"Students have too many distractions like video games and MTV to read."
"Their parents don't read; how can we teach them to read?"

Over the summer she hired a reading specialist to work with 9th graders who had scored below the 25th percentile on the state test. She met with every department chair and discussed their views of candidates in their department who could take on the role of teacher leader. She was looking for teachers who were well regarded by their colleagues and would be willing to integrate literacy support strategies into their instruction. After consulting the department chairs, Jalma assigned one teacher from each department to teach general education classes with a common group of students. She promised extra training and support to help them be successful with these students.

The week before school started, Jalma hired a consultant to work with these specially selected teachers, along with her administrative team, the reading specialist, and the media specialist. They learned about the reading and writing process, tried out several literacy support strategies, and had time to discuss common goals and a vision for the team. They named themselves the Soaring Eagles.

When school began, Jalma and her administrative team gathered data on student performance. As she presented the data to the faculty, she asked them to complete a PMI chart (Pluses, Minuses, Interesting) about the data. There was much to celebrate for the IB students, and the faculty felt satisfied. However, as the teachers looked at the Minus and Interesting columns they noticed how low the scores were for the students in the bottom 18 percent. It became obvious to everyone that something needed to be done to help these students read and write at higher levels. In addition, most teachers admitted that even the students reading on grade level struggled to comprehend their textbooks.

Jalma formed a literacy team, worked closely with the team of teachers focused on the general education students, and arranged for ongoing literacy professional development for all *teachers and administrators. The literacy team worked with Jalma to set improvement goals for all students—not just those in the IB program. They decided that the students in the bottom 18 percent would require additional support, so they purchased a research-based reading program, trained one teacher to implement it, and scheduled an extra period of instruction for these students.*

Professional development sessions helped teachers see the level of literacy challenges inherent in reading complex texts. Teachers met by departments, and the department chairs facilitated the development of agreements to use specific literacy strategies geared toward critical reading, critical thinking, and essay writing. Teachers began to realize that they could adapt the strategies to use with the students in most of their classes—even, in some cases, with the IB students to help them work through the high-level reading and writing demands of the IB curriculum. Not surprisingly, the "students in the middle" benefited, too. The school began to see student test scores rise as early as the next year, and they kept rising as the literacy team continued to meet, to monitor progress, and to revise plans for needed support.

It is important to understand *why* some teachers resist jumping on board with a schoolwide literacy initiative. After all, most teachers do not feel that improving literacy is a bad thing. Sometimes excellent teachers who work hard to support their students' content-area learning are among the most resistant. Figure 8.10 shows some of the reasons why teachers resist and strategies that school leaders can use to get them involved with the literacy improvement effort. Administrators and members of the literacy team may wish to use this chart as a guide for discussion by adding a column with the heading "Possible Action Steps" and brainstorming ways to work with teachers who may resist integrating literacy into their content-area teaching.

8.10 **Responding to Teachers Who Resist Literacy Improvement Efforts**	
Why Teachers May Be Resistant	**Key Messages for Teachers to Hear**
Fear—I am confident about my content knowledge but fearful about the expectation that I should know how to teach reading or writing—what if I do it wrong?	You are not expected to become reading experts, but you *are* the best ones to provide content area literacy support because you understand the reading and writing demands of your content area.
Feeling of being overwhelmed—There are standards to address and assessments to give and committee work to do and too many students and not enough time and now I have to teach reading, too?	Literacy instruction will enable students to learn the content better and be more successful after explicit teaching and modeling. Use of the literacy strategies will actually save time and effort.

Why Teachers May Be Resistant	Key Messages for Teachers to Hear
The comfort of the familiar—I have always done it this way, and it basically works; I am not sure I want to change it.	The stakes are higher, student demographics are changing, and the goals have shifted. We are now attempting to prepare all students for college, career, and citizenship, and that requires new tactics on the part of all of us.
"This, too, shall pass"—So many things come and go in education; if I just lie low, this new literacy fad will pass as well.	Being able to use reading, writing, thinking, and speaking/listening to learn what you want/need to know and communicate it to others is not a *fad*—it is the definition of an independent learner.
Lack of support/resources/time—As usual, they want me to do this but are not giving me adequate training/support/planning time/materials to do it right. Forget it!	This is a really important priority for our school over the next three years, and we will make sure you have the support to do it right. We cannot afford to do it wrong—and students are counting on you to help them.
Unclear expectations/lack of understanding—Now they want us to become reading specialists and stop teaching content, and I am just not going to do that.	We are asking that you provide more content area reading and writing instruction and more opportunities to have students read and write. We are not asking you to become a reading specialist.
Belief systems—Students should have learned to read in elementary school and should come to me as competent readers and writers. My job is to give students the content. It's too late if they get to middle/high school and can't read. I don't assign reading because most students won't do it anyway, but they learn the content through videos and demonstrations and lots of hands-on, so what is the big deal? Anyway, some like to read, some don't—that's the way it is.	Actually, middle and high school are not too late. If students come to you without these skills, are you willing to condemn them for life? When you provide all of those experiences for students, you enable them to evade reading, not develop competence as readers, writers, and learners. Besides, based on what you are saying, you are working harder than they are! The one who works the hardest generally learns the most—and that should be the students! Breaking down resistance to reading and writing means creating a classroom environment that motivates students to engage with reading and writing. You need strategies to do this—that is why we are providing good professional development for all teachers on content area literacy strategies.
Inadequate professional development—We have to go to these one-size-fits-all inservice workshops. The consultant is an elementary specialist who does not understand what works with adolescents; there are no content area examples. I am not sure how these strategies are relevant or how to use them in my classroom. We get two workshops, and we are supposed to be "trained."	We understand that you will need ongoing professional development to make content area teaching and learning rich in literacy support across all classrooms. We are providing a menu of different professional development options. We are not insisting that everyone do the same thing, but we are tying literacy improvement to school improvement goals and professional goals. Our expectation is that everyone will focus on improving their content area reading and writing instruction over the next three years and will put into place grade-level, departmental, and team agreements regarding the use of specific literacy strategies or areas of focus.

Source: J. Meltzer, 2006, Center for Resource Management, Inc. Copyright 2006 by J. Meltzer. Adapted with permission from Center for Resource Management.

As is the case in all other aspects of leading a schoolwide literacy improvement initiative, careful planning for how to build the capacity of teachers and administrators in the school will pay off. Just as teachers are being asked to motivate their students to engage with reading and writing, principals need to motivate their staff to wholeheartedly engage in schoolwide efforts to improve students' literacy habits and skills. It is the role—and responsibility—of the principal to find effective ways to do this because effective collaborative effort is the only way to accomplish the goal of increasing students' proficiency as readers and writers.

Key Messages

Instructional leaders provide the guidance and support necessary for schoolwide change. Although principal leadership is imperative, a schoolwide literacy improvement effort may ultimately require that leadership be distributed throughout the school community to be effective. Distributed leadership involves teachers in the decision-making process, allowing them to take ownership of the effort. A school literacy team, the literacy coach, middle-level leaders, and other teachers can all play important leadership roles. The key messages in this chapter are the following:

• Leaders can build the leadership capacity of their teachers to provide support for literacy improvement efforts.

• Distributing leadership throughout the school community allows for increased knowledge, guidance, and support for a literacy improvement effort.

• The school literacy team is an effective vehicle for developing goals, strategies, and measures to implement literacy improvement across all content areas.

• The school literacy coach and reading specialist provides invaluable expertise to guide and support teachers in developing literacy knowledge and skills.

• All members of the school community have important roles to play so that they can contribute to the literacy initiative.

Principals should consider the formal and informal leadership roles that already exist in their schools. Teachers who currently play a leadership role can continue to do so, and other teachers who have knowledge about the literacy learning process can be brought into a leadership role. By providing these literacy leaders with support and authority to make decisions, the principal can effectively distribute leadership for the literacy improvement effort. When teachers exercise greater autonomy and principals and teachers work together on schoolwide decision making, the potential exists for principals to have fewer interruptions in their work, for teachers to spend less time waiting for permission to make decisions they are capable of making themselves, and for school-improvement planning and monitoring to capture more of the time and attention of all the faculty.

9 | Allocate Resources to Support Literacy

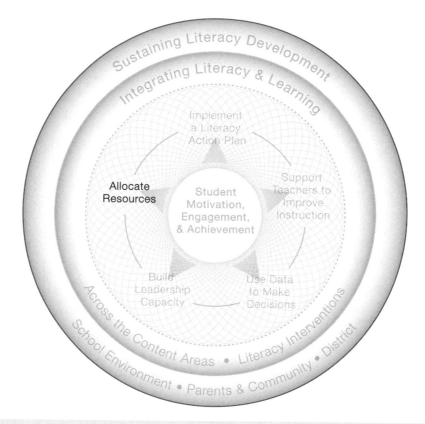

Why is this component important? Various resources are essential to the implementation of an effective literacy improvement effort. Leaders who strategically allocate resources such as time, space, personnel, professional development, funding, technology, and materials are more likely to meet the goals of the school's literacy action plan. Doing so may involve a reallocation of resources or using resources in different ways than in the past.

Strategic allocation of resources is essential to ensure that all students receive the instruction they need. A school's literacy action plan outlines the necessary resources to meet each goal. Finding these resources, however, is never an easy task. School leaders who are dedicated to the goal of improving literacy advocate for resources from the district, the state, and the local business community, and they understand how existing resources might be better used. Important literacy support resources include

- time for literacy learning, assessment, planning, and instruction;
- use of support personnel, such as literacy coaches, reading specialists, tutors, and paraprofessionals, to work with teachers and students;
- professional development for all teachers in content-related literacy instruction;
- instructional materials and technologies to support differentiated literacy instruction; and
- adequate funding to support ongoing literacy initiatives.

These resources are the same ones that leaders are responsible for using wisely to support students' general academic success. The difference that we focus on here is viewing these resources through the lens of literacy.

In this chapter, we address the upper-left point of the star on the graphic of the Leadership Model for Improving Adolescent Literacy, *Allocate Resources*, which represents the fifth *action step*. The chapter begins with a vignette that highlights how one school used their resources to support literacy improvement efforts. The same vignette continues later in the chapter. We discuss each type of resource and provide examples of how each might best be used to support literacy improvement. The chapter concludes with key messages.

Strategic and Creative Use of Resources to Support Literacy

The teachers at Allewan Regional Middle School were discouraged by the state assessment results. Student performance in reading, writing, and math was stagnant, and in some cases lower than the year before. Too many students could not comprehend what they read or substantiate their ideas in writing. Too many disliked reading and were uninterested in learning. Textbooks were typically written at levels too advanced for the students to read, and the teachers used them only to supplement oral instruction or visual media. The majority of students could not or would not complete assigned reading. The teachers did not know what to do.

Recognizing these problems, school administrators initiated discussions with teachers. They determined that the best approach was to hire grade-level curriculum coordinators to work directly with teachers. Despite this enviable resource allocation, the curriculum coordinators encountered much resistance in the first few years. Teachers were angry that the school had hired newcomers with less experience over internal candidates and had eliminated department-head positions and stipends to help fund the new positions. Content teachers were anxious about classroom observations, which might reveal their struggles to help students learn. Clearly, the resource of additional staff was only one part of the solution to improve literacy and academic learning.

The curriculum coordinators realized that a schoolwide literacy action plan for academic improvement was essential. The plan needed to go beyond content area curriculum revisions and include a schoolwide literacy needs assessment that would help teachers enhance student learning. The school needed funding for professional development, instructional materials, student assessments, and technology support. It needed time for many purposes—to assess all students, to schedule targeted interventions for struggling learners, to provide professional development for teachers, to create common periods for team planning, and to meet with teachers and guidance counselors from other schools to ensure curriculum alignment with the feeder elementaries and the high school. Also critical would be changing teachers' mindsets from thinking about reading as a stand-alone subject to reading and writing as primary vehicles for learning across all subject areas.

The work began slowly but quickly gained momentum as the teachers realized that the focus was on increased support for student learning, not top-down administrative control or standardization of instruction, as they had feared. The school provided support to individual teachers in the form of curriculum resources, instructional modeling, and personal coaching. It supported teams through literacy workshops and curriculum revision meetings. Schoolwide committees were established for departmental planning, technology expansion, and curriculum alignment to state standards. The school purchased copies of Strategies That Work *(Harvey & Goudvis, 2000) for every classroom teacher to help establish a common literacy language for all staff. District support included diverting federal grant funding solely to the middle school for one year to jump-start the change process. District leaders also shifted the curriculum review process from individual schools to districtwide K–12 committees so content learning could be effectively spiraled up through the grades.*

At the core of the change process was a "build it and they will come" approach to literacy professional development. Teachers reported that the literacy support strategies they used were largely limited to assigned reading of novels and short stories and testing on literal comprehension. Teachers said that they were not teaching literacy strategies to develop comprehension or higher-order thinking because they did not know how to do this. Many teachers admitted they did not think the students could handle more challenging tasks. The school provided workshops and teacher-sharing seminars in multiple formats during and after school and during district professional development days. Professional development texts and detailed handouts on literacy strategies provided support for classroom applications. Small grant-supported stipends conveyed appreciation for teachers who volunteered to develop their literacy knowledge and skill.

The results after just two years amazed everyone. Seventy-five teachers voluntarily attended more than 2,900 hours of professional development in literacy. State assessment data showed consistent improvement over the next several years. Teachers and administrators gave credit for the improvement to the teachers' voluntary agreement to use the same set of research-based literacy strategies across all content areas. Teachers who had disliked teaching a reading class because of students' lack of interest and poor behavior were surprised by the increasing attentiveness when students learned how to improve their comprehension and were given a choice of texts, materials at appropriate reading levels, and small-group settings in which to talk about what they read. Teachers at each grade level appreciated that entering students came to them with a consistent set of core literacy strategies that they could build on. Teacher evaluation became an opportunity for professional dialogue, and schoolwide committees strengthened and unified the school culture. One teacher spoke for many when she reflected that the schoolwide approach designed by the curriculum coordinators had changed the school culture from "night to day."

The school continues to align literacy with academic learning, and the success story is ongoing. Each year new initiatives systemically link the resources of time, personnel, technology, materials, and school policy to expand and deepen literacy and learning for all students.

School leaders at Allewan Middle School had to make some decisions about the reallocation of resources, and it took time for teachers to get used to the shift. Many schools across the United States face dilemmas when trying to provide resources to support literacy development. Some do not have enough textbooks for content-area instruction or have limited library materials; some lack space to house groups of students for targeted interventions; some lack state or federal grants to support purchase of literacy consultation or texts that describe learning strategies for the content areas; some lack personnel or release days for professional development; some lack a sufficient technology infrastructure. However, in many cases, as discussed in the vignette, school and district leaders can find resources to support literacy by reallocating funds, redefining professional roles and responsibilities, adjusting schedules, clarifying priorities, and applying for grants. In the rest of this chapter, we describe a variety of options for how leaders can best use resources to support and sustain a schoolwide literacy improvement effort.

Time/Space/Personnel for Literacy Development

Providing time, space, and personnel for literacy assessment, action planning, instructional planning, literacy instruction, and systematic monitoring of progress is essential. But there is no single best way to do it. In this section we present a variety of approaches from which school leaders can select. The goal for using these resources is the same for all schools: increasing school and teacher capacity to embed literacy learning in every class, every day, for every student. The key is ensuring that resources for content-area literacy are seen as essential for academic success, not as an intrusion or competitor for scarce resources.

Time

Because of the urgency of concern about poor student performance, high dropout rates, school improvement time lines, or other pressures, schools sometimes implement literacy programs or new approaches on a piecemeal basis without taking the time to assess current capacity or plan a comprehensive approach. Unfortunately, the result is often piecemeal progress. School leaders who think through the various ways that time will need to be spent and who plan accordingly can ensure that adequate time is provided to ensure success. For example, school leaders should plan time for

- literacy team meetings,
- assessment,
- grade-level and content-area meetings,
- the integration of literacy support strategies in content-area instruction,
- literacy interventions, and
- schoolwide or classroom-based sustained silent reading.

Literacy team meetings. Schools need time for a cross-content, schoolwide literacy team to meet and plan a coordinated, comprehensive program of literacy services. Team members need time to learn best practices, visit high-performing schools, research and purchase appropriate materials, discuss assessment needs, and gain substantive input from teachers, administrators, parents, and other stakeholders at all stages of the development of the literacy action plan. Initially the literacy team will benefit from meeting weekly or twice a month to plan the schoolwide literacy improvement initiative. Less frequent meetings may result in substantially less progress and loss of momentum. Many schools have found it effective to dedicate one year to developing a comprehensive three- to five-year literacy action plan. Some schools begin teacher professional development in literacy strategies and implement small-scale pilot implementations of various components of the action plan during the first year to speed up progress. Once the long-term plan is ready, the literacy team may cut back to monthly whole-group meetings with more frequent subcommittee meetings as needed.

Assessment. School leaders should also plan for time to assess student capabilities as readers and writers. The school should develop an assessment calendar so that everyone is clear on when and why specific reading and writing assessments will be given, and by whom. In some cases, teachers will need time not only for administering the assessments but also for scoring them, as is the case with using rubrics to assess student responses to district writing prompts. It is also essential to plan for meetings at which teachers and administrators can review the assessment results to plan appropriate instructional and programmatic responses or to evaluate progress. The timing of these meetings will depend on when the school gets the assessment results. Depending on the assessment, this could be in three to six weeks, in several months, or immediately through computer or manual scoring. Where appropriate, time must also be allotted for a reading specialist or a special education teacher with a reading background to complete individual diagnostic testing of students who are reading or writing substantially below grade level. School leaders should discuss these time demands with the teachers and administrators responsible for coordinating different aspects of assessment and decide with them how schedules will accommodate the time requirements.

Schools and districts have different levels of autonomy over aspects of their testing schedules, depending on whether they are administering state, standardized, or local assessments. Some schools complete leveled reading and writing assessments early in the school year to provide current data, whereas others prefer to test in late spring so the results can be cumulated and distributed over the summer, giving teachers time to plan for individual needs. Schools that rely on a computer-based assessment often test two or three times a year to determine progress and areas that might require additional emphasis. This type of assessment can then serve as both an instructional support and a progress-monitoring tool. Often the school's literacy team proposes the scheduling of literacy assessments (other than state assessments), taking into consideration teacher feedback and buy-in. School administrators then approve and design the actual schedule, with an understanding of the multiple time demands of other school functions.

Grade-level and content-area meetings. Once the school has its assessment data, teachers need time for grade-level and content-area meetings to define methods for embedding literacy within content area instruction. Common planning time for teams is critical but may be scheduled in various ways. Some teachers prefer to allot a certain amount of time at every daily meeting for literacy; some like to allot one full meeting a week to literacy; some prefer to allot one day each month. Some will say they do not have time for any literacy planning at all, which may require a school to establish literacy planning as a school policy. Until all teachers accept their role in advancing literacy for all students, resistance will naturally occur. Teachers often use complaints about lack of time as an excuse for not working to improve instruction. Many schools change their schedules and find the resources to support such things as common planning time for grade-level teams or departments, 20 minutes to share literacy techniques at each faculty meeting, early-release days for reviewing curriculum or examining student work, stipends for work during the summer to integrate literacy within the content curriculum, and time for independent reading of literacy instructional texts or attending literacy conferences as part of the certification renewal process.

Integrating literacy support strategies in content-area instruction. Teachers often insist that they cannot get through their content curriculum, let alone add in "more" reading, writing, or speaking/presenting tasks. Literacy support does not require time away from content area instruction; it can occur during and as an integral part of content acquisition. Through professional development, many teachers discover that using literacy strategies (such as analytical graphic organizers, word walls/sorts, higher-order questioning techniques, and structured after-reading processes for communicating what was learned) actually reduces time spent on review and reinforcement of content materials. Others see how increasing reading engagement through sustained silent reading or peer discussions about student-selected texts results in increased interest in course topics. Some teachers, however, will continue to resist devoting time to literacy instruction until they become accountable for it. As discussed in Chapter 6, monitoring can occur through administrators' use of literacy walk-throughs, inclusion of literacy tasks in classroom evaluation forms, requirements to include literacy support in lesson plans, or other schoolwide structures that establish expectations for embedding literacy in all content instruction. School leaders can support teachers' effective reconceptualization of their role in teaching literacy support strategies by clearly articulating the literacy components of content standards, district curriculum guides, local assessments, and school goals.

Literacy interventions. Often the most challenging time issue is the time needed for literacy interventions for struggling learners, because these interventions should occur in addition to—not instead of—content-area classes. Students and parents are sometimes resistant if compensatory instruction occurs during elective periods, unified arts periods, or after school, especially if the student receives literacy support in isolation from core content studies. Schools that provide a variety of options seem to fare best. Options can include

- differentiated small-group instruction within the regular classroom;
- small-group pullout for literacy support during English class on set days each week;
- reading and writing instruction instead of foreign language instruction for below-grade-level learners;
- lunchtime tutoring;
- literacy software programs used in differentiated computer technology classes;
- required literacy courses in place of electives;
- Saturday or after-school peer-tutoring groups; and
- summer enrichment programs for literacy.

When schools provide an array of options, they find they can fulfill the individual education plans for special education students as well as assist non—special education students who have specific learning needs.

Sustained silent reading (SSR). SSR should not replace explicit instruction in reading, but it does provide time for students to apply and practice the strategies they have learned. Finding time for scheduling a schoolwide sustained silent reading period or more time for content-area reading is often a challenge. Ideally, to be effective, SSR periods need to be scheduled daily or at least three times per week for 15 to 30 minutes each, for a total of 90 to 100 minutes per week. Schools have successfully scheduled SSR periods first thing in the morning, as part of a midmorning content block, or instead of homeroom or advisory periods after lunch. Another creative way to schedule additional SSR time is to require teachers to have students spend 10 to 15 minutes of each instructional block actively reading something relevant to the topic of study—a section of the textbook, a short article, or a poem. This text forms the basis for further learning by serving as the focus for discussion, functioning as a review, or extending thinking about a concept that students have previously studied.

The vignette below is an illustration of how Allewan Regional Middle School addressed time issues.

Allewan Regional Middle School responded to time issues in a number of creative ways. Initially the school had struggling readers and writers attend pullout classes. But, in an otherwise heterogeneous school, this led to a socially damaging stigma for students who missed unified arts classes. To address this issue, the grade-level teams decided to create one class of learners who were significantly below grade level and met at the same time that all team students had reading class. Initially teams tried a revolving schedule of small-group instruction for these students while others worked independently on a differentiated reading software program. After assessing the first year's progress, the teachers realized that this configuration worked for students who were one to three years below grade level, but that those who were four or more years behind needed different, more intensive classroom interventions. They kept the original revolving-group model, while adding two days of pullout services in a nearby classroom for those needing support in decoding, fluency, and basic comprehension. The intensive-support classroom offered a reading "lounge" area on the floor, many high-interest books, interactive learning activities, and an enthusiastic teacher. Pullout students became envied by their peers. Struggling students no longer felt penalized for their deficiencies and were able to thrive in unified arts classes where teachers used literacy support strategies to address topics that more readily engaged these students.

Space

Each school has different space needs and must assess its current space to find room for literacy instruction, equipment, and materials. Involving teachers in these discussions will often result in innovative ideas. Ideas for creative use of space include

- providing small-group, differentiated instruction within the classroom to offset classroom space required for pullout programs;
- using computer labs during the computer teacher's planning periods for whole-group literacy tasks such as writing, Internet research, or Web quests;
- storing high-interest or parallel curriculum materials on rolling carts so they can circulate between classrooms in schools with insufficient library space;
- housing teacher literacy resources in the teacher's lounge for easy checkout;
- placing newspapers in racks in the cafeteria;
- posting examples of student writing in hallways; and
- placing book-swap boxes in classroom corners.

Personnel

Qualified school personnel are undoubtedly the most valuable resource in any educational system. In fact, for a literacy improvement effort to move forward, people with expertise in literacy need to be involved in making decisions and in developing and implementing the literacy action plan. Classroom teachers are not always able to meet all of the literacy needs of students for a variety of reasons. They may not have the training they need to implement literacy strategies effectively, or they may not have the time required to work with students independently. School leaders might find that one of the best ways they can support their classroom teachers is to hire other professionals who specialize in literacy.

Hiring a full-time literacy coach to guide the schoolwide literacy plan, provide professional development, model strategy use with students, coach individual teachers, and give feedback after classroom observations will strongly influence literacy development across the school. If funding makes it impossible to hire a full-time person, schools may share a literacy coach position with other district schools or provide a stipend and release time to a classroom teacher with strong literacy expertise. Developing a cross-content literacy team that designs and leads the implementation of a schoolwide literacy action plan is also a particularly effective use of current personnel to support literacy development. Another important step is making sure there are reading specialists or special education teachers with reading backgrounds on staff in middle and high schools with large numbers of struggling readers and writers. Using those who are knowledgeable in specific aspects of literacy to coteach, peer-coach, and provide workshops works well in the interim while a school or district seeks funding for new literacy personnel. Ensuring teacher knowledge of literacy through professional development extends literacy capacity. When hiring new teachers, administrators can ask questions to determine each applicant's literacy knowledge. They can enlist retired teachers to provide after-school literacy support or help with small groups in the classroom. The goal is to build on current personnel capacity while planning to expand over time the number of personnel with knowledge about literacy support strategies.

Troubleshooting Time, Space, and Personnel Issues

As issues arise, school leaders can facilitate collaborative brainstorming about ways to address the problems. In Figure 9.1 we provide some solutions to common issues related to time and personnel.

9.1　Addressing Time and Personnel Issues		
Area	Issue	Possible Solutions
Time	Social studies and science teachers are willing to try differentiated project- and unit-based instruction but lack time to develop sets of materials at different reading levels to match student needs.	The library/media specialist creates carts that hold parallel curriculum resources. The parents or a student service group can be enlisted to stock the resource carts.
	Teachers feel they have no time to work with students in a multiperiod schedule, or some students in block schedules need literacy instruction on a daily basis instead of a single-semester course.	Teachers form differentiated small groups and coteach with the special education teacher or aides. The existing schedule is changed to offer more flexible time blocks.
Personnel	Teachers have many students with reading, learning, and organizational disabilities and do not know how, or have time, to help them on a one-to-one basis to address their individual needs.	Special education personnel with expertise in reading consult with content area teachers regarding the design and use of graphic organizers. Special education teachers or guidance/office staff serve as one-to-one tutors during the homeroom period.
	Teachers have students with limited English proficiency but are not familiar with strategies to help them develop language and content learning skills.	An ELL or bilingual teacher is regularly paired in a coteaching situation with a mainstream content area teacher.

Professional Development

At Allewan Regional Middle School, teachers did not respond well to a video series for the whole faculty that had preset questions to answer in the follow-up study groups. They complained that the materials were too general and did not relate to instruction in different content areas. The curriculum coordinators created a professional development assessment that all teachers completed. Then the school developed a differentiated professional development model to respond to teachers' different needs and readiness levels. Those who wanted university courses were guided to an on-site course with the modeling and practice activities they sought. Those who wanted small-group sharing were grouped by content or grade levels for monthly seminars at which everyone was asked to bring and discuss any materials related to that month's literacy topic. Those who requested technology support were invited to the computer lab to try out different software, often with students assisting the computer lab instructor. Those who wanted to read independently attended informal, after-school book club meetings to discuss the concepts and applications with others who had read the same text. Those who asked to visit places such as art museums or science discovery centers to talk about how those institutional resources could be applied to literacy were granted flexible release days. The school offered literacy workshops during planning time, after school, and during summers. Textbook representatives visited to share strategies for struggling learners. The school established a tracking system to ensure that all teachers achieved at least 12 hours in literacy professional development across the school year. The results were beyond what anyone had anticipated—on average, teachers completed more than 30 hours in literacy professional development plus nearly 90 hours each in content-area professional development as documented by the teacher recertification process.

At the beginning of a literacy improvement effort, professional development that stresses consistent use of literacy strategies across content disciplines and grade levels is often effective. Teachers who participate often find that they know more about literacy support than they realized. In any case, they soon learn that literacy support strategies enhance content learning and academic success. As discussed in Chapter 6, professional learning communities are developed when teachers have ongoing opportunities to engage in literacy dialogue with other teachers and to share ideas, observe one another, and provide feedback.

Reluctance to undertake literacy instruction sometimes stems from a teacher's own lack of knowledge about how to teach reading, writing, listening/viewing, thinking, or speaking/presenting strategies explicitly. Some teachers' beliefs that the elementary or middle school teachers before them should have taught literacy skills often reflect the middle or high school teachers' own sense of inadequacy about being expected to teach literacy strategies while also trying to cover extensive content-area curricula. Just as students need carefully sequenced learning activities that move them forward on the continuum of academic learning, teachers also need a carefully scaffolded plan for literacy development. As described in Chapter 5, it is important that the literacy team complete a thorough assessment of what the school's teachers know about literacy strategies and which ones they use. The school can use this information, coupled with information about students' reading and writing skills, to define and design the content of professional development.

Many options for teacher professional development are available; deciding which options works best will depend on the school and district structures for teacher professional development. Figure 9.2 shows various formats that can be effective in improving teachers' content-area literacy skills and the resources needed to support their implementation.

9.2 Formats and Resource Support for Professional Development in Content-Area Literacy	
Format	**Resource Support**
Individual teachers attend conferences, take university courses, conduct action research, enroll in online courses	Travel, tuition reimbursement, time to report back to faculty
All or selected teachers attend activities on early-release or workshop days, with time to learn, apply, and share by team, grade level, or department	Release days, stipends for workshop leaders
Individual teachers observe other teachers, visit best-practice schools, peer coach	Substitute teachers
The literacy coach leads workshops, coplans, coteaches, models, observes/provides feedback, and provides content area literacy resources	Individual meetings with teachers/teams/departments
All teachers meet during faculty, team, grade-level, or department meetings	Time at meetings
Members of the literacy team meet and attend additional training with consultant, coleading faculty workshops with the consultant	Release time and substitute teachers for team to meet, funding for the consultant, use of workshop days

Some school leaders resist literacy professional development, feeling that they cannot afford to hire an outside literacy consultant. School leaders who do hire outside consultants to work with them over time often reflect afterward that the cost was well worth it because the result was a substantial increase in teacher knowledge and motivation to use the strategies. Some less expensive ways for teachers to develop literacy knowledge and expertise are also available but require more leadership and initiative by school personnel to implement successfully. Instructional videos are available that blend facilitated instruction with classroom vignettes that show literacy strategies in actual use. The school can establish teacher study groups in which the group selects and independently reads a literacy strategy text, with meetings held to discuss a few chapters at a time and to plan how to apply the strategies in the classroom (see Appendix D for a list of good books to read and discuss). Many universities offer "learning through teaching" courses on-site at schools: the professor teaches the strategies in short, after-school sessions and spends additional time modeling the applications with actual students while other teachers observe during planning periods or with substitute coverage. Some schools purchase online courses for the entire school or provide tuition reimbursement for teachers who take advantage of professional development available through distance learning. Others ask their own teachers to hold informal seminars with their peers to share classroom methods. Still others create and distribute literacy newsletters; route literacy journals around the school, noting important articles; and purchase multiple copies of literacy texts for teachers to check out. The goal is to flood teachers with opportunities to learn, apply, and share literacy techniques with their peers as well as their students.

Figure 9.3 presents three broad approaches to professional development for literacy. The approaches vary in terms of whether the initial offerings are geared to certain groups of teachers (such as teachers of particular grade levels or content areas, or cross-content-area teacher mentors) or are incorporated into broader configurations, such as departments or the entire faculty.

9.3 **Approaches to Professional Development for Content Area Literacy Support**	
If ...	**Then ...**
The school literacy team first defines the literacy strategies to be taught at certain grade levels or content areas	Professional development can be provided for specific teachers on the specific strategies that those teachers will be accountable for
Professional development is first offered to a smaller group of cross-content teacher mentors who learn the strategies and practice them in the classroom	They can cofacilitate activities during whole-faculty workshops that show how the strategies apply to content area instruction, sharing their experiences so that other teachers see the strategies' effectiveness in their specific content area
Time at each faculty and department meeting, or one team meeting each week, is allotted to learning literacy support strategies	Literacy learning becomes part of the regular school schedule, and the perception that literacy is yet another "add-on" is put to rest

Materials and Technology

Careful selection of materials and technology to support a school's literacy improvement effort is essential. Without these resources, instruction and assessment may be hampered. Materials and technology to support literacy development include commercial programs, materials associated with a specific approach, multiple copies of texts, software to support reading and writing, reading assessments, parallel curriculum materials, and individual texts. In this section of the chapter, we discuss some of these in detail so that leaders can better understand how they specifically relate to a schoolwide literacy improvement effort. Equipped with such an understanding, leaders can advocate for funding to purchase materials and technology that are applicable or for using existing materials and technology differently so that they support literacy development more effectively. Leaders should consider the following items:

- assessment instruments,
- leveled texts,
- literacy-related software,
- Internet resources,
- technology infrastructure, and
- high-interest reading material.

Assessment Instruments

As discussed earlier, monitoring literacy development requires the use of different types of assessments. School leaders choose assessments based on what they feel is necessary to know about students' reading and writing abilities so that the school can provide appropriate instruction and intervention. Assessments that provide lexile scores or indicate a level of performance that can be connected to grade level help teachers understand each student's instructional reading level and areas of strength and weakness in literacy. These results are useful when choosing leveled texts and parallel curriculum materials (see next section). Other literacy assessments include informal reading inventories; group-administered comprehension tests; computerized assessments of reading comprehension, writing, or language usage; assessments that focus on one aspect of literacy such as fluency or vocabulary; or writing assessments that use prompts and rubrics. Several resource issues are associated with assessment. Obviously commercially available assessment instruments cost money for consumable test materials or licenses and scoring, and they may require technology infrastructure to administer. As discussed earlier, costs in time are associated with administering, and in some cases scoring, assessments and in reviewing results. Assessment results, in conjunction with curriculum requirements, should be used to drive decisions about purchase of other print and electronic resources.

Leveled Texts

Once teachers know students' reading levels, they can then use the two approaches described in Chapter 2 to differentiate instruction: (1) use parallel content texts that match students' lexile or reading levels, and (2) help students learn and use strategies to read texts that are above their lexile or reading level. Teachers can use students' reading levels and book lists that are coded by grade level or lexile score to match students to texts. Teachers as well as students can use sources such as an online database or the Web site at www.lexile.com to locate resources at multiple reading levels for most content areas. Additionally, an increasing number of publishers now provide leveled collections of nonfiction materials, themed sets of books, and software.

In the past few years, publishers have been increasingly responsive to the need for parallel resources to support content area texts. However, school leaders may be unaware of these new resources. One way to expand literacy resources is to contact the publishers of all content-area textbooks to learn about any supplemental materials that have been published. These often include study guide workbooks, glossaries of content-area vocabulary, transparencies of analytical graphic organizers that can be used for instruction, parallel readings that range from comic book formats to higher-level primary source documents, and audio-video resources to provide background knowledge before content-area instruction begins.

Literacy Software

Many computer programs are now available that use streaming video and audio enhancements to motivate struggling readers to tackle text. Most are individually self-paced and differentiated according to pre-assessment of students' reading abilities. Data-management software tracks student progress over time, giving periodic feedback to students as they finish various modules and providing a wide array of teacher reports to track individual, small-group, and whole-class progress. Several software programs that help students plan, compose, revise, and edit their writing are also available. School leaders should be cautioned that the software differs in terms of the specific needs it is designed to address and that students need to be matched with appropriate programs.

Internet Resources

Internet resources are also playing an increasingly important part in developing student literacy. Many school librarians offer information-literacy courses for all students in the school, helping students learn how to navigate the Web to access information, analyze accuracy and quality of text, compare information across multiple sources, and learn how to use the information without plagiarizing. Web quests allow teachers to enhance comprehension of content through interactive instruction that students can complete independently or in small groups. Other online resources are available that provide guided practice in decoding, vocabulary, and comprehension or that help students create, edit, share, and publish their writing.

Technology Infrastructure

Because technology is a medium of literacy as well as a tool for improving it, it is imperative that schools provide classroom computers, laptops for teachers, computer labs for group instruction, and software that parallels that used in colleges and workplaces. Because virtually all 21st-century careers demand computer literacy, what was once an extra resource in schools is rapidly becoming a minimum requirement for student preparation for future careers. Yet many schools do not have the funds to adequately meet this need for technology. Some approaches to working with insufficient technology resources are

- having teachers use presentation software (such as PowerPoint) with one computer for whole-class instruction;
- having teachers rotate students in learning stations so everyone has some opportunity to use a small bay of classroom computers; and
- partnering with local businesses to receive donated computers when companies upgrade their computer system, and avidly seeking local, state, or federal grants to support increased technology.

Troubleshooting Materials and Technology Issues

As with time, space, and personnel, school leaders can facilitate brainstorming with the literacy team to address problems about materials and technology as they arise. Figure 9.4 shows some common problems and how they might be addressed.

Funding for Literacy Development

Funding for resources is scarce, with schools facing increased community, state, and national pressures to do more with less. School leaders can easily become discouraged as they find themselves constantly dealing with the unpleasant reality that lack of funding hinders student learning and growth. Sometimes it feels as though "the light at the end of the tunnel has temporarily gone out." Although overcoming funding limitations is by no means an easy task, school leaders who look for possible opportunities often find them.

Within the school, leaders can review requests for all content areas simultaneously during the annual budgetary process to ensure that the resource funds are distributed

9.4 Addressing Issues on Materials and Technology		
Area	**Issue**	**Possible Solutions**
Materials	Teachers do not know how to locate parallel resources for content study, and students do not know how to locate interesting materials for their individual reading levels.	Have the library/media specialist offer a workshop on lexiles to show teachers and students how to access parallel resources. Mark library books with a lexile number on the inside front cover.
	Teachers know that students benefit when lessons are preceded by presentations of background information but they do not have varied types of supplemental materials related to their textbooks or time to locate them.	Hold a professional development workshop in the library, with time provided for content area teachers to locate supplemental materials. Content area or special education teachers can be given substitute coverage to search the Internet for lesson plans already created by others.
Technology	Teachers do not get the reading assessment scores of their students, or they get them too late to be useful.	Set up electronic systems so teachers can receive reading assessment results for their students in a timely way.
	The school has only a few computers per classroom, so teachers cannot do whole-group research or writing activities that require computers.	Set up each team's computers in one classroom so teachers can flexibly use that room for whole-group computer use. The library can house a mobile cart of computers, using a classroom checkout system.

equitably and appropriately, not according to the status quo from previous years. Measures to select the best texts and other materials will help to ensure that students will actively use them, and having teachers involved in the selection process will strengthen use of the materials in the classroom. Publishers can often provide a wide array of supplemental resources at little or no cost; these often include materials that support literacy development.

Schools can acquire many literacy resources by requesting them within the community. For example, classroom sets of newspapers may be available free or at nominal cost. Parents and community members can provide used magazines, books, and audiotapes; local office supply companies may donate pencils, notebooks, sticky notes, and other classroom writing supplies; parents and retirees can volunteer to offer after-school tutoring; chambers of commerce can locate and provide classroom speakers; nearby schools or colleges can provide interlibrary loans, substitute teachers, mentors, teacher professional development, tutoring, and research resources; community agencies can purchase class sets of books; and so forth.

Within the district and state, school leaders who persistently seek budgetary support for literacy often find the funding they seek. A district may have enough funds at year-end to get one additional computer or to buy literacy texts for teachers. Community and state grants can be written to support purchases of books or technology. Many publishing companies cite state and local grant opportunities on their Web sites. Many corporations offer free resources or grants for teacher professional development. Free samples of materials are often available at literacy conferences.

The key for school leaders is dedicating time in their busy daily schedule to look for these opportunities and to keep literacy development in the forefront of every discussion about resources within and beyond the school. Just one hour of targeted Internet research can reveal multiple grant possibilities that teachers, office staff, or committee members can explore. School press releases and newsletters can include mention of needed resources. Word-of-mouth discussions at sports or community events can result in needed donations. School Web sites can include a link for parent volunteers. Districts can work together to share the costs of professional development. The time expended to locate supplemental funding for literacy support can have a dramatic impact, but only when school leaders keep literacy in the forefront of their thinking throughout the year.

Key Messages

Resource allocation for literacy development is an essential factor in the success of the schoolwide literacy improvement process. Creative approaches are necessary to overcome issues related to limited time, space, personnel, materials, and technology. Resource allocations work best when they are aligned with and integrated within the current curriculum, culture, and pedagogy of each school. The key messages of this chapter are the following:

• School leaders may need to think about resources differently than they have in the past to support literacy efforts.

• Schools need to allocate time for meetings, for professional development for teachers and administrators, for coaching and mentoring in the classroom, and for students to read during the school day.

• Space needs to be considered creatively to "make room" for a focus on literacy.

• Personnel decisions are critical to the success of a literacy improvement effort.

• An effective literacy coach can accomplish much to move the literacy focus forward.

• Professional development can occur in a variety of formats.

• Materials, including technology, can enhance a literacy effort.

• School leaders may have to be creative and persistent in finding funding sources to support the literacy effort.

When teachers see that school leaders are exploring avenues to support literacy development, they are more motivated to focus on literacy assessment, planning, and instruction. Students see that literacy is a schoolwide priority when they experience explicit literacy instruction and have access to motivational materials and technology support to help them improve content comprehension and enhance their academic success. When this is the case, students become more willing to engage in content learning and develop their toolbox of strategies for self-directed learning. When community members see that schools are focusing on literacy and that progress is indicated through consistently improved assessment scores, they will be more willing to contribute time, resources, and tax dollars to the school. Strategic allocation of resources is a tool for achieving teacher, student, parent, and community support for literacy. Each school and district will choose to use resources for literacy development in different ways. Leaders who allocate resources wisely have a greater chance of seeing students prepared to meet the literacy demands of postsecondary education, careers, and productive citizenship.

CONCLUSION

Middle and high school leaders face growing demands to improve student performance. Raising student achievement and truly preparing all students for careers, options in higher education, and active citizenship are daunting challenges. However, as described in this book, a systemic focus on improving students' reading, writing, and thinking skills can be a lever for improving student achievement. If educators carry out this focus as a collaborative, schoolwide literacy improvement effort, success is much more probable.

As educators, we must work together to develop approaches to meet the literacy needs of every student and to increase schools' capacities to improve adolescent literacy overall. If we do not, the future choices and quality of life for many of our students will be diminished. Inaction or inadequate response has negative consequences for our society on many levels. It is the job of our schools to educate all of our students. Ongoing focused attention to literacy development in middle and high schools is an integral part of this charge.

The Leadership Model for Improving Adolescent Literacy provides school leaders with the guidance and support to implement a schoolwide literacy improvement effort. In creating this model, we assumed that school improvement requires a systems approach and collaborative, informed leadership that is focused, active, and supportive. This type of systemic leadership can take place when principals use the model to understand their critical role as instructional leader through the lens of literacy. When leaders take actions as defined by the points of the star in the model in service of the goals shown in the center and on the outer bands of the model, improved student motivation, engagement, and achievement—for all students—is possible.

APPENDIX A:
FOUR VIGNETTES

Middle School Vignette

Enter Hope Middle School and you are immediately barraged with words. A large photo-mosaic mural covers the entry wall proclaiming "READ TO SUCCEED." When you look closer, the letters of the sign are made from hundreds of tiny photos of book covers. A sign next to the mural says that the mural was made by the 8th grade art classes in 2005-2006 and that the book covers represent all of the books read by students during Sustained Silent Reading that year.

On the TV mounted in the corner of the entry way, two students are doing a commercial about Ben Mikaelsen's *Touching Spirit Bear*. They have obviously planned their two minute pitch—they read two excerpts fluently and with gusto and tell potential readers that to find out the ending "they will just have to read the book!" Then the screen is filled with a blog where comments are typed in from those who have and have not read the book. Furious typing continues for five minutes. The principal notices you standing in the hallway reading the screen. "Oh yes! It is our daily blogging about a book—kids are selected at random across grades to be the day's bloggers, and they are in the computer lab waiting to blog as soon as the commercial is aired. We have to make sure there are at least ten copies of whatever book gets featured because they just fly out of the library. It's been pretty successful!"

Two students show up in the entry just as the blogging winds down and introduce themselves as Cassie and Brett. The principal indicates that they are both seventh graders and will serve as your tour guides. You are led to the 7th grade wing to a common area where 50 students are gathered, all with laptops. Two student teams are debating the pros and cons of nuclear power, both showing their PowerPoint presentations. The first team presents. The presentation is articulate, clearly rehearsed, and backed by considerable evidence and citation. The students listening send comments and requests for fact checks and rebuttals to the team, which appear on the screen. Active interest and engagement are evident. Your guides explain that there will be several rounds of each debate and that debate issues have to do with various forms of energy. Since all 7th graders have laptops at the school through a grant, the laptops are used extensively in all classes. You ask your guides how they have used their laptops during the past week. "Well," Cassie says, "on my team we have been working on the National Geographic JASON Project on *Monster Storms*, preparing for our debates, doing a math Web quest, putting together a multimedia presentation for our author study and using it to finish our short stories."

"Yeah, we're doing a lot of the same stuff only we finished the math Webquest on probability and we're putting together a digital collage with narration about historic areas in our town that we are afraid might get lost. They want us to do that for the Historical Society Web site. That's a pretty cool project," adds Brett.

Cassie begins to lead us back towards the media center. You ask if all the students have laptops. "No, 6th and 8th graders need to use the lab or the laptop cart," Cassie says. You figure that the high level of engagement and literacy you just observed will not be as apparent in the 6th and 8th grade wings—but you are wrong.

When you walk by the library, you notice small groups of students and adults sitting in circles throughout the library intently discussing what appears to be an article. When you ask what is going on, Cassie says, "Oh that's *Controversy Circles*. There's an article that everyone reads who is in the circle—you can pick the article you want but they are all about the same topic—and then you discuss it and then you get into groups with people who read all of the articles and do a—what's that called, Brett?"

"A Jigsaw."

"Yeah, a Jigsaw and then you do a Discussion Web— its pretty cool. Sometimes the adults are people who work in the school or people from different businesses. And the topics are sometimes really interesting like about gun control and medical ethics and dilemmas like if it is good to have economic development if it causes pollution and stuff like that." The library is full of discussion and students reading, researching, using the computers, working together on projects.

You get to the 6th grade wing and walk into a science class. Students are working in pairs doing research on chemical solutions and planning demonstrations that illustrate key concepts related to salinity and saturation. In another science classroom, after completing their bellwork, students are reading intently on computers and coding the articles they are reading using highlighting. The teacher explains they are reading about chemical reactions to determine if the information confirms or contradicts the experiment they just did. In a third science classroom, students are working in small groups to create chapters for a lab manual. In one 6th grade English/language arts classroom, students are doing a nonfiction study and everyone in the room is reading, writing, or conferencing with a peer or with the teacher. In another, students are discussing different Gary Paulsen novels in literature circles. In a third, students are creating Reader's Theatre pieces based on various science fiction books—one group is working on their selection of key scenes from *The Green Book* by Jill Paton Walsh. You notice three students discussing and looking at books in the classroom library.

In one math classroom, a four corners activity about geometric concepts is underway; in another, students are using a graphic organizer to solve word problems. In the third, students are doing a paired reading of the chapter in the textbook, questioning, summarizing, and clarifying as needed. In social studies classes, students are writing *A Day in the Life* papers for Greek or Roman times, preparing for talk show interviews of famous Greeks and Romans, and doing compare and contrast charts around cultural aspects of today's Greece vs. ancient Greece.

The 8th grade wing is similarly active—students are reading and classifying letters from soldiers from different eras, working on an interdisciplinary unit on roller coaster design, and using Reciprocal Teaching to understand a chapter in the textbook. Students are designing their own poetry anthologies, analyzing the pond water they collected and entering the data into a database that an environmental agency has created, and deciding how to write up the experiments they just completed. Word Walls throughout the school tell you what is being studied, and you see students using the words and teachers asking them to refer to the words. Many of the words on the walls are "team words" which are reinforced by all teachers on each team. You see "change," "solution," "division," "parallel," "force," and "stress" under the heading "multiple meaning words." You now remember seeing these words in other 8th grade classes.

In every class you notice teachers modeling or teaching literacy support strategies —students are practicing them or using them independently. What strikes you is the high level of student engagement, collaboration, critical thinking, and discussion—and the amount of reading and writing you see. This continues to be the case in the Allied Arts wing where art is accompanied by writing, students in Physical Education class are critiquing basketball plays captured on video, and Health students are using Reciprocal Teaching to read about contagious diseases. Student work is posted everywhere—when you pause to read some of it, the level of the work impresses you favorably and you think that many high school students cannot do what these middle schoolers are expected—and are able—to do.

As you head back to the office, you notice two boys and two girls working in a small room. They are reading and making sound effects and using a variety of voices. Cassie explains that they make books on tape for the elementary students and that they work hard to read it "perfectly." In a computer lab, students are working on a program to develop reading comprehension. You pass a conference room where a group of teachers is having an intense discussion about student performance data and how they will use specific literacy support strategies to address students' needs. Cassie explains that one of the teachers is the literacy coach who helps teachers teach. You catch the words "before," "during," and "after" from their conversation.

Once back at the office, you thank the guides and they leave to go back to class. The principal asks how the tour went. You mention that in many schools you don't think you would have seen this much reading, writing, presentation, and discussion in a week, much less a day! The principal smiles and says that three years ago, you wouldn't have seen this much at Hope Middle School either. "At first, both teachers and students resisted. Students were asked to work harder and teachers had to learn a how to integrate literacy into learning. When we finally managed to hire a literacy coach, teachers began slowly to open their classrooms to her, and that helped a lot. I arranged for the coach to attend each team meeting once a month for several months and once they got to know what she had to offer, the teachers realized she was a real resource to them. They had to know that I was serious about this literacy effort as well. Each teacher has to have an Individual Professional Development Plan and I make sure it contains work on literacy improvement. But now, it is just part of the way we do business. It took clear expectations, lots of professional development and coaching, and lots of focus but I think we're getting there. My assistant principal and I spent a lot of time in classrooms talking to teachers about literacy support and content learning. I think it is fair to say that most teachers provide literacy support before, during, and after reading. The scores look better and everyone has really taken it on as a collective responsibility. I think we're getting there, slowly but surely." Reflecting on what you observed, you can't help but agree.

Literacy Support in the English Classroom*

In Alan Hessin's English class, students are beginning a unit study of Greek drama. To build students' background knowledge, activate their prior knowledge, connect their out-of-school literacies to the subject at hand, and build their interest in the upcoming unit, Alan begins by showing three clips of television commercials and sets up a Venn diagram on the board to record answers about what the commercials have in common. Students realize that all share a quality that Alan labels as "dramatic irony." After the discussion, Alan asks students to do a quick-write on the idea of dramatic irony. He asks volunteers to share what they have written, and he responds to each student's work in a way that continues to refine students' understanding of the term. Alan hands out several cartoons he has pulled off of the Web and asks the students to examine the cartoons in pairs and jot down any and all examples of dramatic irony that they see.

Alan writes three terms on the board—*astrology*, *Tarot cards*, and *fortune cookies*—and asks students what the three terms have in common. Kali says that they are all used to predict the future. Alan broadens the discussion to include ways in which ancient peoples prophesied the future. He mentions the ancient Roman practice of interpreting the entrails of animal sacrifices and the ancient Greek practice of consulting oracles. He asks: Does anyone in the class believe in prophesies? Would they have believed them if they had lived more then 2,000 years ago? A lively discussion ensues.

Then Alan asks if students know any people who are so full of themselves that they ignored warning signs and got themselves into trouble. Several students share examples of people like this. He asks students if they can name any political leaders who have made a mistake that cost them their career or their life. What motivated them to these actions? Was pride a major factor? Jamie mentions Richard Nixon, who assumed that he had the right to bug people's conversations because he was the president. Alan

---

* *Authors' note:* This lesson example is based on a PBS teacher lesson: www.pbs.org/empires/thegreeks/ educational/lesson4.html.

introduces the ancient Greek concept of *hubris*, meaning overconfident pride and arrogance. Alan writes three terms on the board—*fate*, *dramatic irony*, and *hubris*—and summarizes the discussion by saying that these three concepts would be essential to their study of the Greek play *Oedipus Rex*. He tells the students that the play was written nearly 2,500 years ago and that many people consider it one of the greatest tragedies ever written.

To build students' background knowledge about ancient Greece and Greek theater, Alan shows a clip of the documentary on Greek drama found at the PBS Web site. Then he shows a five-minute clip from the play, just so students can get a sense of what the characters may have looked and dressed like. Then Alan does a dramatic reading of the prologue with the students following along. Next, Alan indicates a stack of handouts and tells students that he has two versions of the *Oedipus Rex* play—the original (in translation) and a reader's theater version by Rick Bartel that is shorter and easier to read. He asks students to select which text they will use for the unit. About a third of the students choose the original play, and the rest choose the reader's theater version—about what Alan predicted. Then he hands out a character grid so that students can keep track of characters as they read and models how he wants them to fill it out as they read. He asks students to begin coding the text they have chosen by placing an exclamation point (!) where they think a character makes a good point or where they can clearly visualize the action, a question mark (?) where they are confused, and a "greater than" sign (>) beside lines where there are words they do not understand. Alan gives them some "heads up" notes about the Prologue. He tells them what Oedipus means when he calls the citizens of Thebes "the children of Cadmus" and why Oedipus calls on Apollo. He also suggests that they look for all references to "sight." Students begin reading and coding and filling out the character grid.

After students finish rereading the prologue, Alan says that tomorrow they will begin reading sections aloud, with students rotating speaking roles and all others in the group reading the lines of the chorus. He assigns parts for the first scenes so that students can practice reading aloud their lines for the next day. Alan tells students that they will alternate texts for each scene and discuss examples of fate, hubris, and dramatic irony as found throughout the play. He offers extra points for noticing these during the unit. Tim asks if wearing togas will be permitted. Alan laughs and stresses that students may wear togas only *over* regular clothes! The class is dismissed, but Alan hears many of the students still talking about Greek theater as they leave the room.

Literacy Support in the Math Classroom*

Andrea Bouchard hands out a list of mathematical terms and a five-step problem-solving graphic organizer to the 7th grade students in her pre-algebra class. Most barely look up as she walks around the groups of desks and distributes the sheets; they are too busy reviewing and discussing the board work. Sounds unlikely? That's what Andrea thought before she tried the strategy, but the students know that on Mondays and Fridays class will begin with a silly problem related to real-life dilemmas and a flawed solution that needs to be corrected. Today's problem begins with someone spilling Pepsi onto a keyboard and concerns whether the owner of the laptop made a mistake by not buying an extended warranty. The problem requires careful reading about depreciation, replacement costs, interest rates, and warranty details and combines application of math knowledge, higher-order thinking, and critical reading of mathematically dense text—all lifelong mathematical literacy habits that Andrea wants her students to develop.

Andrea rings a chime to indicate that each group has five minutes to complete their response, including a mathematical presentation and a rationale statement for why the solution presented in the problem is flawed. She rings the chime again in five minutes. She picks a number from a hat and announces that student #2 in each group will be doing the presentations today. Students do not know in advance who will be chosen, so all need to prepare.

As a member of each of the six groups presents the group's response, the others rate the mini-presentation using a short rubric that gets handed back to the presenters. Andrea notes that the presentations are much clearer, more mathematically specific, and more concise and to the point than they were earlier in the year, and she commends the students before asking them to look at the list of terms and the graphic organizer that she handed out at the beginning of class.

Andrea projects the graphic organizer on the Smartboard and asks students to look at the terms on the list. She tells the class that they are going to continue with their problem-solving unit by beginning to do word problems that describe one variable in relation to another, just like the equations they were working on earlier in the week. She says that she will demonstrate how she wants the students to use the problem-solving graphic organizer to set up and solve the word problems they will be doing. As she models what to do, she wants the students to listen for the vocabulary terms on the sheet. Every time they hear her say a term, they should check it off.

---

* *Authors' note:* We wish to thank Marshalyn Baker for her contribution to this vignette.

Andrea uses the words *equation, variable, unknown,* and other words on the list as she explains how to use the graphic organizer to solve the first problem: *Anna is twice as old as Tia. Their combined age is 24 years. How old is each girl?* After she finishes explaining, she asks the students to compare with a partner which terms they heard and to try to define the terms in their own words. Then she asks students to share which terms they do not know. She asks other students to provide answers, or, when no one is sure, she provides a definition and an example. Then she asks for three to five nominees from the list to be added to the class word wall. Marcus thinks *unknown* should be added because it means something else most of the time but has a specific meaning when you do math problems. Ellie agrees and suggests *variable* for the same reason. The class seems satisfied with the terms chosen to support their work in this unit, and the students add the terms to their three-column math vocabulary journals, where they note the word in context, a definition in their own words, and a strategy for remembering what the term means. Andrea asks that students who are having trouble coming up with a memory strategy consult the others in their group for ideas.

Andrea then returns to the problem-solving organizer and models how to do another problem: *Two CDs cost $26. One CD costs $4 more than the other. How much does each CD cost?* She directs students' attention to how to set up the problem and how to use the organizer to guide their thinking. After modeling a third problem, which she asks the students to do with her and complete so they have an example to guide their work, Andrea asks students to work in pairs and use the organizer to do three more problems in the math textbook. She points to a thick stack of blank graphic organizers on her desk and asks that one person in each pair get three organizers.

Students quickly get to work. There is a low conversational buzz in the room. Andrea addresses confusion as it occurs. The students work steadily, and most pairs make it through two problems before the end of the period. Andrea asks students to contribute tips they have discovered about using the graphic organizer and asks how it helps or does not help when trying to solve this type of word problem. Steven says he likes it because it makes him go through the problem step by step and think about it. Dani says she thinks it made her more organized, which she guesses is the point! There is good-natured laughter as Andrea asks students to pick up two blank organizers on their way out the door and to complete problems 4 and 5 for homework. "Just try them," she says. "See what you can do. We will go over them tomorrow. We will be working on problems like this for the next week, so you will get plenty of practice. Good work today!"

Literacy Support in the Science Classroom

True or false: In Washington State alone, glaciers provide 470 billion gallons of water each summer. That is the first of five questions on the anticipation-reaction guide that Glen Oshima hands out to his students as they come into class, along with an article on glaciers. Reading about the significance of glaciers could be a meaningless and disconnected activity unless Glen gives students a purpose for reading. Students fill out the anticipation-reaction guide and begin reading the article to see if their initial response is right or if the article provides evidence to the contrary. Previously Glen has modeled and had the students practice how to fill out an anticipation-reaction guide, so students are able to complete the activity on their own. But Glen has differentiated the activity to meet the needs of different readers in his class. Proficient readers like Alesha get a more challenging article to read and more challenging prompts after the first one, which is the same on both sheets. For example, in the article Cody reads, the answer to the question is explicit; in Alesha's article, the answer will need to be inferred from the information provided.

When the students have completed their guides based on the reading, Glen works with the class to begin filling out a KWL-plus chart on glaciers. Glen asks students what they already know (K) about the topic and writes down answers in the first column. Because the students have all read one of the articles, they all know something about the topic, and the list grows quickly. Then Glen asks students to work in pairs to begin to identify what they would like to learn about glaciers. After five minutes of brainstorming, the class compiles a list under the "want to learn" (W) column.

Glen passes out a knowledge-rating guide with the following terms:

ice worms	archaeologists	freshwater
Ice Age	climate	accumulation
topography	sediment	crevasses
ridges	air pocket	compression

Students mark each term as "I know it," "I have heard of it," or "Never heard of it." Again in pairs, they try to explain to each other terms that are not known, using the glossary in the textbook to look up words neither knows and adding them and the definition in their own words to their notebooks.

Glen then draws their attention to a picture of a glacier in the textbook. He asks the students to read the section of chapter in the textbook that relates to glaciers, writing down five ideas that strike them as important or interesting on index cards he hands out. Students read the text, jot quotations down on the cards, and on the other side of each card write down why the statement struck them as interesting or important. After all of the students are finished reading, they quickly form groups of four and discuss the chapter section using another strategy they have used before: Save the Last Word for Me. Discussion is animated as students respond to the quotations each selected.

Glen asks the students to tell him the answer to the question: *Why are glaciers important to the earth's ecology?* As they talk, he constructs a concept map on the board. The students use this map to write their summary statement. At the end of the class session, Glen leads a class discussion to ensure that everyone understands the reading and the lesson and can summarize the major concepts. He concludes by connecting the study of ice worms and their importance to space travel, advances in tissue preservation for organ transplants, and insight into the possibility of life on other planets.

APPENDIX B: GLOSSARY

academic literacy—types of literacy that students need in order to succeed in school

aliterate—having the ability to read and write adequately but typically choosing not to read or write

alternative assessment—form of assessment designed to assess the literacy skills of students with special needs, through alternative methods such as systematic review of samples of student work or documented observation of students' reading behaviors

authentic literacy tasks—literacy tasks that play into adolescents' needs to do things that are real, often prompting new effort for rehearsal, comprehension, discussion of content, planning, or other literacy skills

bell work—activity, related to the content area, that the teacher assigns as the bell rings and that students work on while the teacher takes roll and gets class started

cognitive strategies—strategies that allow students to use higher-order thinking skills

comprehension—the construction of meaning for the reader

context—words surrounding a particular word that can assist in determining meaning

criterion-referenced assessment—assessment designed to measure student performance in reference to established performance or content standards related to reading and writing

critical reading—a high-level reading skill that involves evaluation

decoding—the process of taking in oral or written language (listening and reading) and determining the meaning of individual components of that language

diagnostic assessment—assessment designed to measure the literacy skills of students in a variety of areas against a set of criteria in each area to determine the difference between students' demonstration of skills and the expected skills for their grade/ability level

dialogue journal—notebook kept jointly by two people, usually a student and a teacher, with each writing entries as messages to the other and exchanging the notebook after each entry

differentiated instruction—teaching students at their own levels of instruction by allowing some students to work on their own and pulling others into a small group for explicit instruction

distributed leadership—shared leadership responsibilities based on areas of expertise and knowledge

during-reading activity—an activity done while reading to help monitor comprehension

engagement-instruction cycle—cycle of engagement and instruction that increases students' confidence and competence as readers and writers

English language learners (ELLs)—students who come to English-speaking schools with different degrees of literacy in their own language, which affects the acquisition of literacy skills in English

explicit instruction—instruction guided by the teacher, who uses various strategies to help students understand what they are reading

expository text—informational texts such as those found in science, social studies, music, art, and technology classes

fluency—the speed of reading and the ability to pause at the right places to understand the meaning of the text accurately

formative assessment—assessment designed to measure the literacy skills of students as a part of instruction so that the results can inform what additional types of instruction (review, reteaching, additional guided practice, enrichment) teachers should use

guided practice—practice of literacy skills, by students, with support and instruction

independent learners—learners who are able to use cognitive and metacognitive strategies independently as needed to strengthen and deepen literacy and learning

independent practice—practice of literacy skills by students working on their own

independent reading level—the level at which a student can read with 95 percent accuracy

individualized instruction—instruction in which students work at their own pace on material based on their needs, interests, and abilities

inquiry project—task designed around a unit of study to encourage students individually, in pairs, or in small groups to carry out an investigation, to answer questions of importance and interest to them about a particular topic, or to generate a solution to a problematic situation

leveled texts—books or readings that match the reading levels of different students

lexile score—a scientific approach to text leveling based on semantic difficulty and syntactic complexity and set on a scale that ranges from 200L for beginning readers to above 1700L for advanced texts

literacy—the communication modes of reading, writing, listening, speaking, viewing, and representing

literacy action plan—a schoolwide plan to improve literacy that includes data-driven goals, action steps, time lines, responsible persons, indicators of effectiveness, and resources needed

literacy coach—teachers who work primarily with other teachers and who do not have a student assignment

literacy intervention—a class, tutoring program, pullout session, or summer program for students who score below the grade level on standardized reading tests

literacy support strategy—instructional strategy that supports weaker readers, writers, speakers, and thinkers as they develop the skills and strategies that competent communicators use

literacy team—team that is representative of the school community and that works on schoolwide efforts to improve literacy

literacy walk-through—a walk through the school building or individual classrooms to collect real-time data that reveal the literacy instructional practices being used

metacognition—ability to self-regulate one's thoughts and use strategies to aid learning

metacognitive awareness—ability to know when material being read makes sense and what to do when it lacks clarity

metacognitive strategies—strategies that allow students to monitor their comprehension

narrative text—text that follows a story pattern

norm-referenced assessment—assessment designed to measure student performance in reference to a peer group's performance normative curve on the same assessment of reading and writing

norms—average scores for a given group of students, which allow comparisons of different students or groups of students

percentile rank—score that indicates where a student stands in comparison with others who took the test

phonics—way of teaching reading and spelling that stresses sound-symbol relationship, especially in beginning reading instruction

postreading activity—activity done after reading to summarize, reinforce, and extend new information

prereading activity—activity completed before reading to activate prior knowledge

professional learning community—educators who come together to form a supportive group and commit themselves to continuous learning

questioning strategies—strategies students can use to ask questions of text to improve comprehension

quick-write—literacy strategy that gives students an opportunity to reflect on their learning, consisting of a piece of writing on a particular topic or question completed in three to five minutes

reading specialist—teacher who works in intervention classes with students

scaffolding instruction—building a support structure for students so that they can tackle increasingly complex tasks

schema—a person's prior knowledge coupled with attitudes, beliefs, and cultural background

screening data—data that help determine which students are in need of extra support

semantics—meaning of words or phrases

sight vocabulary—words that students should know and be able to read automatically

student performance data—data that provide information about student academic achievement

summative assessment—assessment designed to measure the literacy skills of students at a particular point in time, at the end of a unit of study or annually at the same time of year, to determine what reading and writing skills they demonstrate relative to their peers

syntax—word order or position of a word in a sentence

text structure—the way an author organizes a text to communicate the content, such as compare/contrast, sequence, cause/effect, and so forth

think-alouds—teaching strategy in which teachers share their own thinking processes out loud so that students can observe the thinking processes of a strong reader

trade books—books distributed through bookstores, such as those found in a school library, as opposed to textbooks sold to schools

vocabulary development strategies—strategies students can use to learn and remember the many technical terms, key concepts, and academic vocabulary words that they encounter in the study of various disciplines

APPENDIX C:
TOOLS FOR LEADERS TAKING ACTION

Teacher Knowledge Inventory

Schools can use the Teacher Knowledge Inventory (Figure C.1) to assess teachers' perceptions of their knowledge about literacy process and support strategies. Based on the results, school leaders can plan effective professional development to improve the collective knowledge base of literacy learning. The inventory is helpful for identifying in-house expertise that can be used to support the school's literacy improvement efforts. Some teachers may not know all of the terms in the inventory, or some teachers might overrate their literacy knowledge. Likewise, the survey does not cover everything effective teachers need to know. But this inventory, or one like it, can be a productive starting point for discussion and planning.

C.1 **Teacher Knowledge Inventory**

Use the following scale to indicate your level of knowledge about each item below.

1 — I know **nothing** about this aspect of literacy learning.
2 — I know **a little bit** about this aspect of literacy learning.
3 — I know **a fair amount** about this aspect of literacy learning.
4 — I know **a great deal** about this aspect of literacy learning.

Primary content area you teach: _____

What do you know about …

• Connecting the prior knowledge of learners to content (schema)	1	2	3	4
• Having students evaluate their own learning (metacognition)	1	2	3	4
• Implementing methods to promote reading fluency	1	2	3	4
• Implementing methods to promote writing fluency	1	2	3	4
• Implementing methods to promote speaking/presentation fluency	1	2	3	4
• Improving students' listening skills	1	2	3	4
• Improving students' vocabulary in the content areas	1	2	3	4
• Improving students' note-taking skills	1	2	3	4
• Teaching reading comprehension	1	2	3	4
• Supporting weaker students to develop the learning skills and strategies used by stronger students (scaffolding)	1	2	3	4
• Differentiating instruction to meet the needs of all students	1	2	3	4
• Engaging students in varying tasks and texts	1	2	3	4
• Offering students choices when they read in the content area	1	2	3	4
• Providing students with choices when they write in the content area	1	2	3	4
• Grouping students for maximum literacy development	1	2	3	4
• Engaging students to express what they understand about content learning	1	2	3	4
• Teaching students to recognize and use text structure in reading and writing	1	2	3	4

What are one or two areas you would like to learn more about?

Name three literacy support strategies you frequently use as part of classroom teaching.

Classroom Observation Guide

Some school districts have their own format for observation guides. The guide presented in Figure C.2 focuses on how literacy support is incorporated into instruction. It asks that leaders notice what students are doing as well as the teacher's instruction. This particular guide was developed by education consultant Jan Mickler and field-tested in numerous classrooms. Of course, a pre- and post-observation conference is necessary in conjunction with the use of the guide.

C.2 Classroom Observation Guide

Materials/Texts Used (textbooks, workbooks, activity sheets, short texts, etc.)

What is the teacher doing?

What are the students doing?

Level of student engagement (To what extent are *most* of the students attentive to the teacher and to the task?)

1	2	3	4	5	6

(Low) **(High)**

What behaviors do the nonengaged students exhibit?

What else do you notice? (learning/classroom climate, teacher/student talk, student comments, etc.)

Exemplary practice	Rating: 3 = yes; 2 = sort of; 1 = no	Comments
Teacher models strategies to show students how to comprehend and apply what they read.		
Students and teacher ask a variety of questions, make connections and predictions, and discuss concepts, creating a balance of student and teacher talk.		
Students engage in guided practice and receive feedback from the teacher.		
Teacher uses strategies such as think-pair-share to involve all students in classroom discussions.		
Students are actively engaged in doing the learning, talking, and collaborating.		
Students spend time reading and responding to texts.		
Students provide evidence of what they have learned.		
Students use time effectively for processing of and reflection on information.		
Students engage in highly critical thinking.		
Students produced quality work.		

Source: Developed by M. Jan Mickler, *Strategic Literacy Consulting*™. Used with permission from Strategic Literacy Consulting.

Literacy Assessment Review Tool

Many school leaders are responsible for selecting a reading assessment for students. As described in Chapter 7, a variety of types of reading and writing assessments are available for purchase from publishers. Figure C.3, the Literacy Assessment Review Tool, provides school leaders with a systematic process for reviewing them.

C.3 **Literacy Assessment Review Tool**

What information do you want the assessment to provide? (Check one):

Reading

• Level
(holistic score)   _____

• Stanine or percentile—score in comparison with peers
(norm referenced)   _____

• Level of proficiency—score against standards
(criterion referenced)   _____

Writing

• Level
(holistic score)   _____

• Stanine or percentile—score in comparison with peers
(norm referenced)   _____

• Level of proficiency—score against standards
(criterion referenced)   _____

For each assessment you are reviewing that matches the type of assessment you have checked above, complete the following:

Name of the assessment: _____

Publisher: _____

Web site and contact info: _____

Cost per student to administer (cost per consumable booklet/form or registration/account fee): _____

Cost per student to score: _____

Cost of reusable forms (if applicable) or required software/license: _____

First, rank the assessment features in order of importance. Circle 1 for the most important features, 2 for desirable features, and 3 for features that are not of concern to you. Then, for each feature marked with a 1 or a 2, review the documentation regarding this assessment to find out whether a check should be put in the "yes" or "no" column for that feature:

Rank of Feature (circle one)	Assessment Feature	Why This Feature Might Be Important	Yes	No	Notes
1 2 3	Pre- and post-testing and alternate forms are available.	Students can be pre- and post-tested to monitor individual growth and program effectiveness.			
1 2 3	Reports are back within 3–5 weeks.	Allows assessment information to influence instruction.			
1 2 3	Provides information in electronic form.	Allows school/teachers to get information more quickly and to query and sort the data.			
1 2 3	Provides individual and disaggregated group reports.	Provides information for individual students as well as group progress.			
1 2 3	Reliable for population and age of students.	Important to get information that is accurate and relevant.			
1 2 3	Uses only narrative passages or personal prompts.	May provide inflated scores because most students do better with these than with expository passages or essays; does not match content area demands of school.			
1 2 3	Normed recently with a group that is demographically comparable.	Out-of-date norms or norms that are far different than a school's demographic profile may provide invalid comparisons.			
1 2 3	Can be administered in a group.	This is far easier than individual assessment; if individual assessment is required, it is important to know how long the test takes to administer.			
1 2 3	Can be administered within a class period.	If not, longer time periods must be provided.			
1 2 3	Provides off-year/off-month norms.	This is helpful when different forms of the test are used for different "grade levels" but some students score substantially higher or lower than their peers; also helpful when assessment is given midyear.			

Rank of Feature (circle one)	Assessment Feature	Why This Feature Might Be Important	Yes	No	Notes
1 2 3	Is consistent with school and community expectations around literacy.	Otherwise there is a disconnect between what is measured and what is valued.			
1 2 3	Can be administered by teachers without substantial training.	If not, make certain training is provided, or scores may be invalid.			
1 2 3	Option for in-house scoring.	Allows school to do the scoring, which is typically faster and less expensive for larger schools but requires personnel, time, and, sometimes, technology support.			
1 2 3	Requires technology support to administer.	May require technology support that school does not have; on the other hand, makes reporting much faster.			
1 2 3	Provides option for continuous assessment.	Allows teachers to retest as often as every six weeks; does not require guessing the correct level of test to administer; usually requires technology support.			
1 2 3	Available in Spanish or other languages.	If reading or writing skills are being assessed, as opposed to reading or writing skills in *English,* this could be important.			
1 2 3	Teacher training is included if it is required to do the assessment, and technical support is available as part of the purchase cost.	Many extra costs may be "hidden," that is, required teacher training is expensive, administration materials are consumable, or technical support is charged by the hour and involves travel fees.			

APPENDIX D:
RESOURCES FOR FURTHER LEARNING

Conferences

Association for Supervision and Curriculum Development (www.ascd.org) provides resources
for teachers, administrators, coaches, policymakers, and researchers. At state,
regional, and national conferences, participants can choose the topics that interest
them the most out of more than 600 sessions; many of these sessions focus on
issues of adolescent literacy and school reform.

International Reading Association (www.ira.org) meets the professional needs of all grade
levels, and its secondary strand is growing and playing a more prominent role in its
conferences. State affiliates, provinces, and regions offer conferences yearly.

National Council of Teachers of English (NCTE) (www.ncte.org) offers nearly 400 sessions
at its annual conference for middle and high school teachers. Many of these
address issues in adolescent literacy. In addition, NCTE offers other professional
development opportunities in adolescent literacy through online and face-to-face
delivery formats.

School- and District-Based Professional Development

CReating Independence Through Student-Owned Strategies (CRISS) (www.projectcriss.com) is a project designed to help all students read, write, and learn more effectively. The project is based on the premise that teaching reading is everyone's responsibility and that such teaching can be done very effectively within the content areas.

National Literacy Project (www.nationalliteracyproject.org) is a nonprofit organization that works with school districts in long-term relationships and offers summer institutes to build conceptual and pedagogical knowledge of teachers and school and district leaders. Additionally, they help literacy teams develop and implement a literacy action plan using a Literacy Planning Tool—a step-by-step guide for developing a literacy plan.

National Writing Project (NWP) (www.writingproject.org) is a nonprofit organization and the premier effort to improve writing in the United States. Through its professional development model, NWP builds the leadership, programs, and research needed for teachers to help their students become successful writers and learners.

School-Wide Program for Improving Reading and Learning (SPIRAL) (www.crminc.com/adlit3.aspx) is an approach that builds school and teacher capacity to address the literacy needs of all students.

Strategic Literacy Initiative (SLI) (www.wested.org/cs/we/view/pj/179) is a professional development and research program of WestEd, serving middle and high school educators, teacher leaders, and teacher educators. SLI has developed the National Institute in Reading Apprenticeship, designed for staff developers, curriculum leaders, literacy specialists, and others charged with providing ongoing professional development at the school, district, or regional level.

Strategic Instruction Model (SIM) (www.kucrl.org/sim) promotes effective teaching and learning of critical content in schools. SIM strives to help teachers make decisions about what is of greatest importance, what to teach students to help them to learn, and how to teach them well. SIM encompasses learning strategies (explicit steps students follow when confronted with a specific learning task); content enhancement routines (instructional methods for teachers to use in inclusive classrooms); and supporting interventions (such as goal setting, self-advocacy, social skills, and community-building skills).

Web Sites with Resources on Adolescent Literacy

International Reading Association—www.reading.org/resources/issues/focus_adolescent.
    html
Knowledge Loom—knowledgeloom.org/adlit
National Council of Teachers of English—www.ncte.org/collections/adolescentliteracy
ReadWriteThink—www.readwritethink.org

Case Studies of Schools Undertaking Literacy Reform

Middle School

Freeport Intermediate School, Freeport, TX. In *Creating a Culture of Literacy: A Guide
    for Middle and High School Principals*, published by the National Association of
    Secondary School Principals
Hopkins West Junior High School, Minnetonka, MN. In *Creating a Culture of Literacy: A
    Guide for Middle and High School Principals*, published by the National Association of
    Secondary School Principals

High School

Buckhorn High School, New Market, AL. In *Creating a Culture of Literacy: A Guide
    for Middle and High School Principals*, published by the National Association of
    Secondary School Principals
Duncan Polytechnical High School, Fresno, CA. In *Creating a Culture of Literacy: A Guide
    for Middle and High School Principals*, published by the National Association of
    Secondary School Principals
Fenway High School, Boston, MA. http://knowledgeloom.org/adlit
Hoover High School, San Diego, CA. In *Bridging the Literacy Achievement Gap Grades
    4–12*, D. Strickland and D. E. Alvermann (Eds.)
J. E. B. Stuart High School, Falls Church, VA. In *Creating a Culture of Literacy: A Guide
    for Middle and High School Principals*, published by the National Association of
    Secondary School Principals
Muskegon High School, Muskegon, MI. http://knowledgeloom.org/adlit
University Park Campus School, Worcester, MA. http://knowledgeloom.org/adlit

District

Union City Public Schools, Union City, NJ. In *Bridging the Literacy Achievement Gap Grades 4–12*, D. Strickland and D. E. Alvermann (Eds.)

Working with Parents and Community Members

Jackson, A. W., & Andrews, P. G. (2004). *Making the most of middle school: A field guide for parents and others.* New York: Teachers College Press.

National Coalition for Parent Involvement in Education (www.ncpie.org) provides the names of both organizations and individuals who have resources available for parents and schools that wish to improve literacy.

Rotary Club International (www.rotary.org/programs) has made literacy improvement its top goal and provides grants and assistance to schools.

Other organizations with materials for community and parent involvement include the following:

- National Center for Family Literacy (www.famlit.org)
- National Community Education Association (www.ncea.com)
- National Middle School Association (www.nmsa.org)
- National PTA (www.pta.org)
- National Urban League (www.nul.org)
- U.S. Department of Education (www.ed.gov/index.jhtml)

Working with School Districts

Marsh, J. A., Kerr, K. A, Ikemoto, G. S., Darilek, H., Suttorp, M., Zimmer, R. W., & Barney, H. (2005). *The role of districts in fostering instructional improvement: Lessons from three urban districts partnered with the Institute for Learning.* Santa Monica, CA: RAND Corporation.

Togneri, W., & Anderson, S. E. (2003). *Beyond islands of excellence: What districts can do to improve instruction and achievement in all schools.* Washington, DC: Learning First Alliance and the Association for Supervision and Curriculum Development.

Additional Print Resources

General

Irvin, J. L., Buehl, D. R., & Klemp, R. M. (2007). *Reading and the high school student: Strategies to enhance literacy.* Boston: Allyn and Bacon.

Irvin, J. L., Buehl, D. R., & Radcliffe, B. J. (2007). *Strategies for integrating literacy and learning in the middle school content area classroom* (3rd ed.). Boston: Allyn and Bacon.

Rycik, J. A., & Irvin, J. L. (2005). *Teaching reading in the middle grades: Understanding and supporting literacy development.* Boston: Allyn and Bacon.

Strickland, D., & Alvermann, D. E. (Eds.). (2004). *Bridging the literacy achievement gap grades 4–12.* New York: Teachers College Press.

Tovani, C. (2000). *I read it, but I don't get it: Comprehension strategies for adolescent readers.* York, ME: Stenhouse Publishers.

Tovani, C. (2004). *Do I really have to teach reading? Content comprehension, grades 6–12.* York, ME: Stenhouse Publishers.

Student, Motivation, Engagement, and Achievement (Chapter 1)

Board on Children, Youth, and Families. (2003). *Engaging schools: Fostering high school students' motivation to learn.* Washington, DC: National Academies Press.

Gallagher, K. (2002). *Reading reasons: Motivational mini-lessons for middle and high school.* Portland, ME: Stenhouse.

Guthrie, J. T., & Knowles, K. T. (2001). Promoting reading motivation. In L. Verhoeven & C. Snow (Eds.), *Literacy and motivation: Reading engagement in individuals and groups* (p. 173). Mahwah, NJ: Lawrence Erlbaum.

North Central Regional Educational Laboratory. (2005). *Using student engagement to improve adolescent literacy.* Learning Point Associates. Available: www.ncrel.org/litweb/adolescent/qkey10/

Wilhelm, J. D. (1995). *"You gotta be the book": Teaching engaged and reflective reading with adolescents.* New York: Teachers College Press.

Wilhelm, J. D., & Freidemann, P. D. (1998). *Hyperlearning: Where projects, inquiry and technology meet.* York, ME: Stenhouse.

Integrating Literacy and Learning: Across the Content Areas (Chapter 2)

Buehl, D. (2001). *Classroom strategies for interactive learning.* Newark, DE: International Reading Association.

Lenz, B. K., & Deshler, D. D. (2004). *Teaching content to all: Evidence-based inclusive practices in middle and secondary schools.* Boston: Allyn and Bacon.

National Writing Project, & Nagin, C. (2003). *Because writing matters: Improving student writing in our schools.* San Francisco: Jossey-Bass.

Vacca, R., & Vacca, J. (2002). *Content area reading* (8th ed.). Boston: Allyn and Bacon.

Wilhelm, J. D., Baker, T. N., & Dube, J. (2001). *Strategic reading: Guiding students to lifelong literacy, 6–12.* Westport, CT: Heinemann.

Integrating Literacy and Learning: Interventions for Struggling Readers and Writers (Chapter 3)

Beers, K. (2003). *When kids can't read: What teachers can do.* Portsmouth, NH: Heinemann.

Curtis, M. E., & Longo, A. M. (1999). *When adolescents can't read: Materials and methods that work.* Cambridge, MA: Brookline Books.

Hock, M. F., Deshler, D. D., & Schumaker, J. B. (2000). *Strategic tutoring.* Lawrence, KS: Edge Enterprises.

Peterson, C. L., Caverly, D. C., Nicholson, S. A., O'Neal, S., & Cusenbary, S. (2000). *Building reading proficiency at the secondary level: A guide to resources.* San Marcos, TX: Southwest Texas State University and the Southwest Educational Development Laboratory. Available: www.sedl.org/pubs/reading16/

Schoenbach, C. G., Cziko, C., & Hurwitz, L. (1999). *Reading for understanding: A guide to improving reading in middle and high school classrooms.* San Francisco: Jossey-Bass.

Tomlinson, C. A. (1999). *The differentiated classroom: Responding to the needs of all learners.* Alexandria, VA: Association for Supervision and Curriculum Development.

Tomlinson, C. A. (2003). *Differentiation in practice: A resource guide for differentiating the curriculum, grades 5–9.* Alexandria, VA: Association for Supervision and Curriculum Development.

Tomlinson, C. A. (2005). *Differentiation in practice: A resource guide for differentiating the curriculum, grades 9–12.* Alexandria, VA: Association for Supervision and Curriculum Development.

Sustaining Literacy Development (Chapter 4)

Guth, N. D., & Pettengill, S. S. (2005). *Leading a successful reading program: Administrators and reading specialists working together to make it happen.* Newark, DE: International Reading Association.

McEwan, E. (2001). *Raising reading achievement in middle and high schools: Five simple-to-follow strategies for principals.* Thousand Oaks, CA: Corwin Press.

Pilgreen, J. L. (2000). *The SSR handbook: How to organize and manage a sustained silent reading program.* Portsmouth, NH: Boynton/Cook Publishers.

Develop a Literacy Action Plan (Chapter 5)

Carr, J., & Harris, D. (2001). *Succeeding with standards: Linking curriculum, assessment, and action planning.* Alexandria, VA: Association for Supervision and Curriculum Development.

Danielson, C. (2002). *Enhancing student achievement: A framework for school improvement.* Alexandria, VA: Association for Supervision and Curriculum Development.

Ivey, G., & Fisher, D. (2006). *Creating literacy-rich schools for adolescents.* Alexandria, VA: Association for Supervision and Curriculum Development.

Taylor, R., & Collins, V. D. (2003). *Literacy leadership for grades 5–12.* Alexandria, VA: Association for Supervision and Curriculum Development.

Taylor, R., & Gunter, G. (2005). *The K–12 literacy leadership fieldbook.* Thousand Oaks, CA: Corwin Press.

Support Teachers to Improve Instruction (Chapter 6)

Downie, C. J., Steffy, B. E., English, F. W., Frase, L. E., & Poston, W. K. (2004). *The three-minute classroom walk-through: Changing school supervisory practice one teacher at a time.* Thousand Oaks, CA: Corwin Press.

DuFour, R., & Eaker, R. (1998). *Professional learning communities at work: Best practices for enhancing student achievement.* Alexandria, VA: Association for Supervision and Curriculum Development.

Glickman, C. D. (2002). *Leadership for learning: How to help teachers succeed.* Alexandria, VA: Association for Supervision and Curriculum Development.

National Association of Secondary School Principals. (2005). *Creating a culture of literacy: A guide for middle and high school principals.* Reston, VA: Author.

Zmuda, A., Kuklis, R., & Kline, E. (2004). *Transforming schools: Creating a culture of continuous improvement*. Alexandria, VA: Association for Supervision and Curriculum Development.

Use Data to Make Decisions (Chapter 7)

Holcomb, E. (1999). *Getting excited about data: How to combine people, passion and proof*. Thousand Oaks, CA: Corwin Press.

Johnson, R. (2002). *Using data to close the achievement gap: How to measure equity in our schools*. Thousand Oaks, CA: Corwin Press.

Build Leadership Capacity (Chapter 8)

Bean, R. M. (2004). *The reading specialist: Leadership for the classroom, school, and community (solving problems in teaching of literacy)*. New York: Guilford Press.

International Reading Association. (2004). *The role and qualifications of the reading coach in the United States*. Newark, DE: International Reading Association.

Lambert, L. (2003). *Leadership capacity for lasting school improvement*. Alexandria, VA: Association for Supervision and Curriculum Development.

Moxley, D., & Taylor, R. (2006). *Literacy coaching: A handbook for school leaders*. Thousand Oaks, CA: Corwin Press, in association with the National Association of Secondary School Principals.

Toll, C. A. (2005). *The literacy coach's survival guide: Essential questions and practical answers*. Newark, DE: International Reading Association.

Toll, C. A. (2006). *Literacy coach's desk reference: The processes and perspectives for effective coaching*. Urbana, IL: National Council of Teachers of English.

Walpole, S., & McKenna, M. C. (2004). *The literacy coach's handbook: A guide to research-based practice*. New York: Guilford Press.

Allocate Resources for Literacy (Chapter 9)

Alliance for Excellent Education. (2005). *Literacy: Grants*. Available: www.alliance.brown.edu/topics/literacy.shtml

Murphy, R., Penuel, W., Means, B., Korbak, C., Whaley, A., & Allen, J. (2002). *E-DESK: A review of recent evidence on the effectiveness of discrete educational software*. Planning and Valuation Service, U.S. Department of Education DHHS Contract #282-00-008-Task 3. Menlo Park, CA: SRI International.

National Council of Teachers of English. (2006). *Funding focus: Adolescent literacy*. Available: www.ncte.org/about/grants/topic/116646.htm?source=gs

National Education Commission on Time and Learning. (1994). *Prisoners of time: Schools and programs making time work for students and teachers*. Washington, DC: Author.

National Staff Development Council. (2005). *Resources for high-performing schools*. Available: www.nsdc.org/library/model/highperforming.cfm

APPENDIX E:
RESEARCH REFERENCES

In this appendix, we've included research that informed our thinking in the development of the model and this book. Although we also found individual articles and studies helpful, the following resources focus on position statements, policy reports, and reviews of literature. You may find these materials useful in understanding how the model was developed, or you may wish to use them to strengthen your knowledge of the field and to support your literacy improvement efforts.

Position Statements and Policy Reports

ACT. (2006). *Reading between the lines: What the ACT reveals about college readiness in reading.* (Report). Iowa City, IA: Author.

ACT. (2006). *Reading for college and reading for work: Same or different?* (Report). Iowa City, IA: Author.

Biancarosa, G., & Snow, C. E. (2004). *Reading next: A vision for action and research in middle and high school literacy.* (Report from Carnegie Corporation of New York). Washington, DC: Alliance for Excellent Education.

College Board. (2004). *Writing: A ticket to work or a ticket out.* (Report of the National Commission on Writing for America's Families, Schools, and Colleges). New York: Author.

Graham, S. & Perin, D. (2007). *Writing next: Effective strategies to improve writing of adolescents in middle and high schools.* (Report). Washington, DC: Alliance for Excellent Education.

International Reading Association. (2006). *Standards for middle and high school literacy coaches.* Newark, DE: International Reading Association.

Jackson, A. W., & Davis, G. A. (2000). *Turning points 2000: Educating adolescents in the 21st century.* New York: Teachers College Press.

Kamil, M. L. (2004). *Adolescents and literacy: Reading for the 21st century.* Washington, DC: Alliance for Excellent Education.

Moore, D. W., Bean, T., Birdyshaw, D., & Rycik, J. (1999). *Adolescent literacy: A position statement.* Newark, DE: International Reading Association.

National Association of Secondary School Principals. (1996). *Breaking ranks: Changing an American institution.* Reston, VA: Author.

National Association of Secondary School Principals. (2006). *Adolescent literacy position statement.* Reston, VA: Author.

National Association of State Boards of Education. (2005). *Reading at risk: The state response to the crisis in adolescent literacy.* Alexandria, VA: Author.

National Council of Teachers of English. (2004). *A call to action: What we know about adolescent literacy and ways to support teachers in meeting students' needs.* Urbana, IL: Author.

National Council of Teachers of English. (2006). *NCTE principles of adolescent literacy reform.* Urbana, IL: Author.

National Governors Association. (2006). *Reading to achieve: A governor's guide to adolescent literacy.* Washington, DC: Author.

National Reading Panel. (2000). *Teaching children to read: An evidence-based assessment of the scientific research literature on reading and its implications for reading instruction.* Available: www.nichd.nih.gov/publications/nrp/smallbook.cfm

Partnership for 21st Century Skills. (2004). *Learning for the 21st century. Retrieved May 8, 2006, from* www.21stcenturyskills.org/images/stories/otherdocs/P21_Report.pdf

Short, D. J., & Fitzsimmons, S. (2007). *Double the work: Challenges and solutions to acquiring language and academic literacy for adolescent English language learners.* [Report]. Washington, DC: Alliance for Excellent Education.

Sturtevant, E. G. (2003, November). *The literacy coach: A key to improving teaching and learning in secondary schools* [Report commissioned by the Alliance for Excellent Education]. Available: www.all4ed.org

Research Reviews

Alvermann, D. (2002). *Effective literacy instruction for adolescents.* Commissioned paper for the National Reading Conference, Chicago. Available: www.coe.uga.edu/lle/faculty/alvermann/effective2.pdf

Curtis, M. E. (2002, May 20). *Adolescent reading: A synthesis of research.* Paper presented at the National Institute for Literacy/The National Institute of Child Health and Human Development Adolescent Literacy Workshop II. Baltimore, MD.

Davis, S., Darling-Hammond, L., LaPointe, M., & Meyerson, D. (2005). *School leadership study: Developing successful principals.* Stanford, CA: Stanford Educational Leadership Institute. Available: www.seli.stanford.edu/research/documents/SELI_sls_research-review.pdf

Farstrup, A. E., & Samuels, S. J. (Eds.). (2002). *What research has to say about reading instruction* (3rd ed.). Newark, DE: International Reading Association.

Harvey, S., & Goudvis, A. (2000). *Strategies that work: Teaching comprehension to enhance understanding.* York, ME: Stenhouse.

Hoachlander, G., Alt, M., & Beltranena, R. (2001). *Leading school improvement: What research says.* Atlanta, GA: Southern Regional Education Board. Available: www.sreb.org/main/Leadership/pubs/01V04_LeadingSchool_Improvement.pdf

Institute for Educational Leadership. (2000). *Leadership for student learning: Reinventing the principalship.* Washington, DC: Author. Available: www.iel.org

Kamil, M. L., Mosenthal, P. B., Pearson, P. D., & Barr, R. (2000). *Handbook of reading research* (Vol. III). Mahwah, NJ: Lawrence Erlbaum.

Lachat, M. A. (2001). *Data-driven high school reform: The breaking ranks model.* Providence, RI: The LAB at Brown University. Available: www.alliance.brown.edu/pubs/hischlrfm/datdrv_hsrfm.pdf

Langer, J. A. (2001). Beating the odds: Teaching middle and high school students to read and write well. *American Educational Research Journal, 38*(4), 837–880.

Langer, J. A. (2002). *Effective literacy instruction: Building successful reading and writing programs.* Urbana, IL: National Council for the Teachers of English.

Leithwood, K. A., & Riehl, C. (2003). *What do we already know about successful school leadership?* Paper presented at the annual meeting of the American Educational Research Association, Chicago. Available: www.cepa.gse.rutgers.edu/What%20We%20Know%20_long_%202003.pdf

Marzano, R. J. (2003). *What works in schools: Translating research into action.* Alexandria, VA: Association for Supervision and Curriculum Development.

Marzano, R. J. (2004). *Building background knowledge for academic achievement: Research for what works in schools.* Alexandria, VA: Association for Supervision and Curriculum Development.

Marzano, R. J., Pickering, D. J., & Pollock, J. E. (2001). *Classroom instruction that works: Research-based strategies for increasing student achievement.* Alexandria, VA: Association for Supervision and Curriculum Development.

Marzano, R. J., Waters, T., & McNulty, B. A. (2005). *School leadership that works: From research to results.* Alexandria, VA: Association for Supervision and Curriculum Development.

Meltzer, J. (2002). *Adolescent literacy resources: Linking resources with practice.* Providence, RI: The LAB at Brown University. Available: www.alliance.brown.edu/pubs/adlit/alr_lrp.pdf

Meltzer, J., & Hamann, E. (2004). *Meeting the needs of adolescent English language learners for literacy development and content area learning, part one: Focus on motivation and engagement.* Providence, RI: The Education Alliance at Brown University.

Meltzer, J., & Hamann, E. (2005). *Meeting the needs of adolescent English language learners through content area learning, part two: Focus on classroom teaching and learning strategies.* Providence, RI: The Education Alliance at Brown University.

Samuels, S. J., & Farstrup, A. E. (2006). *What research has to say about fluency instruction.* Newark, DE: International Reading Association.

Spillane, J. P. (2006). *Distributed leadership.* San Francisco: Jossey-Bass.

Sturtevant, E., Boyd, F., Brozo, W., Hinchman, K., Moore, D., & Alvermann, D. (2006). *Principled practices for adolescent literacy: A framework for instruction and policy.* Mahwah, NJ: Lawrence Erlbaum.

REFERENCES

ACT. (2006a). *Reading between the lines: What the ACT reveals about college readiness in reading.* [Report]. Iowa City, IA: Author.

ACT (2006b). *Reading for college and reading for work: Same or different?* (Report). Iowa City, IA: Author.

Allen, J. (1999). *Words, words, words: Teaching vocabulary in grades 4–12.* York, ME: Stenhouse.

Alliance for Excellent Education. (2005). *Teacher attrition: A costly loss to the nation and to the states.* Washington, DC: Author.

Alvermann, D. E. (2001, October). *Effective literacy instruction for adolescents.* (Executive summary and paper). Chicago: National Reading Conference. Retrieved August 5, 2004, from www.nrconline.org/publications/alverwhite2.pdf

Alvermann, D. E. (2003). *Seeing themselves as capable and engaged readers: Adolescents and remediated instruction.* Naperville, IL: Learning Point Associates.

Alvermann, D. E. (2004). *Adolescent literacies in a digital world.* New York: Peter Lang.

Anderson, S. E. (2003). *The school district role in educational change: A review of literature.* ICEC Working Paper #2.

Armbruster, B., Lehr, F., & Osborn, J. (2001). *Put reading first: The research building blocks for teaching children to read.* Washington, DC: U.S. Department of Education.

Balfanz, R., McPartland, J., & Shaw, A. (2002, April). *Re-conceptualizing extra help for high school students in a high standards era.* Washington, DC: Office of Vocational and Adult Education, U.S. Department of Education.

Biancarosa, G., & Snow, C. E. (2004). *Reading next: A vision for action and research in middle and high school literacy.* Washington, DC: Alliance for Excellent Education.

Buehl, D. R. (2001). *Classroom strategies for interactive learning* (2nd ed.). Newark, DE: International Reading Association.

College Board. (2004). *Writing: A ticket to work or a ticket out.* (Report of the National Commission on Writing for America's Families, Schools and Colleges). New York: Author.

Cooney, S. (1999). *Leading the way: State actions to improve student achievement in the middle grades.* Atlanta, GA: Southern Regional Education Board.

Curtis, M. E. (2002, May). *Adolescent reading: A synthesis of research.* Paper presented at the U.S. Department of Education and the National Institute of Child Health and Human Development Conference on Adolescent Literacy, Baltimore, MD. Retrieved December 3, 2002, from http://216.26.160.105/conf/nichd/synthesis.asp

Daggett, W. (2005). *Achieving academic excellence through rigor and relevance.* Rexford, NY: International Center for Leadership in Education.

Downey, C. J., Steffy, B. E., English, F. W., Frase, L. E., & Poston, W. K. (2004). *The three-minute classroom walk-through: Changing school supervisor practice one teacher at a time.* Thousand Oaks, CA: Corwin Press.

Eaker, R., DuFour, R., & Burnette, R. (2002). *Getting started: Reculturing schools to become professional learning communities.* Bloomington, IN: National Educational Service.

Elkins, J., & Luke, A. (1999). Redefining adolescent literacies. *Journal of Adolescent & Adult Literacy, 43*(3), 212–215.

Elmore, R. F. (2002). *Bridging the gap between standards and achievement: The imperative for professional development in education.* Washington, DC: Albert Shanker Institute.

Fullan, M. (2001). *Leading in a culture of change.* San Francisco: Jossey-Bass.

Gamoran, A., & Kelly, S. (2003). Tracking, instruction, and unequal literacy in secondary school English. In M. T. Hallinan, A. Gamoran, W. Kubitschek, & T. Loveless (Eds.), *Stability and change in American education: Structure, process, and outcomes* (pp. 109–126). Clinton Corners, NY: Eliot Werner Publications.

Garcia, G. E. (2000). Bilingual children's reading. In M. L. Kamil, P. B. Mosenthal, P. D. Pearson, & R. Barr (Eds.), *Handbook of reading research* (Vol. 3, pp. 813–834). Mahwah, NJ: Lawrence Erlbaum.

Graham, S., & Perin, D. (2007). *Writing next: Effective strategies to improve writing of adolescents in middle and high schools.* [Report]. Washington, DC: Alliance for Excellent Education.

Guthrie, J. T. (2001). Contexts for engagement and motivation in reading. *Reading Online.* Retrieved August 11, 2004, from www.readingonline.org/articles/handbook/guthrie/index.html

Guthrie, J. T., & Knowles, K. T. (2001). Promoting reading motivation. In L. Verhoeven & C. Snow (Eds.), *Literacy and motivation: Reading engagement in individuals and groups* (p. 173). Mahwah, NJ: Lawrence Erlbaum.

Guthrie, J. T., & Wigfield, A. (Eds.). (1997). *Reading engagement: Motivating readers through integrated instruction.* Newark, DE: International Reading Association.

Guthrie, J. T., & Wigfield, A. (2000). Engagement and motivation in reading. In M. L. Kamil, P. B. Mosenthal, P. D. Pearson, & R. Barr (Eds.), *Handbook of reading research* (Vol. 3, pp. 403–422). Mahwah, NJ: Lawrence Erlbaum.

Harvey, S., & Goudvis, A. (2000). *Strategies that work: Teaching comprehension to enhance understanding.* Portland, ME: Stenhouse.

Honig, M. I., & Hatch, T. C. (2004). Crafting coherence: How schools strategically manage multiple, external demands. *Educational Researcher, 33*(8), 16–30.

International Reading Association. (2004). *The role and qualifications of the reading coach in the United States.* Newark, DE: Author.

International Reading Association. (2006). *Standards for middle and high school literacy coaches.* Newark, DE: International Reading Association.

Irvin, J. L., Buehl, D., & Klemp, R. (2007). *Reading and the high school student: Strategies to enhance literacy* (2nd ed.). Boston: Allyn and Bacon.

Joftus, S. (2002). *Every child a graduate: A framework for an excellent education for all middle and high school students.* Washington, DC: Alliance for Excellent Education.

Kamil, M. L. (2003). *Adolescents and literacy: Reading for the 21st century.* Washington, DC: Alliance for Excellent Education.

Lachat, M. A., & Smith, S. (2004). *Data use in urban high schools.* Providence, RI: Northeast and Islands Regional Educational Laboratory.

Lachat, M. A., & Smith, S. (2005). Practices that support data use in urban high schools. *Journal of Education for Students Placed at Risk (JESPAR), 10*(3), 333–349.

Langer, J. (2002). *Effective literacy instruction: Building successful reading and writing programs.* Urbana, IL: National Council of Teachers of English.

Lee, C. D. (2005). Bridging home and school literacies: Models for culturally responsive teaching: A case for African-American English. In J. Flood, S. B. Heath, & D. Lapp (Eds.), *Handbook of research on teaching literacy through the communicative and visual arts* (pp. 334–345). Mahwah, NJ: Lawrence Erlbaum Associates.

Leithwood, K. A., & Riehl, C. (2003). *What do we already know about successful school leadership?* Paper presented at the annual meeting of the American Educational Research Association, Chicago.

Leithwood, K., Louis, K. S., Anderson, S., & Wahlstrom, K. (2004). *How leadership influences student learning.* New York: Wallace Foundation.

Loup, K. S., Garland, J. S., Ellett, C. D., & Rugutt, J. K. (1996). Ten years later: Findings from a replication of a study of teacher evaluation practices in our 100 largest school districts. *Journal of Personnel Evaluation in Education, 10*(3), 203–206.

Marsh, J. A., Kerr, K. A, Ikemoto, G. S., Darilek, H., Suttorp, M., Zimmer, R. W., & Barney, H. (2005). *The role of districts in fostering instructional improvement: Lessons from three urban districts partnered with the institute for learning.* Santa Monica, CA: RAND Corporation.

Meltzer, J. (with Smith, N., & Clark, H.). (2002). *Adolescent literacy resources: Linking research and practice.* Providence, RI: Northeast and Islands Regional Educational Laboratory at Brown University.

Meltzer, J., & Hamann, E. (2004). *Meeting the needs of adolescent English language learners for literacy development and content area learning; Part One: Focus on motivation and engagement.* Providence, RI: Education Alliance at Brown University.

Metcalfe, C. (1999). Developmental classroom observation as a component of monitoring and evaluating the work of subject departments in secondary schools. *Journal of In-Service Education, 25*(3), 447–454.

Moore, D. W., Bean, T. W., Birdyshaw, D., & Rycik, J. A. (1999). *Adolescent literacy: A position statement.* Newark, DE: International Reading Association.

National Governors Association. (2006). *Reading to achieve: A governor's guide to adolescent literacy.* Washington, DC: Author.

National Middle School Association. (2001). *Supporting young adolescents' literacy learning: A joint position paper of the International Reading Association and the National Middle School Association.* Westerville, OH: Author.

National Writing Project. (2006). *Supporting good writing instruction.* Available: www.writingproject.org/encourage/supporting.csp

National Writing Project, & Nagin, C. (2003). *Because writing matters: Improving student writing in our schools.* San Francisco: Jossey-Bass.

Partnership for 21st Century Skills. (2006). *Learning for the 21st century.* Retrieved May 8, 2006, from www.21stcenturyskills.org/images/stories/otherdocs/P21_Report.pdf

Pearson, P. D., & Gallagher, M. (1983). The instruction of reading comprehension. *Contemporary Educational Psychology, 8,* 317–344.

Peterson, C. L., Caverly, D. C., Nicholson, S. A., O'Neal, S., & Cusenbary, S. (2000). *Building reading proficiency at the secondary school level: A guide to resources.* San Marcos, TX: Southwest Texas State University and the Southwest Educational Development Laboratory.

Putnam, R. T., & Borko, H. (2000). What do new views of knowledge and thinking have to say about research on teaching learning? *Educational Researcher, 29*(1), 4–15.

Roe, M. (2001). Combining enablement and engagement to assist students who do not read and write well. In J. A. Rycik & J. L. Irvin (Eds.), *What adolescents deserve: A commitment to students' literacy learning* (pp. 10–19). Newark, DE: International Reading Association.

Schmoker, M. (2006). *Results now: How we can achieve unprecedented improvements in teaching and learning.* Alexandria, VA: Association for Supervision and Curriculum Development.

Schoenbach, R., Greenleaf, C., Cziko, C., & Hurwitz, L. (1999). *Reading for understanding: A guide to improving reading in middle and high school classrooms.* San Francisco: Jossey-Bass.

Short, D. J., & Fitzsimmons, S. (2007). *Double the work: Challenges and solutions to acquiring language and academic literacy for adolescent English language learners.* [Report]. Washington, DC: Alliance for Excellent Education.

Smith, M., & Wilhelm, J. (2002). *Reading don't fix no Chevys: Literacy in the lives of young men.* Portsmouth, NH: Heinemann.

Smith, T., & Ingersoll, R. (2004). What are the effects of induction and mentoring on beginning teacher turnover? *American Educational Research Journal, 41*(3), 681–714.

Snow, C. (2002). *Reading for understanding: Toward an R&D program in reading comprehension.* Santa Monica, CA: Rand Education.

Southern Regional Education Board. (2002). *Launching your school's literacy campaign*. Unpublished paper.

Spillane, J. P. (2006). *Distributed leadership*. Somerset, NJ: Jossey-Bass.

Spillane, J. P., Diamond, J. B., Burch, P., Hallett, T., Jita, L., & Zoltners, J. (2002). Managing in the middle: School leaders and the enactment of accountability policy. *Educational Policy, 16*(5), 731–762.

Spillane, J. P., Halverson, R., & Diamond, J. B. (2004). Towards a theory of leadership practice: A distributed perspective. *Journal of Curriculum Studies, 36*(1), 3–34.

Strong, M., Fletcher, S., & Villar, A. (2004). *An investigation of the effects of teacher experience and teacher preparedness on the performance of Latino students in California*. Santa Cruz, CA: New Teacher Center.

Sturtevant, E., Boyd, F., Brozo, W., Hinchman, K., Moore, D., & Alvermann, D. E. (2006). *Principled practices for a literate America: A framework for literacy and learning in the upper grades*. Mahwah, NJ: Lawrence Erlbaum.

Symonds, K. W. (2003). *Literacy coaching: How school districts can support a long-term strategy in a short-term world*. San Francisco: Bay Area School Reform Collaborative.

Thelen, J. (1986). Vocabulary instruction and meaningful learning. *Journal of Reading, 29*(7), 603–609.

Togneri, W., & Anderson, S. E. (2003). *Beyond islands of excellence: What districts can do to improve instruction and achievement in all schools*. Washington, DC: Learning First Alliance and the Association for Supervision and Curriculum Development.

Torgesen, J. K., & Hudson, R. F. (2006). Reading fluency: Critical issues for struggling readers. In S. J. Samuels & A. Farstrup (Eds.), *What research has to say about fluency instruction* (pp. 130–158). Newark, DE: International Reading Association.

Tovani, C. (2000). *I read it, but I don't get it: Comprehension strategies for adolescent readers*. Portland, ME: Stenhouse.

Tyack, D. (2002). *Forgotten players: How local school districts shaped American education*. In A. M. Hightower, M. S. Knapp, J. A. Marsh, & M. W. McLaughlin (Eds.), *School districts and instructional reform* (pp. 9–24). New York: Teachers College Press.

Vygotsky, L. (1962). *Thought and language*. Cambridge, MA: MIT Press.

Wilhelm, J. D., Baker, T., & Dube, J. (2001). *Strategic reading: Guiding students to lifelong literacy 6–12*. Portsmouth, NH: Heinemann.

Williams, J. D. (2003) *Preparing to teach writing: Research, theory and practice*. Mahwah, NJ: Lawrence Erlbaum Associates.

INDEX

sustained silent reading (SSR), 101, 103, 207
sustaining literacy development
　about, 19–20, 98–101
　district support for, 108–113
　parental and community involvement,
　　104–108
　school leaders' roles, 101–103

teacher evaluation, 154–155
Teacher Knowledge Inventory, 136, 237–238*f*
teachers. *See also* content-area teachers/teaching;
　teacher support
　assessing capacity to improve literacy,
　　132–134
　collaborative implementation, 127, 148
　developing literacy expertise, 9–10
　leadership capacity of, 123–124*f*, 180–184,
　　183*f*
　preparation of, 5
　professional development opportunities,
　　125*f*–126*f*, 150, 151*f*, 188, 210–213*f*,
　　212*f*
　resistance of, 194–198, 196*f*–197*f*
　special education, 86–87, 191, 192*f*
　student dependence on, 6
　understanding current practices of, 135–137
teacher support, by administration
　classroom observations, 152–153, 239*f*–
　　240*f*
　importance of, 20–21, 145–146
　literacy coaching, 149–150
　literacy walk-throughs, 153–154
　making the work public, 148–149
　methods of, 71–73
　monitoring program implementation,
　　150–156
　new faculty induction, 155–156*f*
　professional development opportunities,
　　150, 151*f*
　professional learning communities, 147
　teacher evaluation, 154–155
technology, and literacy, 7–8, 43, 213–216, 217*f*
texts
　complexity levels of, 61
　differentiation in, 66–68
　interacting with, and through, 41–42
tutoring programs, 92–93

Union City Public Schools, 247
University Park Campus School, 246
urban school districts, 111–112
use data to make decisions, 21

vignettes
　breaking cycle of failure, 34–36
　content-area teachers and literacy support,
　　62–65
　creating literacy-rich environment, 101–103
　data-driven literacy planning, 129–137,
　　160–163
　district efforts, 108–110
　English classroom literacy support, 226–227
　high school literacy vision, 11–15
　literacy coaching, 184–188
　literacy teams, 180–185, 184*f*
　Math classroom literacy support, 228–229
　middle school literacy, 222–226
　motivating and supportive environment,
　　37–39
　professional development, 210–213*f*, 212*f*
　proficient readers, 56–58
　resource allocation, 201–204, 208
　school leaders' roles, 89–91
　Science classroom literacy support, 230
　struggling readers in content-area
　　classrooms, 77–80
　teacher resistance, 194–198, 196*f*–197*f*
　teacher support by leaders, 71–73, 146–
　　147, 151–152
vision, creating a, 10–16, 46–48, 127
vocabulary development, 44–45, 60, 86–87

Web sites, school, 107
word processing, 68
writing
　content-area instruction in, 83
　elements of improving achievement,
　　68–69
　formats and genres of, 70–71
writing-to-learn strategies, 69

ABOUT THE AUTHORS

Judith L. Irvin is a professor at Florida State University. Dr. Irvin's career includes chairing the Research Committee for the National Middle School Association for six years and serving as executive director of the National Literacy Project, a nonprofit organization dedicated to improving middle and high school literacy. She has written and edited numerous books, chapters, and articles on adolescent literacy, most notably *Reading and the High School Student: Strategies to Enhance Literacy* (with Buehl & Klemp, 2007), *Strategies for Enhancing Literacy and Learning in Middle School Content Area Classrooms* (with Buehl & Radcliffe, 2007), and *Teaching Middle School Reading* (with Rycik, 2005). She is a speaker and consultant to school systems and professional organizations throughout the United States and served on the Commission on Adolescent Literacy of the International Reading Association and on the board of the National Middle School Association. She spent eight years as a middle and high school social studies and reading teacher. She can be reached at irvin@coe.fsu.edu.

Julie Meltzer is the director of literacy research and development at the Public Consulting Group's Center for Resource Management, Inc. (CRM), in Portsmouth, New Hampshire. Dr. Meltzer is the codeveloper of CRM's *School-Wide Program for Improving Reading and Learning* (SPIRAL), which supports middle and high school educators to systemically address improving adolescent literacy. As director of the Adolescent Literacy Project at the LAB at Brown University, Dr. Meltzer developed the Adolescent Literacy Support Framework and authored *Adolescent Literacy Resources: Linking Research and Practice* (2002) and other research-based resources for professional development and technical assistance. A sought-after keynote speaker, author, reviewer, conference presenter, and workshop leader, Dr. Meltzer consistently seeks to help educators build their capacity to effectively apply promising research-based practices to support the literacy development and learning needs of adolescents. A key focus of her current work is helping school leaders to understand the roles, responsibilities, and actions associated with academic literacy development at the middle and high school levels. Dr. Meltzer can be reached at jmeltzer@pcgus.com.

Melinda Dukes is a doctoral candidate in the Department of Educational Leadership and Policy Studies at Florida State University and holds two advanced degrees: specialist of education in educational administration and master of education in reading. She has received professional certifications in educational leadership, program evaluation, human resource development, and policy planning and analysis. She has more than a decade of experience as a classroom teacher, district reading specialist, and regional reading consultant. Ms. Dukes has worked with many school districts in Florida to develop strategic reading initiatives and has guided and supported these districts throughout their implementation efforts.

Related ASCD Resources: Literacy and Adolescents

At the time of publication, the following resources were available; for the most up-to-date information about ASCD resources, go to www.ascd.org. ASCD stock numbers are noted in parentheses.

Audio

Improving Reading Is Everyone's Business by Brenda Hunter (Audiotape #203122S25; CD #503215S25)

Literacy Matters Across the Curriculum by Robin Fogarty and Brian Pete (Audiotape #204280S25; CD #504414S25)

Mixed Media

The Multiple Intelligences of Reading and Writing: Making the Words Come Alive Books-in-Action Package (10 Books and 1 Video) by Thomas Armstrong (#703381S25)

Using Data to Assess Your Reading Program (Book and CD-ROM) by Emily Calhoun (#102268S25)

Networks

Visit the ASCD Web site (www.ascd.org) and click on About ASCD. Go to the section on Networks for information about professional educators who have formed groups around topics such as "Language, Literacy, and Literature" and "Middle Grades." Look in the Network Directory for current facilitators' addresses and phone numbers.

Online Courses

Visit the ASCD Web site (www.ascd.org) for the following professional development opportunities:

Helping Struggling Readers by Kathy Checkley (#PD04OC42)

Successful Strategies for Literacy and Learning by Angelika Machi (#PD03OC27)

Print Products

Building Student Literacy Through Sustained Silent Reading by Steve Gardiner (#105027S25)

Educational Leadership, March 2004: What Research Says About Reading (Entire Issue #104028S25)

Educational Leadership, April 2005: The Adolescent Learner (Entire Issue #105034S25)

Educational Leadership, October 2005: Reading Comprehension (Entire Issue #106037S25)

Literacy Leadership for Grades 5–12 by Rosemarye Taylor and Valerie Doyle Collins (#103022S25)

Literacy Strategies for Grades 4–12: Reinforcing the Threads of Reading by Karen Tankersley (#104428S25)

Video

Implementing a Reading Program in Secondary Schools Video (One 30-Minute Videotape with a Facilitator's Guide #402033S25)

The Lesson Collection: Literacy Strategies Tapes 49–56 (Eight 10- to 20-Minute Videotapes #405160S25)

For more information, visit us on the World Wide Web (www.ascd.org), send an e-mail message to member@ascd.org, call the ASCD Service Center (1-800-933-ASCD or 703-578-9600, then press 2), send a fax to 703-575-5400, or write to Information Services, ASCD, 1703 N. Beauregard St., Alexandria, VA 22311-1714 USA.